HAND BOOK
OF AUTOMOBILES

1915-1916

BY THE ASSOCIATION OF
LICENSED AUTOMOBILE MANUFACTURERS
(NATIONAL AUTOMOBILE CHAMBER OF COMMERCE)

Dover Publications, Inc., New York

Published in Canada by General Publishing
Company, Ltd., 30 Lesmill Road, Don Mills, Toronto,
Ontario.

Published in the United Kingdom by Constable
and Company, Ltd., 10 Orange Street, London WC 2.

This Dover edition, first published in 1970, is an
unabridged republication of the *Hand Book of
Automobiles* as published in 1915 and 1916 by the
National Automobile Chamber of Commerce (suc-
cessor to the Association of Licensed Automobile
Manufacturers) .

International Standard Book Number: 0-486-22689-1
Library of Congress Catalog Card Number: 70-141892

Manufactured in the United States of America
Dover Publications, Inc.
180 Varick Street
New York, N. Y. 10014

HAND BOOK
OF
AUTOMOBILES

1915

NATIONAL AUTOMOBILE
CHAMBER OF COMMERCE
INCORPORATED

TWELFTH ANNUAL ANNOUNCEMENT

A S THE standard authority on the products of American automobile manufacturers, the Twelfth Annual Hand Book is offered in the belief that it will be as well received and as useful as previous issues. Its illustrations and specifications describe in detail the products of the principal manufacturers of automobiles in the United States.

That comparison by buyers of motor cars may be easy and accurate, all cars shown herein have been subjected to a uniform investigation as to details of construction.

Individual manufacturers listed in this Hand Book will be glad to send complete catalogues descriptive of their product upon request, and catalogues may also be obtained from dealers in the principal cities and towns.

January, 1915.

ORGANIZATION OF

NATIONAL AUTOMOBILE CHAMBER OF COMMERCE

(INCORPORATED)

OFFICERS

Charles Clifton, *President* . . . Pierce-Arrow Motor Car Company

Wilfred C. Leland, *Vice-President* . . . Cadillac Motor Car Company

Hugh Chalmers, *Second Vice-President* . . Chalmers Motor Company
Gasoline Passenger Vehicle Division

Windsor T. White, *Second Vice-President* . . . The White Company
Commercial Vehicle Division

H. H. Rice, *Second Vice-President* . . . . The Waverley Company
Electric Vehicle Division

R. D. Chapin, *Secretary* . . . . . . Hudson Motor Car Company

George Pope, *Treasurer* . . . . . Pope Manufacturing Company

Alfred Reeves, *General Manager*
National Automobile Chamber of Commerce

S. A. Miles, *Show Manager* National Automobile Chamber of Commerce

BOARD OF DIRECTORS

Charles Clifton . . . . . . Pierce-Arrow Motor Car Company

Wilfred C. Leland . . . . Cadillac Motor Car Company

C. C. Hanch . . . . Nordyke & Marmon Company

Hugh Chalmers . . . . Chalmers Motor Company

Alvan Macauley . . . . Packard Motor Car Company

S. T. Davis, Jr. . . . . Locomobile Company of America

Windsor T. White . . . . The White Company

William E. Metzger . . . . . Argo Electric Vehicle Company

H. O. Smith . . . . . Premier Motor Manufacturing Company

L. H. Kittredge . . . . Peerless Motor Car Company

R. D. Chapin . . . . Hudson Motor Car Company

E. R. Benson . . . . Studebaker Corporation

H. H. Rice . . . . The Waverley Company

John N. Willys . . . . Willys-Overland Company

C. W. Churchill . . . . Winton Motor Car Company

PATENTS COMMITTEE

C. C. Hanch . . . .   Nordyke & Marmon Company
William H. Van Dervoort . . . . .   Moline Automobile Company
Windsor T. White . . . .   The White Company
Wilfred C. Leland . . . . . .   Cadillac Motor Car Company
Howard E. Coffin . . . .   Hudson Motor Car Company

TRAFFIC COMMITTEE

William E. Metzger . . . . . .   Argo Electric Vehicle Company
E. R. Benson . . . .   Studebaker Corporation
R. E. Olds . . . .   Reo Motor Car Company

SHOW COMMITTEE

George Pope . . . .   Pope Manufacturing Company
H. O. Smith . . . .   Premier Motor Manufacturing Company
Wilfred C. Leland . . . . . .   Cadillac Motor Car Company

LEGISLATIVE COMMITTEE

H. H. Rice . . . .   The Waverley Company
J. I. Farley . . . .   Auburn Automobile Company

ELECTRIC VEHICLE COMMITTEE

H. H. Rice . . . .   The Waverley Company
F. R. White . . . .   Baker Motor Vehicle Company
W. C. Anderson . . . .   Anderson Electric Car Company

COMMERCIAL VEHICLE COMMITTEE

Windsor T. White . . . .   The White Company
Alvan Macauley . . . .   Packard Motor Car Company
H. Kerr Thomas . . . . .   Pierce-Arrow Motor Car Company
P. D. Wagoner . . . .   General Vehicle Company
M. L. Pulcher . . . .   Federal Motor Truck Company

GOOD ROADS COMMITTEE

R. D. Chapin . . . .   Hudson Motor Car Company
S. D. Waldon . . . .   Packard Motor Car Company
E. R. Benson . . . .   Studebaker Corporation

ALPHABETICAL INDEX

GASOLINE PASSENGER VEHICLES

ALPHABETICAL INDEX—Continued

ELECTRIC VEHICLES

GASOLINE COMMERCIAL VEHICLES

INDEX OF TRADE NAMES

GASOLINE PASSENGER VEHICLES

INDEX OF TRADE NAMES—Continued

ELECTRIC VEHICLES

GASOLINE COMMERCIAL VEHICLES

N. A. C. C. HORSE-POWER RATING

The standard horse-power rating, formerly known as the A. L. A. M. Rating, has been officially adopted by the National Automobile Chamber of Commerce, Inc.

The formula adopted is $\frac{D^2 x N}{2.5}$. D is the cylinder bore in inches, N the number of cylinders, and 2.5 a constant, based on the average view of eminent engineers as to a fair, conservative rating for a four-cycle motor at one thousand feet per minute piston speed.

TABLE OF HORSE-POWER FOR USUAL SIZES OF MOTORS

Bore		Horse-power			
INS.	M/M.	1 CYL.	2 CYLS.	4 CYLS.	6 CYLS.
2 1/2	64	2 1/2	5	10	15
2 5/8	68	2 3/4	5 1/2	11	16 1/2
2 3/4	70	3	6	12 1/10	18 1/5
2 7/8	73	3 5/16	6 5/8	13 1/4	19 7/8
3	76	3 3/5	7 1/5	14 2/5	21 3/5
3 1/8	79	3 15/16	7 13/16	15 5/8	23 7/16
3 1/4	83	4 1/4	8 1/2	16 9/10	25 2/5
3 3/8	85	4 9/16	9 1/8	18 1/4	27 2/5
3 1/2	89	4 9/10	9 4/5	19 3/5	29 2/5
3 5/8	92	5 1/4	10 1/2	21 1/12	31 3/5
3 3/4	95	5 5/8	11 1/4	22 1/2	33 3/4
3 7/8	99	6	12	24	36 1/16
4	102	6 2/5	12 4/5	25 3/5	38 2/5
4 1/8	105	6 13/16	13 5/8	27 1/4	40 9/10
4 1/4	108	7 1/4	14 1/2	28 9/10	43 3/10
4 3/8	111	7 5/8	15 5/16	30 5/8	45 15/16
4 1/2	114	8 1/10	16 1/5	32 2/5	48 3/5
4 5/8	118	8 9/16	17 1/8	34 1/4	51 3/5
4 3/4	121	9	18	36 1/10	54 1/10
4 7/8	124	9 1/2	19	38	57
5	127	10	20	40	60
5 1/8	130	10 1/2	21	42	63
5 1/4	133	11	22	44 1/10	66 1/5
5 3/8	137	11 9/16	23	46	69 1/10
5 1/2	140	12 1/10	24 1/5	48 2/5	72 3/5
5 5/8	143	12 5/8	25 5/16	50 5/8	75 15/16
5 3/4	146	13 1/4	26 1/2	53	79 1/2
5 7/8	149	13 13/16	27 5/8	55 1/4	82 9/10
6	152	14 2/5	28 4/5	57 3/5	86 2/5

To simplify reading of the above, the horse-power figures are approximate, but correct within one-sixteenth.

ILLUSTRATIONS AND SPECIFICATIONS GASOLINE PASSENGER VEHICLES

CHALMERS MOTOR COMPANY

DETROIT MICHIGAN

Price $1650
Six-Passenger Touring 1725
Two- or Three-Passenger Coupelet . 1900
Five-Passenger Sedan 2750
Seven-Passenger Limousine . . . 3200

CHALMERS "LIGHT SIX" TOURING CAR "26-B"

COLOR	Body, blue; chassis, black	CAST	En bloc	
SEATING CAPACITY	Five persons	BORE	3½ inches	
CLUTCH	Multiple disc	STROKE	5½ inches	
WHEELBASE . .	126 inches	COOLING . . .	Water	
GAUGE	56 inches	RADIATOR . . .	Cellular	
TIRE DIMENSIONS:		IGNITION . . .	Jump spark	
FRONT . . .	34 x 4½ inches	ELECTRIC SOURCE .	Storage battery	
REAR	34 x 4½ inches	DRIVE	Shaft	
BRAKE SYSTEMS	Contracting and expanding on both rear wheels	TRANSMISSION . .	Selective sliding gear	
HORSE-POWER . .	N. A. C. C. (formerly A.L.A.M.) rating 29.4	GEAR CHANGES .	Three forward, one reverse	
CYLINDERS . . .	Six	POSITION OF DRIVER	Left-side drive and center control	
ARRANGED . . .	Vertically, under hood			

Price includes top, top hood, electric lighting, electric self-starter, windshield, speedometer and demountable rims

CHALMERS
MOTOR
COMPANY

DETROIT
MICHIGAN

Price	$1900
Five-Passenger Touring . .	1650
Six-Passenger Touring . .	1725
Five-Passenger Sedan . . .	2750
Seven-Passenger Limousine .	3200

CHALMERS "LIGHT SIX" COUPELET "26-B"

COLOR	Body panels, blue; chassis, black
SEATING CAPACITY	Two or three persons
CLUTCH	Multiple disc
WHEELBASE . .	126 inches
GAUGE	56 inches
TIRE DIMENSIONS:	
FRONT . . .	34 x 4½ inches
REAR	34 x 4½ inches
BRAKE SYSTEMS .	Contracting and expanding on both rear wheels
HORSE-POWER . .	N. A. C. C. (formerly A.L.A.M.) rating 29.4
CYLINDERS . . .	Six

ARRANGED . . .	Vertically, under hood
CAST	En bloc
BORE	3½ inches
STROKE	5½ inches
COOLING . . .	Water
RADIATOR . . .	Cellular
IGNITION . . .	Jump spark
ELECTRIC SOURCE .	Storage battery
DRIVE	Shaft
TRANSMISSION . .	Selective sliding gear
GEAR CHANGES .	Three forward, one reverse
POSITION OF DRIVER	Left-side drive and center control

Price includes electric lighting, electric self-starter, speedometer and demountable rims

CHALMERS
MOTOR
COMPANY

DETROIT
MICHIGAN

Price $3200
Five-Passenger Touring 1650
Six-Passenger Touring . . . 1725
Two- or Three-Passenger Coupelet . 1900
Five-Passenger Sedan 2750

CHALMERS "LIGHT SIX" LIMOUSINE "26-B"

COLOR	Body panels, blue; chassis, black	ARRANGED . . .	Vertically, under hood	
SEATING CAPACITY	Seven persons	CAST	En bloc	
CLUTCH	Multiple disc	BORE	3½ inches	
WHEELBASE . .	132 inches	STROKE	5¼ inches	
GAUGE	56 inches	COOLING . . .	Water	
TIRE DIMENSIONS:		RADIATOR . . .	Cellular	
FRONT . . .	35 x 5 inches	IGNITION . . .	Jump spark	
REAR	35 x 5 inches	ELECTRIC SOURCE .	Storage battery	
BRAKE SYSTEMS .	Contracting and expanding on both rear wheels	DRIVE	Shaft	
		TRANSMISSION . .	Selective sliding gear	
HORSE-POWER . .	N. A. C. C. (formerly A.L.A.M.) rating 29.4	GEAR CHANGES .	Three forward, one reverse	
CYLINDERS . . .	Six	POSITION OF DRIVER	Left-side drive and center control	

Price includes electric lighting, electric self-starter, speedometer and demountable rims

CHALMERS
MOTOR
COMPANY

DETROIT
MICHIGAN

Price $2400
Seven-Passenger Touring . 2400

CHALMERS "MASTER SIX" TORPEDO "29"

COLOR	Body, blue or gray; chassis, black	ARRANGED . . .	Vertically, under hood
SEATING CAPACITY	Five persons	CAST	In blocks of thre
CLUTCH	Multiple disc	BORE	4 inches
WHEELBASE . .	132 inches	STROKE	5½ inches
GAUGE	56 inches	COOLING . . .	Water
TIRE DIMENSIONS:		RADIATOR . . .	Cellular
FRONT . . .	36 x 4½ inches	IGNITION . . .	Jump spark
REAR	36 x 4½ inches	ELECTRIC SOURCE .	High-tension magneto
BRAKE SYSTEMS .	Contracting and expanding on both rear wheels	DRIVE	Shaft
		TRANSMISSION . .	Selective sliding gear
HORSE-POWER . .	N. A. C. C. (formerly A.L.A.M.) rating 38.4	GEAR CHANGES .	Four forward, one reverse
CYLINDERS . . .	Six	POSITION OF DRIVER	Left-side drive and center control

Price includes top, top hood, electric lighting, electric self-starter, windshield, speedometer and demountable rims

PREMIER MOTOR MANUFACTURING COMPANY

INDIANAPOLIS
INDIANA

Price $1985
Two-Passenger Roadster . 1985

PREMIER "6-50" TOURING CAR

COLOR	Blue-black		BORE	4 inches
SEATING CAPACITY	Seven persons		STROKE	5½ inches
CLUTCH . . .	Multiple disc		COOLING . . .	Water
WHEELBASE . .	132 inches		RADIATOR . . .	"V"-shaped honeycomb
GAUGE	56½ inches			
TIRE DIMENSIONS:			IGNITION . . .	Jump spark
FRONT . . .	36 x 4½ inches			
REAR	36 x 4½ inches		ELECTRIC SOURCE .	Generator and magneto
BRAKE SYSTEMS .	Contracting and expanding on both rear wheels		DRIVE	Shaft
HORSE-POWER . .	N. A. C. C. (formerly A.L.A.M.) rating 38.4		TRANSMISSION . .	Selective gear
			GEAR CHANGES .	Three forward, one reverse
CYLINDERS . . .	Six			
ARRANGED . . .	Vertically, under hood		POSITION OF DRIVER	Left-side drive and center control
CAST	In blocks of three			

Price includes top, top hood, electric lighting, electric self-
starter, windshield, speedometer and demountable rims

PREMIER MOTOR MANUFACTURING COMPANY

INDIANAPOLIS INDIANA

Price, $1985

PREMIER ROADSTER "6-49"

COLOR	Blue-black		CAST	In blocks of three
SEATING CAPACITY	Two persons		BORE	3⅝ inches
CLUTCH	Multiple disc		STROKE	5½ inches
WHEELBASE . .	132 inches		COOLING . . .	Water
GAUGE	56½ inches		RADIATOR . . .	Honeycomb
TIRE DIMENSIONS:			IGNITION . . .	Jump spark
FRONT . . .	36 x 4½ inches		ELECTRIC SOURCE .	High-tension magneto
REAR	36 x 4½ inches			
BRAKE SYSTEMS .	Contracting and expanding on both rear wheels		DRIVE	Shaft
			TRANSMISSION . .	Selective gear
HORSE-POWER . .	N. A. C. C. (formerly A.L.A.M.) rating 31.6		GEAR CHANGES .	Three forward, one reverse
			POSITION OF DRIVER	Left-side drive and center control
CYLINDERS . . .	Six			
ARRANGED . . .	Vertically, under hood			

Price includes top, top hood, electric lighting, electric self-starter, windshield, speedometer and demountable rims

**NORDYKE &
MARMON
COMPANY**

INDIANAPOLIS
INDIANA

Price	. $3250
Seven-Passenger Touring	. 3350
Four-Passenger Touring	. 3250
Two-Passenger Roadster	. 3250
Two-Passenger Speedster	. 3250

MARMON TOURING CAR "41"

COLOR	Body and running gear, blue-black; wheels, cream yellow	ARRANGED . . .	Vertically, under hood
SEATING CAPACITY	Five or seven persons	CAST	In blocks of three
		BORE	4¼ inches
		STROKE	5½ inches
CLUTCH	Cone	COOLING . . .	Water
WHEELBASE . .	132 inches	RADIATOR . . .	Honeycomb
GAUGE	56½ inches	IGNITION . . .	Jump spark
TIRE DIMENSIONS:		ELECTRIC SOURCE .	High-tension magneto and storage battery
FRONT . . .	36 x 4½ inches		
REAR	36 x 4½ inches	DRIVE	Shaft
BRAKE SYSTEMS .	Contracting and expanding on both rear wheels	TRANSMISSION . .	Selective sliding gear
		GEAR CHANGES .	Three forward, one reverse
HORSE-POWER . .	N. A. C. C. (formerly A.L.A.M.) rating 43.3	POSITION OF DRIVER	Left-side drive and center control
CYLINDERS . . .	Six		

Price includes top, top hood, electric lighting, electric self-starter, windshield, speedometer and demountable rims

NORDYKE &   Price, $5000
MARMON
COMPANY
INDIANAPOLIS
INDIANA

MARMON TOURING CAR "48"

COLOR	Blue-black	CAST	In pairs
SEATING CAPACITY	Seven persons	BORE	4½ inches
CLUTCH	Multiple disc	STROKE	6 inches
WHEELBASE . .	145 inches	COOLING . . .	Water
GAUGE	56½ inches	RADIATOR . . .	Honeycomb
TIRE DIMENSIONS:		IGNITION . . .	Jump spark
FRONT . . .	36 x 4½ inches	ELECTRIC SOURCE .	High-tension
REAR	37 x 5 inches		magneto and storage battery
BRAKE SYSTEMS .	Internal expanding on both rear wheels	DRIVE	Shaft
		TRANSMISSION . .	Selective sliding gear
HORSE-POWER . .	N. A. C. C. (formerly A.L.A.M.) rating 48.6	GEAR CHANGES .	Three forward, one reverse
CYLINDERS . . .	Six	POSITION OF DRIVER	Left-side drive and center control
ARRANGED . . .	Vertically, under hood		

Price includes top, top hood, electric lighting, electric self-starter, windshield, speedometer and demountable rims

APPERSON BROS. AUTOMOBILE COMPANY

KOKOMO INDIANA

Price, $1350

APPERSON JACK-RABBIT "FOUR-40"

COLOR	Elgar dark blue	CAST		En bloc
SEATING CAPACITY	Five persons	BORE		4 inches
CLUTCH	Compression band	STROKE		5 inches
		COOLING		Water
WHEELBASE	116 inches	RADIATOR		"V"-shaped honeycomb
GAUGE	56 inches			
TIRE DIMENSIONS:		IGNITION		Jump spark
FRONT	34 x 4 inches	ELECTRIC SOURCE		High-tension
REAR	34 x 4 inches			
BRAKE SYSTEMS	Contracting and expanding on both rear wheels	DRIVE		Shaft
		TRANSMISSION		Selective sliding gear
HORSE-POWER	N. A. C. C. (formerly A.L.A.M.) rating 25.6	GEAR CHANGES		Three forward, one reverse
CYLINDERS	Four	POSITION OF DRIVER		Left-side drive and center control
ARRANGED	Vertically, under hood			

Price includes top, top hood, electric lighting, electric self-starter, windshield, speedometer and demountable rims

APPERSON BROS.
AUTOMOBILE
COMPANY
KOKOMO
INDIANA

Price, $1485

APPERSON JACK-RABBIT "SIX-45"

COLOR	Elgar dark blue		CAST	En bloc
SEATING CAPACITY	Seven persons		BORE	3½ inches
CLUTCH	Compression band		STROKE	5⅛ inches
WHEELBASE . .	122 inches		COOLING . . .	Water
GAUGE	56 inches		RADIATOR . . .	"V"-shaped honeycomb
TIRE DIMENSIONS:			IGNITION . . .	Jump spark
FRONT . . .	34 x 4 inches		ELECTRIC SOURCE .	High-tension
REAR	34 x 4 inches			
BRAKE SYSTEMS .	Contracting and expanding on both rear wheels		DRIVE	Shaft
			TRANSMISSION . .	Selective sliding gear
HORSE-POWER . .	N. A. C. C. (formerly A.L.A.M.) rating 29.4		GEAR CHANGES .	Three forward, one reverse
CYLINDERS . . .	Six		POSITION OF DRIVER	Left-side drive and center control
ARRANGED . . .	Vertically, under hood			

Price includes top, top hood, electric lighting, electric self-starter, windshield, speedometer and demountable rims

**M c F A R L A N
M O T O R
C O M P A N Y**

C O N N E R S V I L L E
I N D I A N A

Price	$2590
Two-Passenger	2590
Four-Passenger	2590
Five-Passenger	2590
Six-Passenger	2590
Four-Passenger Coupe . .	3300
Seven-Passenger Limousine .	4000

McFARLAN "SIX," SERIES "T"

COLOR	Optional	CAST	En bloc
SEATING CAPACITY	Seven persons	BORE	4 inches
CLUTCH	Cone	STROKE	6 inches
WHEELBASE . .	132 inches	COOLING . . .	Water
GAUGE	56 inches	RADIATOR . . .	Cellular
TIRE DIMENSIONS:		IGNITION . . .	Jump spark
FRONT . . .	36 x 4½ inches	ELECTRIC SOURCE .	Storage battery and generator
REAR	36 x 4½ inches	DRIVE	Shaft
BRAKE SYSTEMS .	Contracting and expanding on both rear wheels	TRANSMISSION . .	Selective sliding gear
HORSE-POWER . .	N. A. C. C. (formerly A.L.A.M.) rating 38.4	GEAR CHANGES .	Three forward one reverse
CYLINDERS . . .	Six	POSITION OF DRIVER	Left-side drive and center control
ARRANGED . . .	Vertically, under hood		

Price includes top, top hood, electric lighting, electric self-
starter, windshield, speedometer and demountable rims

**NATIONAL
MOTOR VEHICLE
COMPANY**

**INDIANAPOLIS
INDIANA**

Price	$2500
Two-Passenger Roadster . . .	2375
Four-Passenger Toy Tonneau .	2375
Five-Passenger Touring . . .	2375
Four-Passenger Coupe	2850
Three-Passenger Cabriolet . .	2700
Four-Passenger "Parlor Car" .	2700

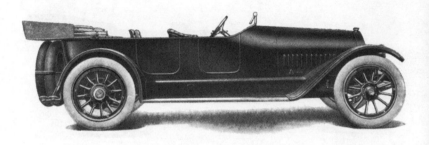

NATIONAL "SIX" TOURING CAR

COLOR	Optional	CAST	En bloc
SEATING CAPACITY	Six persons	BORE	3¾ inches
CLUTCH	Cone	STROKE	5½ inches
WHEELBASE . .	134 inches	COOLING . . .	Water
GAUGE	56 inches	RADIATOR . . .	Honeycomb
TIRE DIMENSIONS:		IGNITION . . .	Jump spark
FRONT . . .	37 x 5 inches	ELECTRIC SOURCE .	Storage battery
REAR	37 x 5 inches		
BRAKE SYSTEMS .	Contracting and expanding on both rear wheels	DRIVE	Shaft
		TRANSMISSION . .	Selective sliding gear
HORSE-POWER . .	N. A. C. C. (formerly A.L.A.M.) rating 33.7	GEAR CHANGES .	Three forward, one reverse
CYLINDERS . . .	Six		
ARRANGED . . .	Vertically, under hood	POSITION OF DRIVER	Left-side drive and center control

Price includes top, top hood, electric lighting, electric self-starter, windshield, speedometer and demountable rims

STUTZ MOTOR CAR COMPANY

INDIANAPOLIS
INDIANA

Price . .	$2000
Bearcat .	2000
Coupe . .	2600
Bulldog .	2250
Touring .	2275
Sedan . .	3675

STUTZ ROADSTER "4-F"

COLOR	Vermilion, Mercedes red or Monitor gray
SEATING CAPACITY	Two persons
CLUTCH	Cone
WHEELBASE . .	120 inches
GAUGE	56 inches
TIRE DIMENSIONS:	
FRONT . . .	34 x 4½ inches
REAR	34 x 4½ inches
BRAKE SYSTEMS .	Internal expanding on both rear wheels
HORSE-POWER . .	N. A. C. C. (formerly A.L.A.M.) rating 36.1
CYLINDERS . . .	Four
ARRANGED . . .	Vertically, under hood

CAST	In pairs
BORE	4¾ inches
STROKE	5½ inches
COOLING . . .	Water
RADIATOR . . .	Cellular
IGNITION . . .	Jump spark
ELECTRIC SOURCE .	High-tension magneto and storage battery
DRIVE	Shaft
TRANSMISSION . .	Selective sliding gear
GEAR CHANGES .	Three forward, one reverse
POSITION OF DRIVER	Right-side drive and right-hand control

Price includes electric self-starter, speedometer and demountable rims

STUTZ MOTOR
CAR COMPANY

INDIANAPLOIS
I N D I A N A

Price . .	$2400
Sedan . .	3800
Touring .	2275
Coupe . .	2850
Roadster .	2250
Bearcat .	2250

STUTZ TOURING CAR "6-F"

COLOR	Blue and maroon	CAST	In blocks of three
SEATING CAPACITY	Six persons	BORE	4 inches
CLUTCH	Cone	STROKE	5 inches
WHEELBASE . .	130 inches	COOLING . . .	Water
GAUGE	56 inches	RADIATOR . . .	Cellular
TIRE DIMENSIONS:		IGNITION . . .	Jump spark
FRONT . . .	34 x 4½ inches	ELECTRIC SOURCE .	High-tension magneto and storage battery
REAR	34 x 4½ inches		
BRAKE SYSTEMS .	Internal expanding on both rear wheels	DRIVE	Shaft
		TRANSMISSION . .	Selective sliding gear
HORSE-POWER . .	N. A. C. C. (formerly A.L.A.M.) rating 38.4	GEAR CHANGES .	Three forward, one reverse
CYLINDERS . . .	Six	POSITION OF DRIVER	Right-side drive and right-hand control
ARRANGED . . .	Vertically, under hood		

Price includes top, top hood, electric lighting, electric self-starter, windshield, speedometer and demountable rims

MOTOR CAR
MANUFACTUR-
ING COMPANY
INDIANAPOLIS
INDIANA

Price $2322
Four-Passenger Roadster . 2222

PATHFINDER TOURING CAR "7-B"

COLOR	Dark blue	CAST	In blocks of three
SEATING CAPACITY	Seven persons	BORE	3¾ inches
CLUTCH	Multiple disc	STROKE	5¼ inches
WHEELBASE . .	124 inches	COOLING . . .	Water
GAUGE	56 inches	RADIATOR . . .	V-shaped cellular
TIRE DIMENSIONS:		IGNITION . . .	Jump spark
FRONT . . .	34 x 4½ inches	ELECTRIC SOURCE .	Storage battery
REAR	34 x 4½ inches	DRIVE	Shaft
BRAKE SYSTEMS .	Expanding on both rear wheels	TRANSMISSION . .	Selective sliding gear
HORSE-POWER . .	N. A. C. C. (formerly A.L.A.M.) rating 33.7	GEAR CHANGES .	Four forward, one reverse
CYLINDERS . . .	Six	POSITION OF DRIVER	Left-side drive and center control
ARRANGED . . .	Vertically, under hood		

Price includes top, top hood, electric lighting, electric self-
starter, windshield, speedometer and demountable rims

MOLINE
AUTOMOBILE
COMPANY

EAST MOLINE
ILLINOIS

Price	.	.	.	$2500
Roadster	.	.	2500
Limousine	.	3800
Sedan	.	.	3250

MOLINE-KNIGHT TOURING CAR

COLOR	Blue-black	CAST	En bloc
SEATING CAPACITY	Five or seven persons	BORE	4 inches
		STROKE	6 inches
CLUTCH	Cone	COOLING . . .	Water
WHEELBASE . .	128 inches	RADIATOR . . .	Tubular
GAUGE	56 inches	IGNITION . . .	Jump spark
TIRE DIMENSIONS:		ELECTRIC SOURCE .	High-tension magneto and dry batteries
FRONT . . .	36 x 4½ inches		
REAR	36 x 4½ inches		
BRAKE SYSTEMS .	Contracting and expanding on both rear wheels	DRIVE	Shaft
		TRANSMISSION . .	Selective sliding gear
HORSE-POWER . .	N. A. C. C. (formerly A.L.A.M.) rating 25.6	GEAR CHANGES .	Four forward, one reverse
CYLINDERS . . .	Four	POSITION OF DRIVER	Left-side drive and center control
ARRANGED . . .	Vertically, under hood		

Price includes top, top hood, electric lighting, electric self-starter, windshield, speedometer and demountable rims

M O L I N E   Price . . $2500
AUTOMOBILE   Touring .   2500
C O M P A N Y   Limousine . 3800
                     Sedan . . 3250
E A S T   M O L I N E
I L L I N O I S

MOLINE-KNIGHT ROADSTER

COLOR	Blue-black
SEATING CAPACITY	Two persons
CLUTCH	Cone
WHEELBASE . .	128 inches
GAUGE	56 inches
TIRE DIMENSIONS:	
FRONT . . .	36 x 4½ inches
REAR	36 x 4½ inches
BRAKE SYSTEMS .	Contracting and expanding on both rear wheels
HORSE-POWER . .	N. A. C. C. (formerly A.L.A.M.) rating 25.6
CYLINDERS . . .	Four
ARRANGED . . .	Vertically, under hood

CAST	En bloc
BORE	4 inches
STROKE	6 inches
COOLING . . .	Water
RADIATOR . . .	Tubular
IGNITION . . .	Jump spark
ELECTRIC SOURCE .	High-tension magneto and dry batteries
DRIVE	Shaft
TRANSMISSION . .	Selective sliding gear
GEAR CHANGES .	Four forward, one reverse
POSITION OF DRIVER	Left-side drive and center control

Price includes top, top hood, electric lighting, electric self-starter, windshield, speedometer and demountable rims

**H. H. FRANKLIN
MANUFACTUR-
ING COMPANY**

**S Y R A C U S E
N E W   Y O R K**

Price .   . $2150
Touring .   2150
Coupe .   . 2600
Sedan .   . 3000
Berlin .   . 3200

FRANKLIN "SIX-30" ROADSTER

COLOR	Brewster green with black mud-guards	
SEATING CAPACITY	Two persons	
CLUTCH	Multiple disc	
WHEELBASE . .	120 inches	
GAUGE	56 inches	
TIRE DIMENSIONS:		
FRONT . . .	34 x 4½ inches	
REAR . . .	34 x 4½ inches	
BRAKE SYSTEMS .	Contracting on transmission and both rear wheels	
HORSE-POWER . .	N. A. C. C. (formerly A.L.A.M.) rating 31.6	
CYLINDERS . . .	Six	
ARRANGED . . .	Vertically, under hood	

CAST	Separately
BORE	3⅝ inches
STROKE	4 inches
COOLING . . .	Air
IGNITION . . .	Jump spark
ELECTRIC SOURCE .	High-tension magneto
DRIVE	Shaft
TRANSMISSION . .	Selective sliding gear
GEAR CHANGES .	Three forward, one reverse
POSITION OF DRIVER	Left-side drive and center control

Price includes top, top hood, electric lighting,
electric self-starter, windshield and speedometer

H. H. FRANKLIN
MANUFACTUR-
ING COMPANY

S Y R A C U S E
N E W   Y O R K

Price   . . $2150
Roadster . 2150
Coupe   . 2600
Sedan . . 3000
Berlin   . 3200

FRANKLIN "SIX-30" TOURING CAR

COLOR . . . . Brewster green, with black mud guards
SEATING CAPACITY Five persons
CLUTCH . . . . Multiple disc
WHEELBASE . . 120 inches
GAUGE . . . . 56 inches
TIRE DIMENSIONS:
  FRONT . . . 34 x 4½ inches
  REAR . . . . 34 x 4½ inches
BRAKE SYSTEMS . Contracting on transmission and both rear wheels
HORSE-POWER . . N. A. C. C. (formerly A.L.A.M.) rating 31.6
CYLINDERS . . . Six

ARRANGED . . . Vertically, under hood
CAST . . . . . Separately
BORE . . . . . 3⅝ inches
STROKE . . . . 4 inches
COOLING . . . Air
IGNITION . . . Jump spark
ELECTRIC SOURCE . High-tension magneto
DRIVE . . . . Shaft
TRANSMISSION . . Selective sliding gear
GEAR CHANGES . Three forward, one reverse
POSITION OF DRIVER Left-side drive and center control

Price includes top, top hood, electric lighting, electric self-starter, windshield and speedometer

LYONS-ATLAS
COMPANY

INDIANAPOLIS
INDIANA

Price $2980
Five-Passenger Touring Car . . 2900
Five-Passenger Sedan 3900
Seven-Passenger Limousine . . 4300
Seven-Passenger Berline Limousine 4300

LYONS-KNIGHT TOURING CAR "K-4"

COLOR	Optional	CAST	In pairs
SEATING CAPACITY	Seven persons	BORE	4½ inches
CLUTCH	Dry plate	STROKE	5½ inches
WHEELBASE . .	130 inches	COOLING . . .	Water
GAUGE	56 inches	RADIATOR . . .	Honeycomb
TIRE DIMENSIONS:		IGNITION . . .	Jump spark
FRONT . . .	37 x 5 inches	ELECTRIC SOURCE .	High-tension magneto and dry batteries
REAR	37 x 5 inches		
BRAKE SYSTEMS .	Contracting and expanding on both rear wheels	DRIVE	Worm
		TRANSMISSION . .	Selective sliding gear
HORSE-POWER . .	N. A. C. C. (formerly A.L.A.M.) rating 32.4	GEAR CHANGES .	Three forward, one reverse
CYLINDERS . . .	Four	POSITION OF DRIVER	Left-side drive and center control
ARRANGED . . .	Vertically, under hood		

Price includes top, top hood, electric lighting, electric self-
starter, windshield, speedometer and demountable rims

HAYNES
AUTOMOBILE
COMPANY
KOKOMO
INDIANA

Price . . $1485
Roadster . 1485

HAYNES TOURING CAR "30"

COLOR	Body, black or green; running gear, black	CAST	En bloc
		BORE	3½ inches
SEATING CAPACITY	Five persons	STROKE	5 inches
CLUTCH	Multiple disc	COOLING . . .	Water
WHEELBASE . .	121 inches		
GAUGE	56 inches	RADIATOR . . .	Cellular
TIRE DIMENSIONS:		IGNITION . . .	Jump spark
FRONT . . .	34 x 4 inches	ELECTRIC SOURCE .	Generator
REAR	34 x 4 inches		
BRAKE SYSTEMS	Internal expanding on both rear wheels	DRIVE	Shaft
		TRANSMISSION . .	Selective sliding gear
HORSE-POWER . .	N. A. C. C. (formerly A.L.A.M.) rating 29.4	GEAR CHANGES .	Three forward, one reverse
CYLINDERS . . .	Six	POSITION OF DRIVER	Left-side drive and center control
ARRANGED . . .	Vertically, under hood		

Price includes top, top hood, electric lighting, electric self-starter, windshield, speedometer and demountable rims

**H A Y N E S
AUTOMOBILE
C O M P A N Y**

**K O K O M O
I N D I A N A**

Price . . . **\$1485**
Touring Car . 1485

HAYNES ROADSTER "30"

COLOR	Body, black or green; running gear, black	ARRANGED . . .	Vertically, under hood
		CAST .	En bloc
SEATING CAPACITY	Two persons	BORE	3½ inches
CLUTCH	Multiple disc	STROKE	5 inches
WHEELBASE . .	121 inches	COOLING . . .	Water
GAUGE	56 inches	RADIATOR . . .	Cellular
TIRE DIMENSIONS:		IGNITION . . .	Jump spark
FRONT . . .	34 x 4 inches	ELECTRIC SOURCE .	Generator
REAR . . .	34 x 4 inches	DRIVE	Shaft
BRAKE SYSTEMS .	Internal expanding on both rear wheels	TRANSMISSION . .	Selective sliding gear
		GEAR CHANGES .	Three forward, one reverse
HORSE-POWER . .	N. A. C. C. (formerly A.L.A.M.) rating 29.4	POSITION OF DRIVER	Left-side drive and center control
CYLINDERS . . .	Six		

Price includes top, top hood, electric lighting, electric self-
starter, windshield, speedometer and demountable rims

HUPP MOTOR
CAR COMPANY

Price . . $1200
Touring . 1200

D E T R O I T
M I C H I G A N

HUPMOBILE ROADSTER "K"

COLOR	Body, blue-black; running gear, maroon		ARRANGED . . .	Vertically, under hood
SEATING CAPACITY	Two persons		CAST	En bloc
CLUTCH	Multiple disc		BORE	3⅜ inches
WHEELBASE . .	119 inches		STROKE	5½ inches
GAUGE	56 or 60 inches		COOLING . . .	Water
TIRE DIMENSIONS:			RADIATOR . . .	Cellular
FRONT . . .	34 x 4 inches		IGNITION . . .	Jump spark
REAR	34 x 4 inches		ELECTRIC SOURCE .	Generator and storage battery
BRAKE SYSTEMS .	Contracting and expanding on both rear wheels		DRIVE	Shaft
			TRANSMISSION . .	Selective sliding gear
HORSE-POWER . .	N. A. C. C. (formerly A.L.A.M.) rating 18.2		GEAR CHANGES .	Three forward, one reverse
CYLINDERS . . .	Four		POSITION OF DRIVER	Left-side drive and center control

Price includes top, top hood, electric lighting, electric self-starter, windshield, speedometer and demountable rims

HUPP MOTOR
CAR COMPANY

Price . . $1200
Roadster . 1200

D E T R O I T
M I C H I G A N

HUPMOBILE TOURING CAR "K"

COLOR	Body, blue-black; running gear, maroon	ARRANGED . . .	Vertically, under hood
SEATING CAPACITY	Five persons	CAST	En bloc
CLUTCH	Multiple disc	BORE	3⅜ inches
WHEELBASE . .	119 inches	STROKE	5½ inches
GAUGE	56 or 60 inches	COOLING . . .	Water
		RADIATOR . . .	Cellular
TIRE DIMENSIONS:		IGNITION . . .	Jump spark
FRONT . . .	34 x 4 inches	ELECTRIC SOURCE .	Generator and storage battery
REAR	34 x 4 inches	DRIVE	Shaft
BRAKE SYSTEMS .	Contracting and expanding on both rear wheels	TRANSMISSION . .	Selective sliding gear
HORSE-POWER . .	N. A. C. C. (formerly A.L.A.M.) rating 18.2	GEAR CHANGES .	Three forward, one reverse
		POSITION OF DRIVER	Left-side drive and center control
CYLINDERS . . .	Four		

Price includes top, top hood, electric lighting, electric self-
starter, windshield, speedometer and demountable rims

CADILLAC
MOTOR CAR
COMPANY

DETROIT
MICHIGAN

Price, $1975

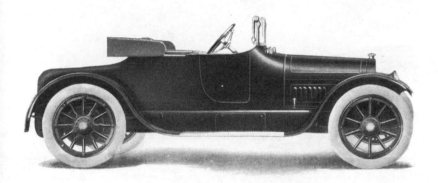

CADILLAC ROADSTER

COLOR	. . . .	Royal green, black trimming	CAST	. . . .	In blocks of four
SEATING CAPACITY		Two persons	BORE	. . . .	3⅛ inches
CLUTCH	. . . .	Multiple disc	STROKE	. . . .	5⅛ inches
WHEELBASE	. .	122 inches	COOLING	. . .	Water
GAUGE	. . . .	56 inches	RADIATOR	. . .	Tubular and plate
TIRE DIMENSIONS:			IGNITION	. . .	Jump spark
FRONT	. . .	36 x 4½ inches	ELECTRIC SOURCE	.	Generator and dry cells
REAR	. . . .	36 x 4½ inches			
BRAKE SYSTEMS	.	Contracting and expanding on both rear wheels	DRIVE	. . . .	Shaft
			TRANSMISSION	. .	Selective sliding gear
HORSE-POWER	. .	N. A. C. C. (formerly A.L.A.M.) rating 31.2	GEAR CHANGES	.	Three forward, one reverse
CYLINDERS	. . .	Eight	POSITION OF DRIVER		Left-side drive and center control
ARRANGED	. . .	V type, 90°, under hood			

Price includes top, top hood, electric lighting, electric self-starter, windshield, speedometer and demountable rims

CADILLAC
MOTOR CAR
COMPANY

DETROIT
MICHIGAN

Price $1975
Seven-Passenger . . . 1975
Five-Passenger Salon . 1975

CADILLAC FIVE-PASSENGER TOURING CAR

COLOR	Royal green, black trimming
SEATING CAPACITY	Five persons
CLUTCH	Multiple disc
WHEELBASE . .	122 inches
GAUGE	56 inches
TIRE DIMENSIONS:	
FRONT . . .	36 x 4½ inches
REAR	36 x 4½ inches
BRAKE SYSTEMS .	Contracting and expanding on both rear wheels
HORSE-POWER . .	N. A. C. C. (formerly A.L.A.M.) rating 31.2
CYLINDERS . . .	Eight
ARRANGED . . .	V type, 90°, under hood

CAST	In blocks of four
BORE	3⅛ inches
STROKE	5⅛ inches
COOLING . . .	Water
RADIATOR . . .	Tubular and plate
IGNITION . . .	Jump spark
ELECTRIC SOURCE .	Generator and dry cells
DRIVE	Shaft
TRANSMISSION . .	Selective sliding gear
GEAR CHANGES .	Three forward, one reverse
POSITION OF DRIVER	Left-side drive and center control

Price includes top, top hood, electric lighting, electric self-
starter, windshield, speedometer and demountable rims

CADILLAC
MOTOR CAR
COMPANY

DETROIT
MICHIGAN

Price, $2500

CADILLAC LANDAULET COUPE

COLOR	Royal green with black trimming		CAST	In blocks of four	
SEATING CAPACITY	Three persons		BORE	3⅛ inches	
CLUTCH	Multiple disc		STROKE	5⅛ inches	
WHEELBASE . .	122 inches		COOLING . . .	Water	
GAUGE	56 inches		RADIATOR . . .	Tubular and plate	
TIRE DIMENSIONS:			IGNITION . . .	Jump spark	
FRONT . . .	36 x 4½ inches		ELECTRIC SOURCE .	Generator and dry cells	
REAR	36 x 4½ inches				
BRAKE SYSTEMS .	Contracting and expanding on both rear wheels		DRIVE	Shaft	
HORSE-POWER . .	N. A. C. C. (formerly A.L.A.M.) rating 31.2		TRANSMISSION . .	Selective sliding gear	
			GEAR CHANGES .	Three forward, one reverse	
CYLINDERS . . .	Eight				
ARRANGED . . .	V type, 90°, under hood		POSITION OF DRIVER	Left-side drive and center control	

Price includes electric lighting, electric self-starter, windshield, speedometer and demountable rims

CADILLAC
MOTOR CAR
COMPANY

DETROIT
MICHIGAN

Price, $2800

CADILLAC SEDAN

COLOR	Royal green with black trimming
SEATING CAPACITY	Five persons
CLUTCH	Multiple disc
WHEELBASE . .	122 inches
GAUGE	56 inches
TIRE DIMENSIONS:	
FRONT . . .	36 x 4½ inches
REAR	36 x 4½ inches
BRAKE SYSTEMS .	Contracting and expanding on both rear wheels
HORSE-POWER . .	N. A. C. C. (formerly A.L.A.M.) rating 31.2
CYLINDERS . . .	Eight
ARRANGED . . .	V type, 90°, under hood

CAST	In blocks of four
BORE	3⅛ inches
STROKE	5⅛ inches
COOLING . . .	Water
RADIATOR . . .	Tubular and plate
IGNITION . . .	Jump spark
ELECTRIC SOURCE .	Generator and dry cells
DRIVE	Shaft
TRANSMISSION . .	Selective sliding gear
GEAR CHANGES .	Three forward, one reverse
POSITION OF DRIVER	Left-side drive and center control

Price includes electric lighting, electric self-starter,
windshield, speedometer and demountable rims

C A D I L L A C
M O T O R   C A R
C O M P A N Y

D E T R O I T
M I C H I G A N

Price $3600
Standard Limousine . 3450

CADILLAC BERLINE LIMOUSINE

COLOR	Royal green, black trimming
SEATING CAPACITY	Seven persons
CLUTCH	Multiple disc
WHEELBASE . .	122 inches
GAUGE	56 inches
TIRE DIMENSIONS:	
FRONT . . .	36 x 4½ inches
REAR	36 x 4½ inches
BRAKE SYSTEMS .	Contracting and expanding on both rear wheels
HORSE-POWER . .	N. A. C. C. (formerly A.L.A.M.) rating 31.2
CYLINDERS . . .	Eight
ARRANGED . . .	V Type, 90°, under hood

CAST	In blocks of four
BORE	3⅛ inches
STROKE	5⅛ inches
COOLING . . .	Water
RADIATOR . . .	Tubular and plate
IGNITION . . .	Jump spark
ELECTRIC SOURCE .	Generator and dry cells
DRIVE	Shaft
TRANSMISSION . .	Selective sliding gear
GEAR CHANGES .	Three forward, one reverse
POSITION OF DRIVER	Left-side drive and center control

Price includes electric lighting, electric self-starter,
windshield, speedometer and demountable rims

SPEEDWELL MOTOR CAR COMPANY

DAYTON, OHIO

Price	$2850
Two-Passenger . .	2850
Four-Passenger . .	2850
Six-Passenger . .	2950
Seven-Passenger .	2950

SPEEDWELL ROTARY TOURING CAR "B," SERIES "I"

COLOR	Body and wheels, Brewster green; chassis, hood and fenders, black	ARRANGED . . .	Vertically, under hood
		CAST	In blocks of three
SEATING CAPACITY	Five persons	BORE	4⅛ inches
CLUTCH	Multiple disc	STROKE	5¼ inches
WHEELBASE . .	135 inches	COOLING . . .	Water
GAUGE	56 inches	RADIATOR . . .	Cellular
TIRE DIMENSIONS:		IGNITION . . .	Jump spark
FRONT . . .	36 x 4½ inches	ELECTRIC SOURCE .	Storage battery and generator
REAR	36 x 4½ inches		
BRAKE SYSTEMS .	Contracting and expanding on both rear wheels	DRIVE	Shaft
		TRANSMISSION . .	Selective sliding gear
HORSE-POWER . .	N. A. C. C. (formerly A.L.A.M.) rating 40.9	GEAR CHANGES .	Three forward, one reverse
		POSITION OF DRIVER	Left-side drive and center control
CYLINDERS . . .	Six		

Price includes top, top hood, electric lighting, electric self-
starter, windshield, speedometer and demountable rims

**PIERCE-ARROW
MOTOR CAR CO.**

B U F F A L O
N E W   Y O R K

Price	**$4300**
Two-Passenger Runabout . . .	4300
Two-Passenger Coupe Runabout .	4575
Coupe	5000
Four-Passenger Touring	4300
Brougham	5200
Landaulet	5200
Sedan	5200
Brougham-Landaulet	5200
Vestibule Brougham	5350
Vestibule Landaulet	5350
Vestibule Brougham-Landaulet .	5350

PIERCE-ARROW TOURING CAR "38-C-3"

COLOR	Optional	CAST	In pairs
SEATING CAPACITY	Five persons	BORE	4 inches
CLUTCH	Cone	STROKE	5½ inches
WHEELBASE . .	134 inches	COOLING . . .	Water
GAUGE	56 inches	RADIATOR . . .	Cellular
TIRE DIMENSIONS:		IGNITION . . .	Jump spark
FRONT . . .	36 x 4½ inches	ELECTRIC SOURCE .	High-tension
REAR	36 x 4½ inches		magneto and
BRAKE SYSTEMS .	Contracting and		storage battery
	expanding on	DRIVE	Shaft
	both rear wheels	TRANSMISSION . .	Selective sliding
HORSE-POWER . .	N. A. C. C. (for-		gear
	merly A.L.A.M.)	GEAR CHANGES .	Four forward,
	rating 38.4		one reverse
CYLINDERS . . .	Six	POSITION OF DRIVER	Right-side drive
ARRANGED . . .	Vertically,		and right-hand
	under hood		control

Price includes top, top hood, electric lighting, electric self-
starter, windshield, speedometer and demountable rims

**PIERCE-ARROW
MOTOR CAR CO.**

**B U F F A L O
N E W   Y O R K**

Price	$4300
Two-Passenger Coupe Runabout	4575
Four-Passenger Touring	4300
Coupe	5000
Five-Passenger Touring	4300
Brougham	5200
Landaulet	5200
Sedan	5200
Brougham-Landaulet	5200
Vestibule Brougham . . .	5350
Vestibule Landaulet	5350
Vestibule Brougham-Landaulet	5350

PIERCE-ARROW RUNABOUT "38-C-3"

COLOR	Optional	CAST	In pairs
SEATING CAPACITY	Two persons	BORE	4 inches
CLUTCH	Cone	STROKE	5½ inches
WHEELBASE . .	134 inches	COOLING . . .	Water
GAUGE	56 inches	RADIATOR . . .	Cellular
TIRE DIMENSIONS:		IGNITION . . .	Jump spark
FRONT . . .	36 x 4½ inches	ELECTRIC SOURCE .	High-tension magneto and storage battery
REAR	36 x 4½ inches		
BRAKE SYSTEMS .	Contracting and expanding on both rear wheels	DRIVE	Shaft
		TRANSMISSION . .	Selective sliding gear
HORSE-POWER . .	N. A. C. C. (formerly A.L.A.M.) rating 38.4	GEAR CHANGES .	Four forward, one reverse
CYLINDERS . . .	Six	POSITION OF DRIVER	Right-side drive and right-hand control
ARRANGED . . .	Vertically, under hood		

Price includes top, top hood, electric lighting, electric self-
starter, windshield, speedometer and demountable rims

**PIERCE-ARROW
MOTOR CAR CO.**

B U F F A L O
N E W   Y O R K

Price	. . . .	$4575
Two-Passenger Runabout	. . .	4300
Four-Passenger Touring	. . .	4300
Coupe	. . . .	5000
Five-Passenger Touring	. . .	4300
Brougham	. . . .	5200
Brougham-Landaulet	. . . .	5200
Vestibule Brougham	. . . .	5350
Vestibule Landaulet	. . . .	5350
Vestibule Brougham-Landaulet	.	5350
Landaulet	. . . . . .	5200
Sedan	. . . .	5200

PIERCE-ARROW COUPE-RUNABOUT "38-C-3"

COLOR	. . . .	Optional
SEATING CAPACITY		Two persons
CLUTCH	. . . .	Cone
WHEELBASE	. .	134 inches
GAUGE	. . . .	56 inches
TIRE DIMENSIONS:		
FRONT	. . .	36 x 4½ inches
REAR	. . . .	36 x 4½ inches
BRAKE SYSTEMS	.	Contracting and expanding on both rear wheels
HORSE-POWER	. .	N. A. C. C. (formerly A.L.A.M.) rating 38.4
CYLINDERS	. . .	Six
ARRANGED	. . .	Vertically, under hood

CAST	. . . .	In pairs
BORE	. . . .	4 inches
STROKE	. . . .	5½ inches
COOLING	. . .	Water
RADIATOR	. . .	Cellular
IGNITION	. . .	Jump spark
ELECTRIC SOURCE	.	High-tension magneto and storage battery
DRIVE	. . . .	Shaft
TRANSMISSION	. .	Selective sliding gear
GEAR CHANGES	.	Four forward, one reverse
POSITION OF DRIVER		Right-side drive and right-hand control

Price includes electric lighting, electric self-starter,
windshield, speedometer and demountable rims

PIERCE-ARROW MOTOR CAR CO.

B U F F A L O
N E W   Y O R K

Price												$5200
Two-Passenger Runabout												4300
Two-Passenger Coupe Runabout												4575
Coupe												5000
Four-Passenger Touring												4300
Five-Passenger Touring												4300
Landaulet												5200
Sedan												5200
Brougham-Landaulet												5200
Vestibule Brougham												5350
Vestibule Landaulet												5350
Vestibule Brougham-Landaulet												5350

PIERCE-ARROW BROUGHAM "38-C-3"

COLOR	Optional	CAST	In pairs
SEATING CAPACITY	Seven persons	BORE	4 inches
CLUTCH	Cone	STROKE	5½ inches
WHEELBASE	134 inches	COOLING	Water
GAUGE	56 inches	RADIATOR	Cellular
TIRE DIMENSIONS:		IGNITION	Jump spark
FRONT	36 x 4½ inches	ELECTRIC SOURCE	High-tension magneto and storage battery
REAR	36 x 4½ inches		
BRAKE SYSTEMS	Contracting and expanding on both rear wheels	DRIVE	Shaft
		TRANSMISSION	Selective sliding gear
HORSE-POWER	N. A. C. C. (formerly A.L.A.M.) rating 38.4	GEAR CHANGES	Four forward, one reverse
CYLINDERS	Six	POSITION OF DRIVER	Right-side drive and right-hand control
ARRANGED	Vertically, under hood		

Price includes electric lighting, electric self-starter, windshield, speedometer and demountable rims

PIERCE-ARROW
MOTOR CAR CO.

B U F F A L O
N E W   Y O R K

Price		$5200
Two-Passenger Runabout	. .	4300
Two-Passenger Coupe Runabout	.	4575
Coupe	. . . .	5000
Four-Passenger Touring	. . .	4300
Five-Passenger Touring	. . . .	4300
Brougham	. . . . . .	5200
Landaulet	. . . . .	5200
Sedan	. . . . . .	5200
Vestibule Brougham	. . . .	5350
Vestibule Landaulet	. . . . .	5350
Vestibule Brougham-Landaulet	.	5350

PIERCE-ARROW BROUGHAM-LANDAULET "38-C-3"

COLOR	Optional
SEATING CAPACITY	Seven persons
CLUTCH	Cone
WHEELBASE . .	134 inches
GAUGE	56 inches
TIRE DIMENSIONS:	
FRONT . . .	36 x 4½ inches
REAR . . .	36 x 4½ inches
BRAKE SYSTEMS .	Contracting and expanding on both rear wheels
HORSE-POWER . .	N. A. C. C. (formerly A.L.A.M.) rating 38.4
CYLINDERS . . .	Six
ARRANGED . . .	Vertically, under hood

CAST	In pairs
BORE	4 inches
STROKE	5½ inches
COOLING . . .	Water
RADIATOR . . .	Cellular
IGNITION . . .	Jump spark
ELECTRIC SOURCE .	High-tension magneto and storage battery
DRIVE	Shaft
TRANSMISSION . .	Selective sliding gear
GEAR CHANGES .	Four forward, one reverse
POSITION OF DRIVER	Right-side drive and right-hand control

Price includes electric lighting, electric self-starter, windshield, speedometer and demountable rims

**PIERCE-ARROW
MOTOR CAR CO.**

**B U F F A L O
N E W   Y O R K**

Price		$6000
Two-Passenger Runabout	. .	4900
Two-Passenger Coupe Runabout	.	5175
Coupe	.	5700
Four-Passenger Touring	. .	4900
Five-Passenger Touring	. .	4900
Seven-Passenger Touring	. .	5000
Landau	.	6000
Brougham . . .	.	5800
Suburban-Landau .	.	6000
Vestibule Suburban	. .	6200
Vestibule Landau	. .	6200
Vestibule Brougham	. .	5950
Vestibule Suburban-Landau	.	6200

PIERCE-ARROW SUBURBAN "48-B-3"

COLOR	Optional		CAST	In pairs
SEATING CAPACITY	Seven persons		BORE	4½ inches
CLUTCH	Cone		STROKE	5½ inches
WHEELBASE . .	142 inches		COOLING . . .	Water
GAUGE	56 inches		RADIATOR . . .	Cellular
TIRE DIMENSIONS:			IGNITION . . .	Jump spark
FRONT . . .	37 x 5 inches		ELECTRIC SOURCE .	High-tension magneto and storage battery
REAR	37 x 5 inches			
BRAKE SYSTEMS .	Contracting and expanding on both rear wheels		DRIVE	Shaft
			TRANSMISSION . .	Selective sliding gear
HORSE-POWER . .	N. A. C. C. (formerly A.L.A.M.) rating 48.6		GEAR CHANGES .	Four forward, one reverse
CYLINDERS . . .	Six		POSITION OF DRIVER	Right-side drive and right-hand control
ARRANGED . . .	Vertically, under hood			

Price includes electric lighting, electric self-starter,
windshield, speedometer and demountable rims

**PIERCE-ARROW
MOTOR CAR CO.**

B U F F A L O
N E W   Y O R K

Price	$4900
Two-Passenger Runabout	4900
Two-Passenger Coupe Runabout	5175
Coupe	5700
Four-Passenger Touring	4900
Seven-Passenger Touring	5000
Suburban	6000
Landau	6000
Brougham	5800
Suburban-Landau	6000
Vestibule Suburban	6200
Vestibule Landau	6200
Vestibule Brougham	5950
Vestibule Suburban-Landau	6200

PIERCE-ARROW TOURING CAR "48-B-3"

COLOR	Optional	CAST	In pairs
SEATING CAPACITY	Five persons	BORE	4½ inches
CLUTCH	Cone	STROKE	5½ inches
WHEELBASE	142 inches	COOLING	Water
GAUGE	56 inches	RADIATOR	Cellular
TIRE DIMENSIONS:		IGNITION	Jump spark
FRONT	37 x 5 inches	ELECTRIC SOURCE	High-tension magneto and storage battery
REAR	37 x 5 inches		
BRAKE SYSTEMS	Contracting and expanding on both rear wheels	DRIVE	Shaft
		TRANSMISSION	Selective sliding gear
HORSE-POWER	N. A. C. C. (formerly A.L.A.M.) rating 48.6	GEAR CHANGES	Four forward, one reverse
CYLINDERS	Six	POSITION OF DRIVER	Right-side drive and right-hand control
ARRANGED	Vertically, under hood		

Price includes top, top hood, electric lighting, electric self-
starter windshield, speedometer and demountable rims

PIERCE-ARROW
MOTOR CAR CO.

B U F F A L O
N E W   Y O R K

Price	$6000
Two-Passenger Runabout . . .	4900
Two-Passenger Coupe Runabout .	5175
Coupe	5700
Four-Passenger Touring	4900
Five-Passenger Touring	4900
Seven-Passenger Touring	5000
Suburban	6000
Landau	6000
Brougham	5800
Vestibule Suburban	6200
Vestibule Landau	6200
Vestibule Brougham	5950
Vestibule Suburban-Landau .	6200

PIERCE-ARROW SUBURBAN-LANDAU "48-B-3"

COLOR	Optional		CAST	In pairs
SEATING CAPACITY	Seven persons		BORE	4½ inches
CLUTCH	Cone		STROKE	5½ inches
WHEELBASE . .	142 inches		COOLING . . .	Water
GAUGE	56 inches		RADIATOR . . .	Cellular
TIRE DIMENSIONS:			IGNITION . . .	Jump spark
FRONT . . .	37 x 5 inches		ELECTRIC SOURCE .	High-tension magneto and storage battery
REAR	37 x 5 inches			
BRAKE SYSTEMS .	Contracting and expanding on both rear wheels		DRIVE	Shaft
HORSE-POWER . .	N. A. C. C. (formerly A.L.A.M.) rating 48.6		TRANSMISSION . .	Selective sliding gear
			GEAR CHANGES .	Four forward, one reverse
CYLINDERS . . .	Six		POSITION OF DRIVER	Right-side drive and right-hand control
ARRANGED . . .	Vertically, under hood			

Price includes electric lighting, electric self-starter,
windshield, speedometer and demountable rims

**PIERCE-ARROW
MOTOR CAR CO.**

**B U F F A L O
N E W   Y O R K**

Price	$6000
Two-Passenger Runabout . .	4900
Two-Passenger Coupe Runabout .	5175
Coupe	5700
Four-Passenger Touring . . .	4900
Five-Passenger Touring . . .	4900
Seven-Passenger Touring . . .	5000
Suburban	6000
Brougham	5800
Suburban-Landau	6000
Vestibule Suburban	6200
Vestibule Landau	6200
Vestibule Brougham	5950
Vestibule Suburban-Landau . .	6200

PIERCE-ARROW LANDAU "48-B-3"

COLOR	Optional	CAST	In pairs
SEATING CAPACITY	Seven persons	BORE	4½ inches
CLUTCH	Cone	STROKE . . .	5½ inches
WHEELBASE . .	142 inches	COOLING . . .	Water
GAUGE	56 inches	RADIATOR . . .	Cellular
TIRE DIMENSIONS:		IGNITION . . .	Jump spark
FRONT . . .	37 x 5 inches	ELECTRIC SOURCE .	High-tension
REAR	37 x 5 inches		magneto and
BRAKE SYSTEMS .	Contracting and		storage battery
	expanding on	DRIVE	Shaft
	both rear wheels	TRANSMISSION . .	Selective sliding
HORSE-POWER . .	N. A. C. C. (for-		gear
	merly A.L.A.M.)	GEAR CHANGES .	Four forward,
	rating 48.6		one reverse
CYLINDERS . . .	Six	POSITION OF DRIVER	Right-side drive
ARRANGED . . .	Vertically,		and right-hand
	under hood		control

Price includes electric lighting, electric self-starter,
windshield, speedometer and demountable rims

PIERCE-ARROW MOTOR CAR CO.

B U F F A L O
N E W   Y O R K

Price	$7200
Two-Passenger Runabout . . .	5900
Two-Passenger Coupe Runabout . .	5175
Coupe	6700
Four-Passenger Touring . . .	5900
Five-Passenger Touring . . .	5900
Seven-Passenger Touring . . .	6000
Suburban	7000
Landau	7000
Brougham	6800
Suburban-Landau	7000
Vestibule Landau	7200
Vestibule Brougham	6950
Vestibule Suburban-Landau . .	7200

PIERCE-ARROW VESTIBULE SUBURBAN "66-A-3"

COLOR	Optional	CAST	In pairs
SEATING CAPACITY	Seven persons	BORE	5 inches
CLUTCH	Cone	STROKE	7 inches
WHEELBASE . .	147½ inches	COOLING . . .	Water
GAUGE	57 inches	RADIATOR . . .	Cellular
TIRE DIMENSIONS :		IGNITION . . .	Jump spark
FRONT . . .	37 x 5 inches	ELECTRIC SOURCE .	High-tension magneto and storage battery
REAR	38 x 5½ inches		
BRAKE SYSTEMS .	Contracting and expanding on both rear wheels	DRIVE	Shaft
		TRANSMISSION . .	Selective sliding gear
HORSE-POWER . .	N. A. C. C. (formerly A.L.A.M.) rating 60	GEAR CHANGES .	Four forward, one reverse
CYLINDERS . . .	Six	POSITION OF DRIVER	Right-side drive and right-hand control
ARRANGED . . .	Vertically, under hood		

Price includes electric lighting, electric self-starter, windshield, speedometer and demountable rims

PIERCE-ARROW MOTOR CAR CO.

B U F F A L O
N E W   Y O R K

Price	**$6000**
Two-Passenger Runabout . . .	5900
Two-Passenger Coupe Runabout .	6175
Coupe	6700
Four-Passenger Touring . . .	5900
Five-Passenger Touring . . .	5900
Suburban	7000
Landau	7000
Brougham	6800
Suburban-Landau	7000
Vestibule Landau	7200
Vestibule Suburban	7200
Vestibule Brougham	6950
Vestibule Suburban-Landau . .	7200

PIERCE-ARROW TOURING CAR "66-A-3"

COLOR	Optional	CAST	In pairs
SEATING CAPACITY	Seven persons	BORE	5 inches
CLUTCH	Cone	STROKE	7 inches
WHEELBASE . .	147½ inches	COOLING . . .	Water
GAUGE	57 inches	RADIATOR . . .	Cellular
TIRE DIMENSIONS:		IGNITION . . .	Jump spark
FRONT . . .	37 x 5 inches	ELECTRIC SOURCE .	High-tension magneto and storage battery
REAR	38 x 5½ inches		
BRAKE SYSTEMS .	Contracting and expanding on both rear wheels	DRIVE	Shaft
HORSE-POWER . .	N. A. C. C. (formerly A.L.A.M.) rating 60	TRANSMISSION . .	Selective sliding gear
		GEAR CHANGES .	Four forward, one reverse
CYLINDERS . . .	Six	POSITION OF DRIVER	Right-side drive and right-hand control
ARRANGED . . .	Vertically, under hood		

Price includes top, top hood, electric lighting, electric self-starter, windshield, speedometer and demountable rims

O L D S
M O T O R
W O R K S
L A N S I N G
M I C H I G A N

Price, $1285

OLDSMOBILE TOURING CAR "42"

COLOR	Body, Orriford lake or Brewster green; chassis, black	CYLINDERS . . .	Four	
		ARRANGED . . .	Vertically, under hood	
		CAST	En bloc	
SEATING CAPACITY	Five persons	BORE	3½ inches	
CLUTCH	Cone	STROKE	5 inches	
WHEELBASE . .	112 inches	COOLING . . .	Water	
GAUGE	56 inches	RADIATOR . . .	Honeycomb	
TIRE DIMENSIONS:		IGNITION . . .	Jump spark	
FRONT . . .	33 x 4 inches	ELECTRIC SOURCE .	Delco system	
REAR	33 x 4 inches	DRIVE	Shaft	
BRAKE SYSTEMS .	Contracting and expanding on both rear wheels	TRANSMISSION . .	Selective gear	
		GEAR CHANGES .	Three forward, one reverse	
HORSE-POWER . .	N. A. C. C. (formerly A.L.A.M.) rating 19.6	POSITION OF DRIVER	Left-side drive and center control	

Price includes top, top hood, electric lighting, electric self-
starter, windshield, speedometer and demountable rims

O L D S
M O T O R
W O R K S
L A N S I N G
M I C H I G A N

Price, $1285

OLDSMOBILE ROADSTER "42"

COLOR	Body, Orriford lake or Brewster green; chassis, black	CYLINDERS . . .	Four
		ARRANGED . . .	Vertically, under hood
		CAST	En bloc
SEATING CAPACITY	Two persons	BORE	3½ inches
CLUTCH	Cone	STROKE	5 inches
WHEELBASE . .	112 inches	COOLING . . .	Water
GAUGE	56 inches	RADIATOR . . .	Honeycomb
		IGNITION . . .	Jump spark
TIRE DIMENSIONS:		ELECTRIC SOURCE .	Delco system
FRONT . . .	33 x 4 inches	DRIVE	Shaft
REAR	33 x 4 inches	TRANSMISSION . .	Selective gear
BRAKE SYSTEMS .	Contracting and expanding on both rear wheels	GEAR CHANGES .	Three forward, one reverse
HORSE-POWER . .	N. A. C. C. (formerly A.L.A.M.) rating 19.6	POSITION OF DRIVER	Left-side drive and center control

Price includes top, top hood, electric lighting, electric self-
starter, windshield, speedometer and demountable rims

O L D S
M O T O R
W O R K S

L A N S I N G
M I C H I G A N

Price, $2975

OLDSMOBILE TOURING CAR "55"

COLOR	Body, Orriford lake or Brewster green; chassis, black	CYLINDERS . . .	Six
		ARRANGED . . .	Vertically, under hood
SEATING CAPACITY	Seven persons	CAST	In pairs
		BORE	4¼ inches
CLUTCH	Cone	STROKE	5¼ inches
WHEELBASE . .	139 inches	COOLING . . .	Water
GAUGE	56 inches	RADIATOR . . .	Honeycomb
		IGNITION . . .	Jump spark
TIRE DIMENSIONS:		ELECTRIC SOURCE .	Delco system
FRONT . . .	36 x 5 inches	DRIVE	Shaft
REAR	36 x 5 inches	TRANSMISSION . .	Selective gear
BRAKE SYSTEMS .	Contracting and expanding on both rear wheels	GEAR CHANGES .	Three forward, one reverse
HORSE-POWER . .	N. A. C. C. (formerly A.L.A.M.) rating 43.3	POSITION OF DRIVER	Left-side drive and center control

Price includes top, top hood, electric lighting, electric self-
starter, windshield, speedometer and demountable rims

MAXWELL
MOTOR COM-
PANY, Inc.

DETROIT
MICHIGAN

Price	$695
With Electric Self-Starter .	750
Roadster	670
Cabriolet	840
Town Car	920

MAXWELL TOURING CAR "25"

COLOR	Black	CAST	En bloc
SEATING CAPACITY	Five persons	BORE	3⅝ inches
CLUTCH	Cone	STROKE	4½ inches
WHEELBASE . .	103 inches	COOLING . . .	Water
GAUGE	56 or 60 inches	RADIATOR . . .	Tubular
TIRE DIMENSIONS:		IGNITION . . .	Jump spark
FRONT . . .	30 x 3½ inches	ELECTRIC SOURCE .	High-tension
REAR	30 x 3½ inches		magneto
BRAKE SYSTEMS .	Contracting and	DRIVE	Shaft
	expanding on	TRANSMISSION . .	Selective gear
	both rear wheels	GEAR CHANGES .	Three forward,
HORSE-POWER . .	N. A. C. C. (for-		one reverse
	merly A.L.A.M.)		
	rating 21	POSITION OF DRIVER	Left-side drive
CYLINDERS . . .	Four		and center con-
ARRANGED . . .	Vertically,		trol
	under hood		

Price includes top, top hood, electric
lighting, windshield and speedometer

JACKSON
AUTOMOBILE
COMPANY

JACKSON
MICHIGAN

Price $1250
Three-Passenger Roadster . 1250

JACKSON "44"

Color	Brewster green		Cast	In pairs
Seating Capacity	Five persons		Bore	4⅛ inches
Clutch	Cone		Stroke	4¾ inches
Wheelbase . .	115 inches		Cooling . . .	Water
Gauge	56 inches		Radiator . . .	Tubular
Tire Dimensions:			Ignition . . .	Jump spark
Front . . .	34 x 4 inches		Electric Source .	Generator
Rear	34 x 4 inches		Drive	Shaft
Brake Systems .	Contracting and expanding on both rear wheels		Transmission . .	Selective sliding gear
Horse-power . .	N. A. C. C. (formerly A.L.A.M.) rating 27.2		Gear Changes .	Three forward, one reverse
Cylinders . . .	Four		Position of Driver	Left-side drive and center control
Arranged . . .	Vertically, under hood			

Price includes top, top hood, electric lighting, electric self-starter, windshield, speedometer and demountable rims

JACKSON
AUTOMOBILE
COMPANY
JACKSON
MICHIGAN

Price, $1650

JACKSON "48-SIX" TOURING CAR

COLOR	Dark blue		CAST	En bloc
SEATING CAPACITY	Five persons		BORE	3½ inches
CLUTCH	Cone		STROKE	5 inches
WHEELBASE . .	125 inches		COOLING . . .	Water
GAUGE	56 inches		RADIATOR . . .	Tubular
TIRE DIMENSIONS:			IGNITION . . .	Jump spark
FRONT . . .	34 x 4½ inches		ELECTRIC SOURCE .	Delco system
REAR	34 x 4½ inches		DRIVE	Shaft
BRAKE SYSTEMS .	Contracting and expanding on both rear wheels		TRANSMISSION . .	Selective sliding gear
HORSE-POWER . .	N. A. C. C. (formerly A.L.A.M.) rating 29.4		GEAR CHANGES .	Three forward, one reverse
CYLINDERS . . .	Six		POSITION OF DRIVER	Left-side drive and center control
ARRANGED . . .	Vertically, under hood			

Price includes top, top hood, electric lighting, electric self-
starter, windshield, speedometer and demountable rims

**JAS. CUNNINGHAM
SON & COMPANY**

R O C H E S T E R
N E W   Y O R K

Price	$3750
Five-Passenger .	3750
Four-Passenger .	3750
Runabout . . .	3500
Limousine . . .	5000
Landaulet . . .	5000

CUNNINGHAM TOURING CAR "S"

COLOR	Optional
SEATING CAPACITY	Seven persons
CLUTCH	Dry disc
WHEELBASE . .	129 inches
GAUGE	56½ inches
TIRE DIMENSIONS:	
FRONT . . .	37 x 5 inches
REAR	37 x 5 inches
BRAKE SYSTEMS .	Contracting and expanding on both rear wheels
HORSE-POWER . .	N. A. C. C. (formerly A.L.A.M.) rating 36.1
CYLINDERS . . .	Four
ARRANGED . . .	Vertically, under hood

CAST	In pairs
BORE	4¾ inches
STROKE	5¾ inches
COOLING . . .	Water
RADIATOR . . .	Cellular
IGNITION . . .	Jump spark
ELECTRIC SOURCE .	High-tension magneto and storage battery
DRIVE	Shaft
TRANSMISSION . .	Selective sliding gear
GEAR CHANGES .	Three forward, one reverse
POSITION OF DRIVER	Left-side drive and center control

Price includes top, top hood, electric lighting, electric self-
starter, windshield, speedometer and demountable rims

**CARTERCAR
COMPANY**

**P O N T I A C
M I C H I G A N**

Price . . $1250
Touring . 1250

CARTERCAR ROADSTER "9-R"

COLOR	Body, blue or gray; running gear, black
SEATING CAPACITY	Two persons
WHEELBASE . .	106 inches
GAUGE	56 or 60 inches
TIRE DIMENSIONS:	
FRONT . . .	33 x 4 inches
REAR	33 x 4 inches
BRAKE SYSTEMS .	Contracting and expanding on both rear wheels
HORSE-POWER . .	N. A. C. C. (formerly A.L.A.M.) rating 19.6
CYLINDERS . . .	Four

ARRANGED . . .	Vertically, under hood
CAST	En bloc
BORE	3½ inches
STROKE	5 inches
COOLING . . .	Water
RADIATOR . . .	Tubular
IGNITION . . .	Jump spark
ELECTRIC SOURCE .	Delco system
DRIVE	Single chain
TRANSMISSION . .	Friction
POSITION OF DRIVER	Right-side drive and right-hand control

Price includes top, top hood, electric lighting, electric self-starter, windshield, speedometer and demountable rims

CARTERCAR
COMPANY

PONTIAC
MICHIGAN

Price   .   . $1250
Roadster .   1250

CARTERCAR TOURING CAR "9-T"

COLOR	Body, blue or gray; running gear, black	ARRANGED . . .	Vertically, under hood
SEATING CAPACITY	Five persons	CAST	En bloc
WHEELBASE . .	106 inches	BORE	3½ inches
GAUGE	56 or 60 inches	STROKE	5 inches
TIRE DIMENSIONS:		COOLING . . .	Water
FRONT . . .	33 x 4 inches	RADIATOR . . .	Tubular
REAR	33 x 4 inches	IGNITION . . .	Jump spark
BRAKE SYSTEMS .	Contracting and expanding on both rear wheels	ELECTRIC SOURCE .	Delco system
		DRIVE	Single chain
HORSE-POWER . .	N. A. C. C. (formerly A.L.A.M.) rating 19.6	TRANSMISSION . .	Friction
		POSITION OF DRIVER	Right-side drive and right-hand control
CYLINDERS . . .	Four		

Price includes top, top hood, electric lighting, electric self-
starter, windshield, speedometer and demountable rims

CHANDLER
MOTOR CAR
COMPANY

CLEVELAND, OHIO

Price . . . $1595
Limousine . 2750
Sedan . . 2750

CHANDLER "SIX" TOURING CAR

COLOR	. . . .	Victoria blue with silver stripe	CAST	. . . .	In blocks of three
			BORE	. . . .	3⅝ inches
SEATING CAPACITY		Five persons	STROKE	. . . .	5 inches
CLUTCH	. . . .	Multiple disc	COOLING	. . .	Water
WHEELBASE	. .	120 inches	RADIATOR	. . .	Honeycomb
GAUGE	. . . .	56 inches	IGNITION	. . .	Jump spark
TIRE DIMENSIONS:			ELECTRIC SOURCE	.	Generator, storage battery and high-tension magneto
FRONT	. . .	34 x 4 inches			
REAR	. . . .	34 x 4 inches			
BRAKE SYSTEMS	.	Expanding on both rear wheels	DRIVE	. . . .	Shaft
			TRANSMISSION	. .	Selective sliding gear
HORSE-POWER	. .	N. A. C. C. (formerly A.L.A.M.) rating 27.4	GEAR CHANGES	.	Three forward, one reverse
CYLINDERS	. . .	Six	POSITION OF DRIVER		Left-side drive and center control
ARRANGED	. . .	Vertically, under hood			

Price includes top, top hood, electric lighting, electric self-starter, windshield, speedometer and demountable rims

CHANDLER
MOTOR CAR
COMPANY

CLEVELAND, OHIO

Price . . $1595
Coupe . . 2200
Coupelet . 1950

CHANDLER "SIX" RUNABOUT

COLOR	Victoria blue with silver stripe	CAST	In blocks of three
SEATING CAPACITY	Two persons	BORE	3⅜ inches
CLUTCH	Multiple disc	STROKE	5 inches
WHEELBASE . .	120 inches	COOLING . . .	Water
GAUGE	56 inches	RADIATOR . . .	Honeycomb
TIRE DIMENSIONS:		IGNITION . . .	Jump spark
FRONT . . .	34 x 4 inches	ELECTRIC SOURCE .	Generator, high-tension magneto and storage battery
REAR	34 x 4 inches		
BRAKE SYSTEMS .	Contracting and expanding on both rear wheels	DRIVE	Shaft
		TRANSMISSION . .	Selective sliding gear
HORSE-POWER . .	N. A. C. C. (formerly A.L.A.M.) rating 27.4	GEAR CHANGES .	Three forward, one reverse
CYLINDERS . . .	Six	POSITION OF DRIVER	Left-side drive and center control
ARRANGED . . .	Vertically, under hood		

Price includes top, top hood, electric lighting, electric self-starter, windshield, speedometer and demountable rims

SAXON MOTOR COMPANY

DETROIT
MICHIGAN

Price, $395

SAXON "A"

COLOR	Body, Richelieu blue; running gear, black
SEATING CAPACITY	Two persons
CLUTCH	Multiple disc
WHEELBASE . .	96 inches
GAUGE	56 or 60 inches
TIRE DIMENSIONS:	
FRONT . . .	28 x 3 inches
REAR	28 x 3 inches
BRAKE SYSTEMS .	Contracting and expanding on both rear wheels
HORSE-POWER . .	N. A. C. C. (formerly A.L.A.M.) rating 12.1
CYLINDERS . . .	Four

ARRANGED . . .	Vertically, under hood
CAST	En bloc
BORE	2⅝ inches
STROKE	4 inches
COOLING . . .	Water
RADIATOR . . .	Cellular
IGNITION . . .	Igniter
ELECTRIC SOURCE .	Dry cells
DRIVE	Shaft
TRANSMISSION . .	Progressive sliding gear
GEAR CHANGES .	Two forward, one reverse
POSITION OF DRIVER	Left-side drive and center control

Price includes top, top hood, lamps and windshield

A U B U R N
A U T O M O B I L E
C O M P A N Y

A U B U R N
I N D I A N A

Price $1075
Two-Passenger Roadster . 1075

AUBURN "4-36"

COLOR	Royal blue	CAST	En bloc
SEATING CAPACITY	Five persons	BORE	3¾ inches
CLUTCH	Cone	STROKE	5 inches
WHEELBASE . .	114 inches	COOLING . . .	Water
GAUGE	56 inches	RADIATOR . . .	Cellular
TIRE DIMENSIONS:		IGNITION . . .	Jump spark
FRONT . . .	32 x 4 inches	ELECTRIC SOURCE .	Storage battery and electric generator
REAR	32 x 4 inches		
BRAKE SYSTEMS .	Contracting and expanding on both rear wheels	DRIVE	Shaft
		TRANSMISSION . .	Selective sliding gear
HORSE-POWER . .	N. A. C. C. (formerly A.L.A.M.) rating 22.5	GEAR CHANGES .	Three forward, one reverse
CYLINDERS . . .	Four	POSITION OF DRIVER	Left-side drive and center control
ARRANGED . . .	Vertically, under hood		

Price includes top, top hood, electric lighting, electric self-
starter, windshield, speedometer and demountable rims

**A U B U R N
AUTOMOBILE
C O M P A N Y**

**A U B U R N
I N D I A N A**

Price $1550
Two-Passenger Roadster . 1550

AUBURN "6-40" TOURING CAR

COLOR	Royal blue	CAST	En bloc
SEATING CAPACITY	Six persons	BORE	3½ inches
CLUTCH	Cone	STROKE	5 inches
WHEELBASE . .	126 inches	COOLING . . .	Water
GAUGE	56 inches	RADIATOR . . .	Cellular
TIRE DIMENSIONS:		IGNITION . . .	Jump spark
FRONT . . .	34 x 4 inches	ELECTRIC SOURCE .	Storage battery and electric generator
REAR	34 x 4 inches		
BRAKE SYSTEMS .	Contracting and expanding on both rear wheels	DRIVE	Shaft
HORSE-POWER . .	N. A. C. C. (formerly A.L.A.M.) rating 29.4	TRANSMISSION . .	Selective sliding gear
		GEAR CHANGES .	Three forward, one reverse
CYLINDERS . . .	Six	POSITION OF DRIVER	Left-side drive and center control
ARRANGED . . .	Vertically, under hood		

Price includes top, top hood, electric lighting, electric self-starter, windshield, speedometer and demountable rims

**PEERLESS
MOTOR CAR
COMPANY**

CLEVELAND, OHIO

Price . .	$2000
Roadster .	2000
Limousine .	3100
Cabriolet .	2300

PEERLESS "ALL-PURPOSE FOUR"

COLOR	Thistle green and black	CAST	En bloc
SEATING CAPACITY	Five persons	BORE	3¾ inches
CLUTCH	Multiple disc	STROKE	5 inches
WHEELBASE . .	113 inches	COOLING . . .	Water
GAUGE	56 inches	RADIATOR . . .	Fin and tube
TIRE DIMENSIONS:		IGNITION . . .	Jump spark
FRONT . . .	34 x 4 inches	ELECTRIC SOURCE .	Dry and storage batteries
REAR	34 x 4 inches	DRIVE	Shaft
BRAKE SYSTEMS .	Contracting and expanding on both rear wheels	TRANSMISSION . .	Selective sliding gear
HORSE-POWER . .	N. A. C. C. (formerly A.L.A.M.) rating 22.5	GEAR CHANGES .	Three forward, one reverse
CYLINDERS . . .	Four	POSITION OF DRIVER	Left-side drive and center control
ARRANGED . . .	Vertically, under hood		

Price includes top, top hood, electric lighting, electric self-starter, windshield, speedometer and demountable rims

PEERLESS
MOTOR CAR
COMPANY

CLEVELAND, OHIO

Price . . $5000
Limousine . 6000

PEERLESS "48-SIX"

COLOR	Optional	CAST	In pairs
SEATING CAPACITY	Seven persons	BORE	4½ inches
CLUTCH	Expanding	STROKE	6 inches
WHEELBASE . .	137 inches	COOLING . . .	Water
GAUGE	56 inches		
TIRE DIMENSIONS:		RADIATOR . . .	Fin and tube
FRONT . . .	37 x 5 inches	IGNITION . . .	Jump spark
REAR	37 x 5 inches	ELECTRIC SOURCE .	High-tension magneto and storage battery
BRAKE SYSTEMS .	Contracting and expanding on both rear wheels		
		DRIVE	Shaft
HORSE-POWER . .	N. A. C. C. (formerly A.L.A.M.) rating 48.6	TRANSMISSION . .	Selective sliding gear
CYLINDERS . . .	Six	GEAR CHANGES .	Four forward, one reverse
ARRANGED . . .	Vertically, under hood	POSITION OF DRIVER	Optional

Price includes top, top hood, electric lighting, electric self-
starter, windshield, speedometer and demountable rims

PEERLESS
MOTOR CAR
COMPANY

CLEVELAND, OHIO

Price . . $2250
Roadster . 2250
Limousine . 3350
Cabriolet . 2550

PEERLESS "ALL-PURPOSE SIX"

COLOR	Thistle green and black		CAST	En bloc
SEATING CAPACITY	Five persons		BORE	3½ inches
CLUTCH	Multiple disc		STROKE	5 inches
WHEELBASE . .	121 inches		COOLING . . .	Water
GAUGE	56 inches		RADIATOR . . .	Fin and tube
TIRE DIMENSIONS:			IGNITION . . .	Jump spark
FRONT . . .	34 x 4 inches		ELECTRIC SOURCE .	Dry cells and storage battery
REAR	34 x 4 inches			
BRAKE SYSTEMS	Contracting and expanding on both rear wheels		DRIVE	Shaft
			TRANSMISSION . .	Selective sliding gear
HORSE-POWER . .	N. A. C. C. (formerly A.L.A.M.) rating 29.4		GEAR CHANGES .	Three forward, one reverse
CYLINDERS . . .	Six		POSITION OF DRIVER	Left-side drive and center control
ARRANGED . . .	Vertically, under hood			

Price includes top, top hood, electric lighting, electric self-starter, windshield, speedometer and demountable rim

HUDSON
MOTOR CAR
COMPANY

DETROIT
MICHIGAN

Price					$1550
Roadster					1550
Convertible Roadster				.	1750
Coupe					2150
Limousine					2550

HUDSON "SIX-40" PHAETON

COLOR	Body and chassis, blue with gold striping; hood, radiator, fenders, etc., black enamel
SEATING CAPACITY	Seven persons
CLUTCH	Multiple disc
WHEELBASE	123 inches
GAUGE	56 inches
TIRE DIMENSIONS:	
FRONT	34 x 4 inches
REAR	34 x 4 inches
BRAKE SYSTEMS	Contracting and expanding on both rear wheels
HORSE-POWER	N. A. C. C. (formerly A.L.A.M.) rating 29.4
CYLINDERS	Six

ARRANGED	Vertically, under hood
CAST	En bloc
BORE	3½ inches
STROKE	5 inches
COOLING	Water
RADIATOR	Vertical flat tube
IGNITION	Jump spark
ELECTRIC SOURCE	Delco system
DRIVE	Shaft
TRANSMISSION	Selective sliding gear
GEAR CHANGES	Three forward, one reverse
POSITION OF DRIVER	Left-side drive and center control

Price includes top, top hood, electric lighting, electric self-starter, windshield, speedometer and demountable rims

H U D S O N
M O T O R   C A R
C O M P A N Y

D E T R O I T
M I C H I G A N

Price . . $2350
Limousine . 3500

HUDSON "SIX-54" PHAETON

COLOR	Body and chassis, coach blue, gold striping; hood, radiator, fenders, etc., black enamel
SEATING CAPACITY	Seven persons
CLUTCH	Multiple disc
WHEELBASE . .	135 inches
GAUGE	56 inches
TIRE DIMENSIONS:	
FRONT . .	36 x 4½ inches
REAR . . .	36 x 4½ inches
BRAKE SYSTEMS .	Contracting and expanding on both rear wheels
HORSE-POWER . .	N. A. C. C. (formerly A.L.A.M.) rating 40.9
CYLINDERS . . .	Six
ARRANGED . . .	Vertically, under hood
CAST	In blocks of three
BORE	4⅛ inches
STROKE	5¼ inches
COOLING . . .	Water
RADIATOR . . .	Vertical flat tube
IGNITION . . .	Jump spark
ELECTRIC SOURCE .	Delco system
DRIVE	Shaft
TRANSMISSION . .	Selective sliding gear
GEAR CHANGES .	Four forward, one reverse
POSITION OF DRIVER	Left-side drive and center control

Price includes top, top hood, electric lighting, electric self-starter, windshield, speedometer and demountable rims

THE F. B.
STEARNS
COMPANY

CLEVELAND
O   H   I   O

Price	.	$1750
Three-Passenger Roadster	.	1750
Three-Passenger Cabriolet	.	2250
Seven-Passenger Limousine	.	2850

STEARNS-KNIGHT TOURING CAR "L-4"

COLOR	Body and running gear, Brewster green with light green stripe; hood and fenders, black
SEATING CAPACITY	Five persons
CLUTCH	Cone
WHEELBASE . .	119 inches
GAUGE	56½ inches
TIRE DIMENSIONS:	
FRONT . . .	34 x 4 inches
REAR	34 x 4 inches
BRAKE SYSTEMS .	Contracting on propeller shaft and expanding on both rear wheels
HORSE-POWER . .	N. A. C. C. (formerly A.L.A.M.) rating 22.5
CYLINDERS . . .	Four

ARRANGED . . .	Vertically, under hood
CAST	En bloc
BORE	3¾ inches
STROKE	5⅝ inches
COOLING . . .	Water
RADIATOR . . .	Honeycomb
IGNITION . . .	Jump spark
ELECTRIC SOURCE .	High-tension magneto and storage battery
DRIVE	Shaft
TRANSMISSION . .	Selective sliding gear
GEAR CHANGES .	Three forward, one reverse
POSITION OF DRIVER	Left-side drive and center control

Price includes top, top hood, electric lighting, electric self-
starter, windshield, speedometer and demountable rims

THE   F.   B.
STEARNS
COMPANY

CLEVELAND
O H I O

Price											$5000
Six-Passenger Touring			.	.	.		5000
Five-Passenger Touring			.	.	.		4850
Four-Passenger Light Touring				.		4850
Three-Passenger Roadster			.	.		4850
Seven-Passenger Limousine			.	.		6100
Seven-Passenger Landaulet			.	.		6200

STEARNS-KNIGHT TOURING CAR

COLOR	Blue, maroon or green
SEATING CAPACITY	Seven persons
CLUTCH	Dry multiple disc
WHEELBASE	140 inches
GAUGE	56½ inches
TIRE DIMENSIONS:	
FRONT	37 x 5 inches
REAR	37 x 5 inches
BRAKE SYSTEMS	Contracting and expanding on both rear wheels
HORSE-POWER	N. A. C. C. (formerly A.L.A.M.) rating 43.3
CYLINDERS	Six
ARRANGED	Vertically, under hood

CAST	In pairs
BORE	4¼ inches
STROKE	5¾ inches
COOLING	Water
RADIATOR	Honeycomb
IGNITION	Jump spark
ELECTRIC SOURCE	High-tension magneto and dry and storage batteries
DRIVE	Shaft
TRANSMISSION	Selective sliding gear
GEAR CHANGES	Four forward, one reverse
POSITION OF DRIVER	Left-side drive and right-hand control

Price includes top, top hood, electric lighting, electric self-
starter, windshield, speedometer and demountable rims

STUDEBAKER
CORPORATION
OF AMERICA
**D E T R O I T
M I C H I G A N**

Price, $985

STUDEBAKER "FOUR" ROADSTER "S-D-R"

COLOR	Optional		CAST	En bloc
SEATING CAPACITY	Three persons		BORE	3½ inches
CLUTCH	Cone		STROKE	5 inches
WHEELBASE . .	108 inches		COOLING . . .	Water
GAUGE	56 inches		RADIATOR . . .	Tubular
TIRE DIMENSIONS:			IGNITION . . .	Jump spark
FRONT . . .	33 x 4 inches		ELECTRIC SOURCE .	Storage battery
REAR	33 x 4 inches		DRIVE	Shaft
BRAKE SYSTEMS .	Contracting and expanding on both rear wheels		TRANSMISSION . .	Selective sliding gear
HORSE-POWER . .	N. A. C. C. (formerly A.L.A.M.) rating 19.6		GEAR CHANGES .	Three forward, one reverse
CYLINDERS . . .	Four		POSITION OF DRIVER	Left-side drive and center control
ARRANGED . . .	Vertically, under hood			

Price includes top, top hood, electric lighting, electric self-
starter, windshield, speedometer and demountable rims

STUDEBAKER
CORPORATION
OF AMERICA

D E T R O I T
M I C H I G A N

STUDEBAKER "FOUR" TOURING CAR "5-D"

COLOR	Body, dark blue with white striping; running gear, black	
SEATING CAPACITY	Five persons	
CLUTCH	Cone	
WHEELBASE . .	108 inches	
GAUGE	56 inches	
TIRE DIMENSIONS:		
FRONT . . .	33 x 4 inches	
REAR	33 x 4 inches	
BRAKE SYSTEMS .	Contracting and expanding on both rear wheels	
HORSE-POWER . .	N. A. C. C. (formerly A.L.A.M.) rating 19.6	
CYLINDERS . . .	Four	
ARRANGED . . .	Vertically, under hood	

CAST	En bloc
BORE	3½ inches
STROKE	5 inches
COOLING . . .	Water
RADIATOR . . .	Tubular
IGNITION . . .	Jump spark
ELECTRIC SOURCE .	Storage battery
DRIVE	Shaft
TRANSMISSION . .	Selective sliding gear
GEAR CHANGES .	Three forward, one reverse
POSITION OF DRIVER	Left-side drive and center control

Price includes top, top hood, electric lighting, electric self-
starter, windshield, speedometer and demountable rims

STUDEBAKER
CORPORATION
OF AMERICA
DETROIT
MICHIGAN

Price, $1385

STUDEBAKER "SIX" TOURING CAR "E-C-V"

COLOR	Body, dark blue; running gear, black	CAST	En bloc
		BORE	3½ inches
SEATING CAPACITY	Five persons	STROKE	5 inches
CLUTCH	Cone	COOLING . . .	Water
WHEELBASE . .	121 inches	RADIATOR . . .	Cellular
GAUGE	56 inches		
TIRE DIMENSIONS:		IGNITION . . .	Jump spark
FRONT . . .	34 x 4 inches	ELECTRIC SOURCE .	Storage battery
REAR	34 x 4 inches		
BRAKE SYSTEMS .	Contracting and expanding on both rear wheels	DRIVE	Shaft
		TRANSMISSION . .	Selective sliding gear
HORSE-POWER . .	N. A. C. C. (formerly A.L.A.M.) rating 29.4	GEAR CHANGES .	Three forward, one reverse
CYLINDERS . . .	Six	POSITION OF DRIVER	Left-side drive and center control
ARRANGED . . .	Vertically, under hood		

Price includes top, top hood, electric lighting, electric self-
starter, windshield, speedometer and demountable rims

**STUDEBAKER
CORPORATION
OF AMERICA**

DETROIT
MICHIGAN

Price,　$1450

STUDEBAKER "SIX" TOURING CAR "E-C"

COLOR	Body, dark blue; running gear, black	CAST	En bloc
		BORE	3½ inches
SEATING CAPACITY	Seven persons	STROKE	5 inches
CLUTCH	Cone	COOLING	Water
WHEELBASE	121 inches	RADIATOR	Cellular
GAUGE	56 inches	IGNITION	Jump spark
TIRE DIMENSIONS:		ELECTRIC SOURCE	Storage battery
FRONT	34 x 4 inches		
REAR	34 x 4 inches	DRIVE	Shaft
BRAKE SYSTEMS	Contracting and expanding on both rear wheels	TRANSMISSION	Selective sliding gear
HORSE-POWER	N. A. C. C. (formerly A.L.A.M.) rating 29.4	GEAR CHANGES	Three forward, one reverse
CYLINDERS	Six	POSITION OF DRIVER	Left-side drive and center control
ARRANGED	Vertically, under hood		

Price includes top, top hood, electric lighting, electric self-starter, windshield, speedometer and demountable rims

G R E A T
W E S T E R N
AUTOMOBILE
C O M P A N Y

PERU, INDIANA

Price	$2500
Four-Passenger Touring	2250
Five-Passenger Touring	2250
Seven-Passenger Touring	2500
Two-Passenger Roadster	2200
Two-Passenger Convertible Coupe .	3200
Four-Passenger Sedan Limousine .	3200
Six-Passenger Berlin Limousine .	3800

GREAT WESTERN TOURING CAR "56-B"

COLOR	Blue-black	CAST	En bloc
SEATING CAPACITY	Six persons	BORE	3¾ inches
CLUTCH	Cone	STROKE	5¾ inches
WHEELBASE . .	122 inches	COOLING . . .	Water
GAUGE	56 inches	RADIATOR . . .	Tubular
TIRE DIMENSIONS:		IGNITION . . .	Jump spark
FRONT . . .	34 x 4 inches	ELECTRIC SOURCE .	High-tension magneto
REAR	34 x 4 inches		
BRAKE SYSTEMS .	Contracting and expanding on both rear wheels	DRIVE	Shaft
		TRANSMISSION . .	Selective sliding gear
HORSE-POWER . .	N. A. C. C. (formerly A.L.A.M.) rating 22.5	GEAR CHANGES .	Three forward, one reverse
CYLINDERS . . .	Four	POSITION OF DRIVER	Left-side drive and center control
ARRANGED . . .	Vertically, under hood		

Price includes top, top hood, electric lighting, electric self-starter, windshield, speedometer and demountable rims

**PACKARD
MOTOR CAR
COMPANY**

**DETROIT
MICHIGAN**

Price	
Salon Touring Car	$4850
Salon Touring Car	4850
Five-Passenger Phaeton	4750
Four-Passenger Phaeton	4750
Runabout	4750
Seven-Passenger Limousine	6000
Seven-Passenger Landaulet	6000
Six-Passenger Limousine	5950
Six-Passenger Landaulet	5900
Six-Passenger Imperial Limousine	6100
Seven-Passenger Imperial Limousine	6150
Seven-Passenger Salon Limousine	6100
Six-Passenger Brougham	6000
Four-Passenger Salon Brougham	5950
Three-Passenger Coupe	5450

PACKARD "5-48" SEVEN-PASSENGER STANDARD TOURING CAR

COLOR	Body and door panels, Packard blue, striped with black; wheels, cream yellow striped with black; chassis black	ARRANGED	Vertically, under hood
		CAST	In blocks of three
		BORE	4¼ inches
		STROKE	5½ inches
		COOLING	Water
SEATING CAPACITY	Seven persons	RADIATOR	Cellular
CLUTCH	Dry plate	IGNITION	Jump spark
WHEELBASE	144 inches	ELECTRIC SOURCE	High-tension magneto, generator and storage battery
GAUGE	56 inches		
TIRE DIMENSIONS:			
FRONT	37 x 5 inches		
REAR	37 x 5 inches	DRIVE	Shaft
BRAKE SYSTEMS	Contracting and expanding on both rear wheels	TRANSMISSION	Sliding gear
		GEAR CHANGES	Three forward, one reverse
HORSE-POWER	N. A. C. C. (formerly A.L.A.M.) rating 48.6	POSITION OF DRIVER	Left-side drive and left-hand control
CYLINDERS	Six		

Price includes top, top hood, electric lighting, electric self-
starter, windshield, speedometer and demountable rims

**PACKARD
MOTOR CAR
COMPANY**

**DETROIT
MICHIGAN**

Price	$3750
Four-Passenger Phaeton	3750
Runabout	3750
Six-Passenger Brougham	5000
Four-Passenger Salon Brougham .	4950
Three-Passenger Coupe	4450

PACKARD "3-38" FIVE-PASSENGER PHAETON

COLOR	Body and door panels, Packard blue, striped with black; wheels, cream yellow striped with black; chassis, black	ARRANGED . . .	Vertically, under hood	
		CAST	In blocks of three	
		BORE	4 inches	
		STROKE	5½ inches	
		COOLING . . .	Water	
SEATING CAPACITY	Five persons	RADIATOR . . .	Cellular	
CLUTCH	Dry plate	IGNITION . . .	Jump spark	
WHEELBASE . .	140 inches	ELECTRIC SOURCE .	High-tension magneto, generator and storage battery	
GAUGE	56 inches			
TIRE DIMENSIONS:				
FRONT . . .	36 x 4½ inches			
REAR	37 x 5 inches	DRIVE	Shaft	
BRAKE SYSTEMS .	Contracting and expanding on both rear wheels	TRANSMISSION . .	Sliding gear	
		GEAR CHANGES .	Three forward, one reverse	
HORSE-POWER . .	N. A. C. C. (formerly A.L.A.M.) rating 38.4	POSITION OF DRIVER	Left-side drive and left-hand control	
CYLINDERS . . .	Six			

Price includes top, top hood, electric lighting, electric
self-starter, windshield and demountable rims

**PACKARD
MOTOR CAR
COMPANY**

**DETROIT
MICHIGAN**

Price									$5100
Standard Touring									3850
Salon Touring									3850
Special Touring									3350
Seven-Passenger Limousine									5000
Seven-Passenger Landaulet									5000
Six-Passenger Limousine									4950
Six-Passenger Landaulet									4900
Seven-Passenger Imperial Limousine									5150
Seven-Passenger Salon Limousine									5100

PACKARD "3-38" SIX-PASSENGER IMPERIAL LIMOUSINE

COLOR	Body, door panels and wheels, Packard blue, striped with black; chassis, black
SEATING CAPACITY	Six persons
CLUTCH	Dry plate
WHEELBASE . .	140 inches
GAUGE	56 inches
TIRE DIMENSIONS:	
FRONT . . .	36 x 4½ inches
REAR . . .	37 x 5 inches
BRAKE SYSTEMS .	Contracting and expanding on both rear wheels
HORSE-POWER . .	N. A. C. C. (formerly A.L.A.M.) rating 38.4
CYLINDERS . .	Six

ARRANGED . . .	Vertically, under hood
CAST	In blocks of three
BORE	4 inches
STROKE	5½ inches
COOLING . . .	Water
RADIATOR . . .	Cellular
IGNITION . . .	Jump spark
ELECTRIC SOURCE .	High-tension magneto, generator and storage battery
DRIVE	Shaft
TRANSMISSION . .	Sliding gear
GEAR CHANGES .	Three forward, one reverse
POSITION OF DRIVER	Left-side drive and left-hand control

Price includes electric lighting, electric self-starter, windshield and demountable rims

PAIGE-DETROIT
MOTOR CAR
COMPANY
DETROIT
MICHIGAN

Price	$1075
Westbrooke Runabout .	1075
Montrose Coupe . . .	1600
Speedway Raceabout .	1275

GLENWOOD TOURING CAR

COLOR	Optional	CAST	En bloc
SEATING CAPACITY	Five persons	BORE	4 inches
CLUTCH	Multiple disc	STROKE	5 inches
WHEELBASE . .	116 inches	COOLING . . .	Water
GAUGE	56 or 60 inches	RADIATOR . . .	Honeycomb
TIRE DIMENSIONS:		IGNITION . . .	Jump spark
FRONT . . .	34 x 4 inches	ELECTRIC SOURCE .	High-tension magneto and storage battery
REAR . . .	34 x 4 inches		
BRAKE SYSTEMS .	Contracting and expanding on both rear wheels	DRIVE	Shaft
		TRANSMISSION . .	Selective sliding gear
HORSE-POWER . .	N. A. C. C. (formerly A.L.A.M.) rating 25.6	GEAR CHANGES .	Three forward, one reverse
CYLINDERS . . .	Four	POSITION OF DRIVER	Left-side drive and center control
ARRANGED . . .	Vertically, under hood		

Price includes top, top hood, electric lighting, electric self-starter, windshield, speedometer and demountable rims

PAIGE-DETROIT
MOTOR CAR
COMPANY

D E T R O I T
M I C H I G A N

Price $1395
Meadowbrooke Runabout . 1395
Dartmore Raceabout . . 1420

FAIRFIELD TOURING CAR

COLOR	Optional	
SEATING CAPACITY	Seven persons	
CLUTCH	Multiple disc	
WHEELBASE . .	123½ inches	
GAUGE	56 or 60 inches	
TIRE DIMENSIONS:		
FRONT . . .	34 x 4 inches	
REAR . . .	34 x 4 inches	
BRAKE SYSTEMS .	Contracting and expanding on both rear wheels	
HORSE-POWER . .	N. A. C. C. (formerly A.L.A.M.) rating 29.4	
CYLINDERS . . .	Six	
ARRANGED . . .	Vertically, under hood	

CAST	En bloc
BORE	3½ inches
STROKE	5¼ inches
COOLING . . .	Water
RADIATOR . . .	Honeycomb
IGNITION . . .	Jump spark
ELECTRIC SOURCE .	High-tension magneto and storage battery
DRIVE	Shaft
TRANSMISSION . .	Selective sliding gear
GEAR CHANGES .	Three forward, one reverse
POSITION OF DRIVER	Left-side drive and center control

Price includes top, top hood, electric lighting, electric self-starter, windshield, speedometer and demountable rims

THE THOMAS
B. JEFFERY
COMPANY

KENOSHA
WISCONSIN

Price $1650
Two-Passenger Roadster . . 1650
Two-Passenger All-Weather . 1950

JEFFERY CHESTERFIELD SIX

COLOR	Chesterfield blue		CAST	En bloc
SEATING CAPACITY	Five persons		BORE . . .	3 inches
CLUTCH	Dry multiple disc		STROKE	5 inches
WHEELBASE . .	122 inches		COOLING . . .	Water
GAUGE	56 inches		RADIATOR . . .	Honeycomb
TIRE DIMENSIONS:			IGNITION . . .	Jump spark
FRONT . . .	34 x 4 inches		ELECTRIC SOURCE .	High-tension magneto
REAR	34 x 4 inches			
BRAKE SYSTEMS .	Internal expanding on both rear wheels		DRIVE	Worm
			TRANSMISSION . .	Selective sliding gear
HORSE-POWER . .	N. A. C. C. (formerly A.L.A.M.) rating 21.6		GEAR CHANGES	Four forward, one reverse
CYLINDERS . . .	Six		POSITION OF DRIVER	Left-side drive and center control
ARRANGED . . .	Vertically, under hood			

Price includes top, top hood, electric lighting, electric self-
starter, windshield, speedometer and demountable rims

IMPERIAL
AUTOMOBILE
COMPANY

JACKSON
MICHIGAN

Price $1085
Two-Passenger Roadster . 1085

IMPERIAL TOURING CAR "64"

COLOR	Black	CAST	En bloc
SEATING CAPACITY	Five persons	BORE	3¾ inches
CLUTCH	Multiple disc	STROKE	5 inches
WHEELBASE . .	115 inches	COOLING . . .	Water
GAUGE	56 inches	RADIATOR . . .	Cellular
TIRE DIMENSIONS:		IGNITION . . .	Jump spark
FRONT . . .	32 x 3½ inches	ELECTRIC SOURCE .	Storage battery
REAR	32 x 3½ inches	DRIVE	Shaft
BRAKE SYSTEMS .	Contracting and expanding on both rear wheels	TRANSMISSION . .	Selective sliding gear
HORSE-POWER . .	N. A. C. C. (formerly A.L.A.M.) rating 22.5	GEAR CHANGES .	Three forward, one reverse
CYLINDERS . . .	Four	POSITION OF DRIVER	Left-side drive and center control
ARRANGED . . .	Vertically, under hood		

Price includes top, top hood, electric lighting, electric self-
starter, windshield, speedometer and demountable rims

WINTON MOTOR CAR COMPANY

CLEVELAND, OHIO

Price	$3250
Four-Passenger Touring . .	3250
Six-Passenger Touring . .	3500
Seven-Passenger Touring . .	3500
Two-Passenger Roadster . .	3250
Three-Passenger Roadster .	3250

WINTON SIX TOURING CAR "21"

COLOR	Optional		BORE	4¼ inches
SEATING CAPACITY	Five persons		STROKE	5½ inches
CLUTCH . .	Multiple disc		COOLING . . .	Water
WHEELBASE . .	136 inches		RADIATOR . . .	Honeycomb
GAUGE	56½ inches		IGNITION . . .	Jump spark
TIRE DIMENSIONS:			ELECTRIC SOURCE .	High-tension magneto and storage battery
FRONT . . .	37 x 5 inches			
REAR . . .	37 x 5 inches			
BRAKE SYSTEMS .	Contracting and expanding on both rear wheels		DRIVE	Shaft
			TRANSMISSION . .	Selective sliding gear
HORSE-POWER . .	N. A. C. C. (formerly A.L.A.M.) rating 48.6		GEAR CHANGES .	Four forward, one reverse
CYLINDERS . . .	Six		POSITION OF DRIVER	Left-side drive and center control
ARRANGED . . .	Vertically, under hood			
CAST	In pairs			

Price includes top, top hood, electric lighting, electric self-starter, windshield, speedometer and demountable rims

**W I N T O N
M O T O R C A R
C O M P A N Y**

CLEVELAND, OHIO

Price	$4600
Landaulet	4600
Sedan	4600
Three-quarter Limousine .	4350

WINTON SIX FULL FOUR-DOOR LIMOUSINE "21"

COLOR	Optional	CAST	In pairs
SEATING CAPACITY	Seven persons	BORE	4½ inches
CLUTCH	Multiple disc	STROKE	5½ inches
WHEELBASE . .	136 inches	COOLING . . .	Water
GAUGE	56½ inches	RADIATOR . . .	Honeycomb
TIRE DIMENSIONS:		IGNITION . . .	Jump spark
FRONT . . .	37 x 5 inches	ELECTRIC SOURCE .	High-tension magneto and storage battery
REAR	37 x 5 inches		
BRAKE SYSTEMS .	Contracting and expanding on both rear wheels	DRIVE	Shaft
		TRANSMISSION . .	Selective sliding gear
HORSE-POWER . .	N. A. C. C. (formerly A.L.A.M.) rating 48.6	GEAR CHANGES .	Four forward, one reverse
CYLINDERS . . .	Six	POSITION OF DRIVER	Left-side drive and center control
ARRANGED . . .	Vertically, under hood		

Price includes electric lighting, electric self-
starter, speedometer and demountable rims

**KRIT MOTOR
CAR COMPANY**

Price $995
Three-Passenger Cabriolet . 1295

**D E T R O I T
M I C H I G A N**

KRIT TOURING CAR DE LUXE "M"

COLOR	Body, blue; running gear, black; wheels, gray	CAST	En bloc
SEATING CAPACITY	Five persons	BORE	3¾ inches
CLUTCH	Multiple disc	STROKE	4 inches
WHEELBASE . .	108 inches	COOLING . . .	Water
GAUGE	56 inches	RADIATOR . . .	Vertical tube
TIRE DIMENSIONS:		IGNITION . . .	Jump spark
FRONT . . .	32 x 3½ inches	ELECTRIC SOURCE .	High-tension magneto
REAR	32 x 3½ inches		
BRAKE SYSTEMS .	Contracting and expanding on both rear wheels	DRIVE	Shaft
		TRANSMISSION . .	Selective sliding gear
HORSE-POWER . .	N. A. C. C. (formerly A.L.A.M.) rating 22.5	GEAR CHANGES .	Three forward, one reverse
CYLINDERS . . .	Four	POSITION OF DRIVER	Left-side drive and center control
ARRANGED . . .	Vertically, under hood		

Price includes top, top hood, electric lighting, electric self-starter, windshield, speedometer and demountable rims

KRIT MOTOR CAR COMPANY

DETROIT
MICHIGAN

Price . . $850
Roadster . 850

KRIT TOURING CAR "O"

COLOR	Body and wheels, Brewster green; gear, black	ARRANGED . . .	Vertically, under hood
SEATING CAPACITY	Five persons	CAST	En bloc
CLUTCH	Multiple disc	BORE	3¾ inches
WHEELBASE . .	108 inches	STROKE	4 inches
GAUGE	56 inches	COOLING . . .	Water
TIRE DIMENSIONS:		RADIATOR . . .	Vertical tube
FRONT . . .	32 x 3½ inches	IGNITION . . .	Jump spark
REAR	32 x 3½ inches	ELECTRIC SOURCE .	Generator and storage battery
BRAKE SYSTEMS .	Contracting and expanding on both rear wheels	DRIVE	Shaft
		TRANSMISSION . .	Selective sliding gear
HORSE-POWER . .	N. A. C. C. (formerly A.L.A.M.) rating 22.5	GEAR CHANGES .	Three forward, one reverse
		POSITION OF DRIVER	Left-side drive and center control
CYLINDERS . . .	Four		

Price includes top, top hood, electric lighting, electric self-
starter, windshield, speedometer and demountable rims

A V E R Y
C O M P A N Y

PEORIA, ILLINOIS

Price . . $1195
Roadster . 1195

GLIDE TOURING CAR "30"

COLOR	Body and chassis, meteor blue; fenders and hood, black	ARRANGED . . .	Vertically, under hood
SEATING CAPACITY	Five persons	CAST	En bloc
		BORE	3½ inches
CLUTCH	Multiple disc	STROKE	5 inches
WHEELBASE .	114 inches	COOLING . . .	Water
GAUGE	56 inches	RADIATOR . . .	Vertical tube
TIRE DIMENSIONS:		IGNITION . . .	Jump spark
FRONT . . .	32 x 4 inches	ELECTRIC SOURCE .	Generator and storage battery
REAR	32 x 4 inches	DRIVE	Shaft
BRAKE SYSTEMS .	Contracting on propeller shaft and expanding on both rear wheels	TRANSMISSION . .	Selective sliding gear
		GEAR CHANGES .	Three forward, one reverse
HORSE-POWER . .	N. A. C. C. (formerly A.L.A.M.) rating 19.6	POSITION OF DRIVER	Left-side drive and center control
CYLINDERS . . .	Four		

Price includes top, top hood, electric lighting, electric self-
starter, windshield, speedometer and demountable rims

INTER-STATE
M O T O R
C O M P A N Y

M U N C I E
I N D I A N A

Price, $1000

INTER-STATE TOURING CAR "T"

COLOR	Optional
SEATING CAPACITY	Five persons
CLUTCH	Cone
WHEELBASE . .	110 inches
GAUGE	56 inches
TIRE DIMENSIONS:	
FRONT . . .	33 x 4 inches
REAR	33 x 4 inches
BRAKE SYSTEMS .	Contracting and expanding on both rear wheels
HORSE-POWER . .	N. A. C. C. (formerly A.L.A.M.) rating 19.6
CYLINDERS . . .	Four
ARRANGED . . .	Vertically, under hood

CAST	En bloc
BORE	3½ inches
STROKE	5 inches
COOLING . . .	Water
RADIATOR . . .	Cellular
IGNITION . . .	Jump spark
ELECTRIC SOURCE .	Storage battery
DRIVE	Shaft
TRANSMISSION . .	Selective sliding gear
GEAR CHANGES .	Three forward, one reverse
POSITION OF DRIVER	Left-side drive and center control

Price includes top, top hood, electric lighting, electric self-starter, windshield, speedometer and demountable rims

WILLYS -
OVERLAND
COMPANY

TOLEDO, OHIO

Price $850
Two-Passenger Roadster . . 795
Panel Delivery Car . . . 895
Express Delivery Car . . 850

OVERLAND TOURING CAR "81"

COLOR	Brewster green with ivory striping		CAST	Separately
			BORE . . .	4 inches
SEATING CAPACITY	Five persons		STROKE	4½ inches
CLUTCH	Cone		COOLING . . .	Water
WHEELBASE . .	106 inches		RADIATOR . . .	Cellular
GAUGE	56 or 60 inches		IGNITION . . .	Jump spark
TIRE DIMENSIONS:			ELECTRIC SOURCE .	High-tension magneto
FRONT . . .	33 x 4 inches			
REAR	33 x 4 inches		DRIVE	Shaft
BRAKE SYSTEMS .	Contracting and expanding on both rear wheels		TRANSMISSION . .	Selective sliding gear
HORSE-POWER . .	N. A. C. C. (formerly A.L.A.M.) rating 25.6		GEAR CHANGES .	Three forward, one reverse
CYLINDERS . . .	Four		POSITION OF DRIVER	Left-side drive and center control
ARRANGED . . .	Vertically, under hood			

Price includes top, top hood, electric lighting, electric self-starter, windshield, speedometer and demountable rims

WILLYS-OVERLAND COMPANY

TOLEDO, OHIO

Price	$1075
Two-Passenger Roadster .	1050
Four-Passenger Coupe . .	1600

OVERLAND TOURING CAR "80"

COLOR	Brewster green with ivory striping	CAST	Separately
SEATING CAPACITY	Five persons	BORE	4⅛ inches
CLUTCH	Cone	STROKE	4½ inches
WHEELBASE . .	114 inches	COOLING . . .	Water
GAUGE	56 or 60 inches	RADIATOR . . .	Cellular
TIRE DIMENSIONS:		IGNITION . . .	Jump spark
FRONT . . .	34 x 4 inches	ELECTRIC SOURCE .	High-tension magneto
REAR . . .	34 x 4 inches		
BRAKE SYSTEMS .	Contracting and expanding on both rear wheels	DRIVE	Shaft
		TRANSMISSION . .	Selective sliding gear
HORSE-POWER . .	N. A. C. C. (formerly A.L.A.M.) rating 27.2	GEAR CHANGES .	Three forward, one reverse
CYLINDERS . . .	Four	POSITION OF DRIVER	Left-side drive and center control
ARRANGED . . .	Vertically, under hood		

Price includes top, top hood, electric lighting, electric self-starter, windshield, speedometer and demountable rims

WILLYS-OVERLAND COMPANY

Price, $1475

TOLEDO, OHIO

OVERLAND TOURING CAR "82"

COLOR	Overland blue with ivory striping
SEATING CAPACITY	Seven persons
CLUTCH	Cone
WHEELBASE . .	125 inches
GAUGE	56 inches
TIRE DIMENSIONS:	
FRONT . . .	35 x 4½ inches
REAR	35 x 4½ inches
BRAKE SYSTEMS .	Contracting and expanding on both rear wheels
HORSE-POWER . .	N. A. C. C. (formerly A.L.A.M.) rating 29.4
CYLINDERS . . .	Six
ARRANGED . . .	Vertically, under hood
CAST	En bloc
BORE	3½ inches
STROKE	5¼ inches
COOLING . . .	Water
RADIATOR . . .	Cellular
IGNITION . . .	Jump spark
ELECTRIC SOURCE .	High-tension magneto
DRIVE	Shaft
TRANSMISSION . .	Selective sliding gear
GEAR CHANGES .	Three forward, one reverse
POSITION OF DRIVER	Left-side drive and center control

Price includes top, top hood, electric lighting, electric self-starter, windshield, speedometer and demountable rims

THE GARFORD
COMPANY
ELYRIA, OHIO
AND
THE WILLYS-
OVERLAND
COMPANY
TOLEDO, OHIO

Price, $2475

WILLYS-KNIGHT TOURING CAR "K-19"

COLOR	Dark blue
SEATING CAPACITY	Five persons
CLUTCH	Cone
WHEELBASE . .	120 inches
GAUGE	56½ inches
TIRE DIMENSIONS:	
FRONT . . .	36 x 4½ inches
REAR	36 x 4½ inches
BRAKE SYSTEMS .	Contracting and expanding on both rear wheels
HORSE-POWER . .	N. A. C. C. (formerly A.L.A.M.) rating 25.6
CYLINDERS . . .	Four
ARRANGED . . .	Vertically, under hood
CAST	In pairs
BORE	4 inches
STROKE	5½ inches
COOLING . . .	Water
RADIATOR . . .	Cellular
IGNITION . . .	Jump spark
ELECTRIC SOURCE .	High-tension magneto
DRIVE	Shaft
TRANSMISSION . .	Selective gear
GEAR CHANGES .	Four forward, one reverse
POSITION OF DRIVER	Left-side drive and center control

Price includes top, top hood, electric lighting, electric self-
starter, windshield, speedometer and demountable rims

**BRIGGS-
DETROITER
COMPANY**
DETROIT
MICHIGAN

Price, $1050

DETROITER TOURING CAR "C-5"

COLOR	Body, raven blue; running gear, black	BORE	3½ inches	
SEATING CAPACITY	Five persons	STROKE	5 inches	
		COOLING . . .	Water	
CLUTCH	Multiple disc	RADIATOR . . .	Tubular	
WHEELBASE . .	112 inches	IGNITION . . .	Jump spark	
GAUGE	56 inches	ELECTRIC SOURCE .	Generator and storage battery, or high-tension magneto and storage battery	
TIRE DIMENSIONS:				
FRONT . . .	32 x 3½ inches			
REAR	32 x 3½ inches			
BRAKE SYSTEMS .	Expanding on both rear wheels	DRIVE	Shaft	
HORSE-POWER . .	N. A. C. C. (formerly A.L.A.M.) rating 19.6	TRANSMISSION . .	Selective sliding gear	
		GEAR CHANGES .	Three forward, one reverse	
CYLINDERS . . .	Four	POSITION OF DRIVER	Left-side drive and center control	
ARRANGED . . .	Vertically, under hood			
CAST	En bloc			

Price includes top, top hood, electric lighting, electric self-
starter, windshield, speedometer and demountable rims

**B R I S C O E
MOTOR   CO.**
INCORPORATED

**J A C K S O N
M I C H I G A N**

Price $785
Five-Passenger De Luxe Touring   .   785

BRISCOE CLOVER LEAF ROADSTER

COLOR	Body, gray or Brewster green; running gear, black	CAST	En bloc
		BORE	3⅛ inches
		STROKE	5⅛ inches
SEATING CAPACITY	Three persons	COOLING . . .	Water
CLUTCH	Cone	RADIATOR . . .	Honeycomb
WHEELBASE . .	107 inches	IGNITION . . .	Jump spark
GAUGE	56 inches	ELECTRIC SOURCE .	High-tension magneto and storage battery
TIRE DIMENSIONS:			
FRONT . . .	30 x 3½ inches		
REAR	30 x 3½ inches	DRIVE	Shaft
BRAKE SYSTEMS .	Expanding on both rear wheels	TRANSMISSION . .	Selective sliding gear
HORSE-POWER . .	N. A. C. C. (formerly A.L.A.M.) rating 15.6	GEAR CHANGES .	Three forward, one reverse
CYLINDERS . .	Four	POSITION OF DRIVER	Left-side drive and left-hand control
ARRANGED . . .	Vertically, under hood		

Price includes top, top hood, electric lighting,
electric self-starter, windshield and speedometer

**B R I S C O E
MOTOR CO.**
INCORPORATED

**J A C K S O N
M I C H I G A N**

Price $785
Three-Passenger Clover Leaf Roadster 785

BRISCOE DE LUXE TOURING CAR

COLOR	Body, gray or Brewster green; running gear, black	CAST	En bloc
		BORE	3⅛ inches
SEATING CAPACITY	Five persons	STROKE	5⅛ inches
CLUTCH	Cone	COOLING . . .	Water
WHEELBASE . .	107 inches	RADIATOR . . .	Honeycomb
GAUGE	56 inches	IGNITION . . .	Jump spark
TIRE DIMENSIONS:		ELECTRIC SOURCE .	High-tension magneto and storage battery
FRONT	30 x 3½ inches		
REAR	30 x 3½ inches	DRIVE	Shaft
BRAKE SYSTEMS .	Expanding on both rear wheels	TRANSMISSION . .	Selective sliding gear
HORSE-POWER . .	N. A. C. C. (formerly A.L.A.M.) rating 15.6	GEAR CHANGES .	Three forward, one reverse
CYLINDERS . . .	Four	POSITION OF DRIVER	Left-side drive and left-hand control
ARRANGED . . .	Vertically, under hood		

Price includes top, top hood, electric lighting,
electric self-starter, windshield and speedometer

**WESTCOTT
MOTOR CAR
COMPANY**

**RICHMOND
INDIANA**

Price $1185
Three-Passenger . 1185

WESTCOTT TOURING CAR "O-35"

COLOR	Westcott green		CAST	En bloc
SEATING CAPACITY	Five persons		BORE	3½ inches
CLUTCH	Cone		STROKE	5 inches
WHEELBASE . .	113 inches		COOLING . . .	Water
GAUGE	56 inches		RADIATOR . . .	Cellular
TIRE DIMENSIONS:			IGNITION . . .	Jump spark
FRONT . . .	33 x 4 inches		ELECTRIC SOURCE .	Storage battery
REAR	33 x 4 inches		DRIVE	Shaft
BRAKE SYSTEMS	Contracting and expanding on both rear wheels		TRANSMISSION . .	Selective sliding gear
HORSE-POWER . .	35		GEAR CHANGES .	Three forward, one reverse
CYLINDERS . . .	Four		POSITION OF DRIVER	Left-side drive and center control
ARRANGED . . .	Vertically, under hood			

Price includes top, top hood, electric lighting, electric self-
starter, windshield, speedometer and demountable rims

VELIE MOTOR VEHICLE COMPANY
MOLINE ILLINOIS

Price, $1595

VELIE TOURING CAR "15"

COLOR	Velie blue
SEATING CAPACITY	Five persons
CLUTCH	Disc
WHEELBASE . .	124 inches
GAUGE	56 inches
TIRE DIMENSIONS:	
FRONT . . .	34 x 4 inches
REAR	34 x 4 inches
BRAKE SYSTEMS .	Contracting and expanding on both rear wheels
HORSE-POWER . .	N. A. C. C. (formerly A.L.A.M.) rating 29.4
CYLINDERS . . .	Six
ARRANGED . . .	Vertically, under hood

CAST	En bloc
BORE	3½ inches
STROKE	5 inches
COOLING . . .	Water
RADIATOR . . .	Honeycomb
IGNITION . . .	Jump spark
ELECTRIC SOURCE .	Storage battery
DRIVE	Shaft
TRANSMISSION . .	Selective sliding gear
GEAR CHANGES .	Four forward, one reverse
POSITION OF DRIVER	Left-side drive and center control

Price includes top, top hood, electric lighting, electric self-starter, windshield, speedometer and detachable demountable rims

L O Z I E R
M O T O R
C O M P A N Y
D E T R O I T
M I C H I G A N

Price,　$3250

LOZIER TOURING CAR "82"

COLOR	Optional	CAST	In blocks of three
SEATING CAPACITY	Seven persons	BORE	3⅞ inches
CLUTCH	Multiple disc	STROKE	6 inches
WHEELBASE . .	132 inches	COOLING . . .	Water
GAUGE	56 inches	RADIATOR . . .	Tubular
TIRE DIMENSIONS:		IGNITION . . .	Jump spark
FRONT . . .	36 x 4½ inches	ELECTRIC SOURCE .	High-tension magneto
REAR	36 x 4½ inches		
BRAKE SYSTEMS .	Contracting and expanding on both rear wheels	DRIVE	Shaft
		TRANSMISSION . .	Selective gear
HORSE-POWER . .	N. A. C. C. (formerly A.L.A.M.) rating 36	GEAR CHANGES .	Three forward, one reverse
CYLINDERS . . .	Six	POSITION OF DRIVER	Left-side drive and center control
ARRANGED . . .	Vertically, under hood		

Price includes top, top hood, electric lighting, electric self-starter, windshield, speedometer and demountable rims

R E G A L   Price .   . $1085
M O T O R   C A R   Roadster .   1085
C O M P A N Y

D E T R O I T
M I C H I G A N

REGAL TOURING CAR "D"

COLOR	Regal blue		CAST	En bloc
SEATING CAPACITY	Five persons		BORE	3¾ inches
CLUTCH	Cone		STROKE	5 inches
WHEELBASE . .	112 inches		COOLING . . .	Water
GAUGE	56 or 60 inches		RADIATOR . . .	Cellular
TIRE DIMENSIONS:			IGNITION . . .	Jump spark
FRONT . . .	33 x 4 inches		ELECTRIC SOURCE .	Storage battery with dry cells
REAR	33 x 4 inches			
BRAKE SYSTEMS .	Contracting and expanding on both rear wheels		DRIVE	Shaft
			TRANSMISSION . .	Selective sliding gear
HORSE-POWER . .	N. A. C. C. (formerly A.L.A.M.) rating 22.5		GEAR CHANGES .	Three forward, one reverse
CYLINDERS . . .	Four		POSITION OF DRIVER	Optional
ARRANGED . . .	Vertically, under hood			

Price includes top, top hood, electric lighting, electric self-
starter, windshield, speedometer and demountable rims

**B U I C K
M O T O R
C O M P A N Y**

**F L I N T
M I C H I G A N**

Price . . $950
Roadster . 900

BUICK "C-25"

COLOR	Body and hood, blue-black; fenders, black; chassis, black with ivory stripe	ARRANGED . . .	Vertically, under hood
		CAST	In pairs
SEATING CAPACITY	Five persons	BORE	3¾ inches
CLUTCH . . .	Cone	STROKE	3¾ inches
WHEELBASE . .	106 inches	COOLING . . .	Water
GAUGE	56 or 60 inches	RADIATOR . . .	Vertical tube
TIRE DIMENSIONS:		IGNITION . . .	Jump spark
FRONT . . .	32 x 3½ inches	ELECTRIC SOURCE .	Delco system
REAR	32 x 3½ inches	DRIVE	Shaft
BRAKE SYSTEMS .	Contracting and expanding on both rear wheels	TRANSMISSION . .	Selective sliding gear
		GEAR CHANGES .	Three forward, one reverse
HORSE-POWER . .	N. A. C. C. (formerly A.L.A.M.) rating 22.5	POSITION OF DRIVER	Left-side drive and center control
CYLINDERS . . .	Four		

Price includes top, top hood, electric lighting, electric
self-starter, windshield and demountable rims

BUICK
MOTOR
COMPANY

FLINT
MICHIGAN

Price . . $1235
Roadster . 1185

BUICK "C-37"

COLOR	Body and hood, blue-black; fenders, black; chassis, black with ivory stripe	
SEATING CAPACITY	Five persons	
CLUTCH	Cone	
WHEELBASE . .	112 inches	
GAUGE	56 or 60 inches	
TIRE DIMENSIONS:		
FRONT . . .	34 x 4 inches	
REAR	34 x 4 inches	
BRAKE SYSTEMS .	Contracting and expanding on both rear wheels	
HORSE-POWER . .	N. A. C. C. (formerly A.L.A.M.) rating 22.5	
CYLINDERS . . .	Four	
ARRANGED . . .	Vertically, under hood	
CAST	In pairs	
BORE	3¾ inches	
STROKE	5 inches	
COOLING . . .	Water	
RADIATOR . . .	Vertical tube	
IGNITION . . .	Jump spark	
ELECTRIC SOURCE .	Delco system	
DRIVE	Shaft	
TRANSMISSION . .	Selective sliding gear	
GEAR CHANGES .	Three forward, one reverse	
POSITION OF DRIVER	Left-side drive and center control	

Price includes top, top hood, electric lighting, electric self-starter, windshield, speedometer and demountable rims

B U I C K
M O T O R
C O M P A N Y
F L I N T
M I C H I G A N

Price . . $1650
Roadster . 1650

BUICK "C-55"

Color	Body and hood, blue-black; fenders, black; chassis, black with ivory stripe	Arranged . . .	Vertically, under hood
Seating Capacity	Seven persons	Cast	In pairs
Clutch	Cone	Bore	3¾ inches
Wheelbase . .	130 inches	Stroke	5 inches
Gauge	56 inches	Cooling . . .	Water
Tire Dimensions:		Radiator . . .	Vertical tube
Front . .	36 x 4½ inches	Ignition . . .	Jump spark
Rear . . .	36 x 4½ inches	Electric Source .	Delco system
Brake Systems .	Contracting and expanding on both rear wheels	Drive	Shaft
		Transmission . .	Selective sliding gear
Horse-power . .	N. A. C. C. (formerly A.L.A.M.) rating 33.7	Gear Changes .	Three forward, one reverse
Cylinders . . .	Six	Position of Driver	Left-side drive and center control

Price includes top, top hood, electric lighting, electric self-starter, windshield, speedometer and demountable rims

**K I S S E L
MOTOR CAR
C O M P A N Y**

**H A R T F O R D
W I S C O N S I N**

Price	$1650
Detachable Sedan	2000
Seven-Passenger Touring .	1850
Cabriolet	1950
Coupe	2300

KISSEL KAR TOURING "6-42"

COLOR	Blue and black	
SEATING CAPACITY	Five persons	
CLUTCH	Cone	
WHEELBASE . .	126 inches	
GAUGE	56 inches	
TIRE DIMENSIONS:		
FRONT . . .	34 x 4 inches	
REAR	34 x 4 inches	
BRAKE SYSTEMS .	Contracting on both rear wheels	
HORSE-POWER . .	N. A. C. C. (formerly A.L.A.M.) rating 31.6	
CYLINDERS . . .	Six	
ARRANGED . . .	Vertically, under hood	

CAST	En bloc
BORE	3⅜ inches
STROKE	5½ inches
COOLING . . .	Water
RADIATOR . . .	Square tube
IGNITION . . .	Jump spark
ELECTRIC SOURCE .	Generator and storage battery
DRIVE	Shaft
TRANSMISSION . .	Selective sliding gear
GEAR CHANGES .	Three forward, one reverse
POSITION OF DRIVER	Left-side drive and center control

Price includes top, top hood, electric lighting, electric self-starter, windshield, speedometer and demountable rims

K I S S E L
MOTOR CAR
COMPANY

H A R T F O R D
W I S C O N S I N

Price	$1800
Five-Passenger Touring . .	1450
Seven-Passenger Touring .	1550
Roadster	1450
Cabriolet	1750
Coupe	2100

KISSEL KAR DETACHABLE SEDAN "4-36"

COLOR	Blue and black
SEATING CAPACITY	Five persons
CLUTCH	Cone
WHEELBASE . .	121 inches
GAUGE	56 inches
TIRE DIMENSIONS:	
FRONT . . .	34 x 4 inches
REAR	34 x 4 inches
BRAKE SYSTEMS .	Contracting on both rear wheels
HORSE-POWER . .	N. A. C. C. (formerly A.L.A.M.) rating 28.9
CYLINDERS . . .	Four
ARRANGED . . .	Vertically, under hood

CAST	En bloc
BORE	4¼ inches
STROKE	5½ inches
COOLING . . .	Water
RADIATOR . . .	Square tube
IGNITION . . .	Jump spark
ELECTRIC SOURCE .	Generator and storage battery
DRIVE	Shaft
TRANSMISSION . .	Selective sliding gear
GEAR CHANGES .	Three forward, one reverse
POSITION OF DRIVER	Left-side drive and center control

Price includes electric lighting, electric self-starter,
windshield, speedometer and demountable rims

KING MOTOR
CAR COMPANY

DETROIT
MICHIGAN

Price $1075
With Electric Lighting and Starting 1165
Roadster 1075
Cabriolet 1490

KING TOURING CAR "C"

COLOR	Dark blue	
SEATING CAPACITY	Five persons	
CLUTCH	Multiple disc	
WHEELBASE . .	113 inches	
GAUGE	56 or 60 inches	
TIRE DIMENSIONS:		
FRONT . . .	33 x 4 inches	
REAR	33 x 4 inches	
BRAKE SYSTEMS .	Contracting and expanding on both rear wheels	
HORSE-POWER . .	N. A. C. C. (formerly A.L.A.M.) rating 24.8	
CYLINDERS . . .	Four	
ARRANGED . . .	Vertically, under hood	

CAST	En bloc
BORE	3⅛ inches
STROKE	5 inches
COOLING . . .	Water
RADIATOR . . .	Cellular
IGNITION . . .	Jump spark
ELECTRIC SOURCE .	Storage battery and distributor system
DRIVE	Shaft
TRANSMISSION . .	Selective sliding gear
GEAR CHANGES .	Three forward, one reverse
POSITION OF DRIVER	Left-side drive and center control

Price includes top, top hood, windshield, speedometer and demountable rims

**KING MOTOR
CAR COMPANY**

D E T R O I T
M I C H I G A N

Price . . $1490
Touring . 1075
Roadster . 1075

KING CABRIOLET "C"

COLOR	Dark blue
SEATING CAPACITY	Two persons
CLUTCH	Multiple disc
WHEELBASE . .	113 inches
GAUGE	56 or 60 inches
TIRE DIMENSIONS:	
FRONT . . .	33 x 4 inches
REAR	33 x 4 inches
BRAKE SYSTEMS .	Contracting and expanding on both rear wheels
HORSE-POWER . .	N. A. C. C. (formerly A.L.A.M.) rating 24.8
CYLINDERS . . .	Four
ARRANGED . . .	Vertically, under hood

CAST	En bloc
BORE	3$\frac{13}{16}$ inches
STROKE	5 inches
COOLING . . .	Water
RADIATOR . . .	Cellular
IGNITION . . .	Jump spark
ELECTRIC SOURCE .	Storage battery and distributor system
DRIVE	Shaft
TRANSMISSION .	Selective sliding gear
GEAR CHANGES .	Three forward, one reverse
POSITION OF DRIVER	Left-side drive and center control

Price includes electric lighting, electric self-starter, windshield, speedometer and demountable rims

KING MOTOR
CAR COMPANY

D E T R O I T
M I C H I G A N

Price	$1075
With Electric Lighting and Starting	1165
Touring	1075
Cabriolet	1490

KING ROADSTER "C"

COLOR	Dark blue
SEATING CAPACITY	Two persons
CLUTCH	Multiple disc
WHEELBASE . .	113 inches
GAUGE	56 or 60 inches
TIRE DIMENSIONS:	
FRONT . . .	33 x 4 inches
REAR . . .	33 x 4 inches
BRAKE SYSTEMS .	Contracting and expanding on both rear wheels
HORSE-POWER . .	N. A. C. C. (formerly A.L.A.M.) rating 24.8
CYLINDERS . . .	Four
ARRANGED . . .	Vertically, under hood

CAST	En bloc
BORE	3⅛ inches
STROKE	5 inches
COOLING . . .	Water
RADIATOR . . .	Cellular
IGNITION . . .	Jump spark
ELECTRIC SOURCE .	Storage battery and distributor system
DRIVE	Shaft
TRANSMISSION . .	Selective sliding gear
GEAR CHANGES .	Three forward, one reverse
POSITION OF DRIVER	Left-side drive and center control

Price includes top, top hood, windshield, speedometer and demountable rims

A B B O T T
MOTOR CAR
C O M P A N Y

D E T R O I T
M I C H I G A N

Price, $2085

ABBOTT-DETROIT TOURING CAR "L"

COLOR	Black with gold stripe		CAST	In pairs
SEATING CAPACITY	Seven persons		BORE	4½ inches
CLUTCH	Multiple disc		STROKE	5½ inches
WHEELBASE . .	121 inches		COOLING . . .	Water
GAUGE	56 inches		RADIATOR . . .	Honeycomb
TIRE DIMENSIONS:			IGNITION . . .	Jump spark
FRONT . . .	36 x 4½ inches		ELECTRIC SOURCE .	Magneto and storage battery
REAR	36 x 4½ inches			
BRAKE SYSTEMS .	Contracting and expanding on both rear wheels		DRIVE	Shaft
			TRANSMISSION . .	Selective sliding gear
HORSE-POWER . .	N. A. C. C. (formerly A.L.A.M.) rating 32.4		GEAR CHANGES .	Three forward, one reverse
CYLINDERS . . .	Four		POSITION OF DRIVER	Right-side drive and right-hand control
ARRANGED . . .	Vertically, under hood			

Price includes top, top hood, electric lighting, electric self-
starter, windshield, speedometer and demountable rims

A B B O T T
M O T O R   C A R
C O M P A N Y

D E T R O I T
M I C H I G A N

Price	$2290
Roadster	2190
Five-Passenger Touring .	2190

ABBOTT-DETROIT TOURING CAR "F"

COLOR	Black with gold stripe	CAST	In blocks of three
SEATING CAPACITY	Seven persons	BORE	3¾ inches
CLUTCH	Multiple disc	STROKE	5¼ inches
WHEELBASE . .	130 inches	COOLING . . .	Water
GAUGE	56 inches	RADIATOR . . .	Honeycomb
TIRE DIMENSIONS:		IGNITION . . .	Jump spark
FRONT . . .	35 x 4½ inches	ELECTRIC SOURCE .	High-tension magneto and storage battery
REAR	35 x 4½ inches		
BRAKE SYSTEMS .	Contracting and expanding on both rear wheels	DRIVE	Shaft
HORSE-POWER . .	N. A. C. C. (formerly A.L.A.M.) rating 33.7	TRANSMISSION . .	Selective sliding gear
		GEAR CHANGES .	Four forward, one reverse
CYLINDERS . . .	Six	POSITION OF DRIVER	Left-side drive and center control
ARRANGED . . .	Vertically, under hood		

Price includes top, top hood, electric lighting, electric self-starter, windshield, speedometer and demountable rims

STEVENS-
DURYEA
COMPANY
CHICOPEE FALLS
MASSACHUSETTS

Price	$4800
Seven-Passenger Landau-Phaeton .	5600
Seven-Passenger Limousine . . .	6100
Seven-Passenger Berlin	6200
Seven-Passenger Landaulet . . .	6300

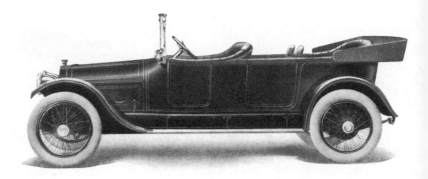

STEVENS-DURYEA TOURING CAR "D-6"

COLOR	English purple lake, lakelet green, olive brown, or sapphire blue
SEATING CAPACITY	Seven persons
CLUTCH . . .	Multiple disc
WHEELBASE . .	138 inches
GAUGE	56 inches
TIRE DIMENSIONS:	
FRONT . . .	37 x 5 inches
REAR . . .	37 x 5 inches
BRAKE SYSTEMS .	Contractng and expanding on both rear wheels
HORSE-POWER . .	N. A. C. C. (formerly A.L.A.M.) rating 47.2
CYLINDERS . . .	Six

ARRANGED . . .	Vertically, under hood
CAST	In pairs
BORE	$4\frac{7}{16}$ inches
STROKE . . .	$5\frac{1}{2}$ inches
COOLING . . .	Water
RADIATOR . . .	Cellular
IGNITION . . .	Jump spark
ELECTRIC SOURCE .	High-tension magneto and storage battery
DRIVE	Shaft
TRANSMISSION . .	Progressive sliding gear
GEAR CHANGES .	Three forward, one reverse
POSITION OF DRIVER	Left-side drive and left-hand control

Price includes top, top hood, electric lighting, electric self-starter, windshield, speedometer and demountable rims

CHEVROLET MOTOR COMPANY

FLINT, MICHIGAN

Price $750
With Electric Lighting and Starting   860

CHEVROLET "ROYAL MAIL" "H-2"

Color	Body and wheels, gun-metal; chassis, black	Arranged . . .	Vertically, under hood	
		Cast	En bloc	
		Bore	3$\frac{11}{16}$ inches	
Seating Capacity	Two persons	Stroke	4 inches	
Clutch	Cone	Cooling . . .	Water	
Wheelbase . .	106 inches	Radiator . . .	Tubular	
Gauge	56 or 60 inches	Ignition . . .	Jump spark	
Tire Dimensions:		Electric Source	High-tension magneto	
Front . . .	32 x 3$\frac{1}{2}$ inches			
Rear	32 x 3$\frac{1}{2}$ inches	Drive	Shaft	
Brake Systems .	Contracting and expanding on both rear wheels	Transmission . .	Selective sliding gear	
		Gear Changes .	Three forward, one reverse	
Horse-power . .	N. A. C. C. (formerly A.L.A.M.) rating 21.7	Position of Driver	Left-side drive and center control	
Cylinders . . .	Four			

Price includes top, top hood, prestolite tank, windshield, speedometer and demountable rims

CHEVROLET MOTOR COMPANY

FLINT, MICHIGAN

Price $875
With Electric Lighting and Starting   985

CHEVROLET "BABY GRAND" TOURING CAR "H-4"

COLOR	Body and wheels, Chevrolet gunmetal or Chevrolet lake red; chassis, black
SEATING CAPACITY	Five persons
CLUTCH	Cone
WHEELBASE . .	106 inches
GAUGE . .	56 or 60 inches
TIRE DIMENSIONS:	
FRONT . . .	32 x 3½ inches
REAR	32 x 3½ inches
BRAKE SYSTEMS .	Contracting and expanding on both rear wheels
HORSE-POWER . .	N. A. C. C. (formerly A.L.A.M.) rating 21.7
CYLINDERS . . .	Four

ARRANGED . . .	Vertically, under hood
CAST	En bloc
BORE	3¹⁵⁄₁₆ inches
STROKE	4 inches
COOLING . . .	Water
RADIATOR . . .	Tubular
IGNITION . . .	Jump spark
ELECTRIC SOURCE .	High-tension magneto
DRIVE	Shaft
TRANSMISSION . .	Selective sliding gear
GEAR CHANGES .	Three forward, one reverse
POSITION OF DRIVER	Left-side drive and center control

Price includes top, top hood, prestolite tank,
windshield, speedometer and demountable rims

CHEVROLET MOTOR COMPANY

FLINT, MICHIGAN

Price, $1425

CHEVROLET "LIGHT SIX" TOURING CAR "L"

COLOR	Body, Chevrolet blue or gunmetal; chassis and wheels, blue
SEATING CAPACITY	Five persons
CLUTCH	Cone
WHEELBASE . .	112 inches
GAUGE	56 inches
TIRE DIMENSIONS:	
FRONT . . .	34 x 4 inches
REAR	34 x 4 inches
BRAKE SYSTEMS .	Contracting and expanding on both rear wheels
HORSE-POWER . .	N. A. C. C. (formerly A.L.A.M.) rating 26.3
CYLINDERS . . .	Six
ARRANGED . . .	Vertically, under hood

CAST	In blocks of three
BORE	$3\frac{5}{16}$ inches
STROKE	$5\frac{1}{4}$ inches
COOLING . . .	Water
RADIATOR . . .	Tubular
IGNITION . . .	Jump spark
ELECTRIC SOURCE .	High-tension magneto
DRIVE . . .	Shaft
TRANSMISSION . .	Selective sliding gear
GEAR CHANGES .	Three forward, one reverse
POSITION OF DRIVER	Left-side drive and center control

Price includes top, top hood, electric lighting, electric self-starter, windshield, speedometer and demountable rims

PULLMAN
MOTOR CAR
COMPANY

YORK, PA.

Price	$2500
Seven-Passenger Touring .	2550
Limousine	3500
Landaulet	3500
Sedan	3200
Cabriolet	2800

PULLMAN TOURING CAR "6-48"

COLOR	Pullman blue
SEATING CAPACITY	Five persons
CLUTCH	Multiple disc
WHEELBASE . .	134 inches
GAUGE	56 inches
TIRE DIMENSIONS:	
FRONT . . .	36 x 4½ inches
REAR	36 x 4½ inches
BRAKE SYSTEMS .	Contracting and expanding on both rear wheels
HORSE-POWER . .	N. A. C. C. (formerly A.L.A.M.) rating 33.7
CYLINDERS . . .	Six
ARRANGED . . .	Vertically, under hood

CAST	In blocks of three
BORE	3¾ inches
STROKE	5¼ inches
COOLING . . .	Water
RADIATOR . . .	Cellular
IGNITION . . .	Jump spark
ELECTRIC SOURCE .	High-tension magneto and storage battery
DRIVE	Shaft
TRANSMISSION . .	Selective sliding gear
GEAR CHANGES .	Four forward, one reverse
POSITION OF DRIVER	Left-side drive
CONTROL . . .	Electric gear shift, center brake

Price includes top, top hood, electric lighting,
electric self-starter, windshield and speedometer

D O D G E
B R O T H E R S

D E T R O I T
M I C H I G A N

Price . . $785
Roadster . 785

DODGE BROTHERS TOURING CAR

COLOR	Black, with blue wheels	CAST	En bloc
SEATING CAPACITY	Five persons	BORE	3⅞ inches
CLUTCH	Cone	STROKE	4½ inches
WHEELBASE . .	110 inches	COOLING . . .	Water
GAUGE	56 or 60 inches	RADIATOR . . .	Tubular
TIRE DIMENSIONS:		IGNITION . . .	Jump spark
FRONT . . .	32 x 3½ inches	ELECTRIC SOURCE .	Generator
REAR	32 x 3½ inches	DRIVE	Shaft
BRAKE SYSTEMS .	Contracting and expanding on both rear wheels	TRANSMISSION . .	Selective sliding gear
HORSE-POWER . .	N. A. C. C. (formerly A.L.A.M.) rating 24	GEAR CHANGES .	Three forward, one reverse
CYLINDERS . . .	Four	POSITION OF DRIVER	Left-side drive and center control
ARRANGED . . .	Vertically, under hood		

Price includes top, top hood, electric lighting, electric self-
starter, windshield, speedometer and demountable rims

OAKLAND
MOTOR CAR
COMPANY

PONTIAC
MICHIGAN

Price, $1685

OAKLAND TOURING CAR "49"

COLOR	Body, blue and gray; running gear, black	CAST	En bloc
		BORE	3½ inches
SEATING CAPACITY	Seven persons	STROKE	5 inches
CLUTCH	Cone	COOLING . . .	Water
WHEELBASE . .	123½ inches	RADIATOR . . .	Cellular
GAUGE	56 inches	IGNITION . . .	Jump spark
TIRE DIMENSIONS:		ELECTRIC SOURCE .	Low-tension magneto with storage battery and dry cells
FRONT . . .	35 x 4½ inches		
REAR	35 x 4½ inches		
BRAKE SYSTEMS .	Contracting and expanding on both rear wheels	DRIVE	Shaft
		TRANSMISSION . .	Selective sliding gear
HORSE-POWER . .	N. A. C. C. (formerly A.L.A.M.) rating 29.4	GEAR CHANGES .	Three forward, one reverse
CYLINDERS . . .	Six	POSITION OF DRIVER	Left-side drive and center control
ARRANGED . . .	Vertically, under hood		

Price includes top, top hood, electric lighting, electric self-
starter, windshield, speedometer and demountable rims

OAKLAND
MOTOR CAR
COMPANY

PONTIAC
MICHIGAN

Price .	. $1200
Roadster .	. 1150
Speedster .	. 1100

OAKLAND TOURING CAR "37"

COLOR	Body, blue and gray; running gear, black	
SEATING CAPACITY	Five persons	
CLUTCH	Cone	
WHEELBASE . .	112 inches	
GAUGE	56 inches	
TIRE DIMENSIONS:		
FRONT . . .	33 x 4 inches	
REAR	33 x 4 inches	
BRAKE SYSTEMS .	Contracting and expanding on both rear wheels	
HORSE-POWER . .	N. A. C. C. (formerly A.L.A.M.) rating 19.6	
CYLINDERS . . .	Four	
ARRANGED . . .	Vertically, under hood	

CAST	En bloc
BORE	3½ inches
STROKE	5 inches
COOLING . . .	Water
RADIATOR . . .	Tubular
IGNITION . . .	Jump spark
ELECTRIC SOURCE .	Low-tension magneto with storage battery and dry cells
DRIVE	Shaft
TRANSMISSION . .	Selective sliding gear
GEAR CHANGES .	Three forward, one reverse
POSITION OF DRIVER	Left-side drive and center control

Price includes top, top hood, electric lighting, electric self-starter, windshield, speedometer and demountable rims

MOON MOTOR
CAR COMPANY

ST. LOUIS
MISSOURI

Price, $1575

MOON "6-40" TOURING CAR

COLOR	Optional		CAST	En bloc
SEATING CAPACITY	Six persons		BORE	3¾ inches
CLUTCH	Multiple disc		STROKE	5¼ inches
WHEELBASE . .	122 inches		COOLING . . .	Water
GAUGE	56 inches			
TIRE DIMENSIONS:			RADIATOR . . .	Honeycomb
FRONT . . .	34 x 4 inches		IGNITION . . .	Jump spark
REAR	34 x 4 inches		ELECTRIC SOURCE .	Delco system
BRAKE SYSTEMS .	Contracting and expanding on both rear wheels		DRIVE	Shaft
HORSE-POWER . .	N. A. C. C. (formerly A.L.A.M.) rating 33.7		TRANSMISSION . .	Selective gear
			GEAR CHANGES .	Three forward, one reverse
CYLINDERS . . .	Six		POSITION OF DRIVER	Left-side drive and center control
ARRANGED . . .	Vertically, under hood			

Price includes top, top hood, electric lighting, electric self-
starter, windshield, speedometer and demountable rims

KLINE MOTOR CAR CORP.

R I C H M O N D
V I R G I N I A

Price	$1750
Two-Passenger Runabout . . .	1750
Seven-Passenger Touring	1850
Two-Passenger Detachable Coupe .	2400
Five-Passenger Limousine . . .	2850
Seven-Passenger Limousine . . .	2850

KLINE KAR FIVE-PASSENGER TOURING

COLOR	Blue or green	CAST	In pairs
SEATING CAPACITY	Five persons	BORE	3½ inches
CLUTCH	Multiple disc	STROKE	5⅛ inches
WHEELBASE . .	123 inches	COOLING . . .	Water
GAUGE	56 inches	RADIATOR . . .	Honeycomb
TIRE DIMENSIONS :		IGNITION . . .	Jump spark
FRONT . . .	34 x 4 inches	ELECTRIC SOURCE .	Generator
REAR	34 x 4 inches	DRIVE	Shaft
BRAKE SYSTEMS .	Internal expanding on both rear wheels	TRANSMISSION . .	Selective sliding gear
HORSE-POWER . .	N. A. C. C. (formerly A.L.A.M.) rating 29.4	GEAR CHANGES .	Three forward, one reverse
CYLINDERS . . .	Six	POSITION OF DRIVER	Left-side drive and center control
ARRANGED . . .	Vertically, under hood		

Price includes top, top hood, electric lighting, electric self-starter, windshield, speedometer and demountable rims

MARION
MOTOR
COMPANY

INDIANAPOLIS
INDIANA

Price	**$2150**
Two-Passenger Roadster	2150
Four-Passenger Coupe .	2650
Five-Passenger Sedan . .	2950

MARION "G-5"

COLOR	Marion blue	CAST	In blocks of three
SEATING CAPACITY	Five persons		
CLUTCH	Multiple disc	BORE	3¾ inches
WHEELBASE . .	124 inches	STROKE	5¼ inches
GAUGE	56 inches	COOLING . . .	Water
TIRE DIMENSIONS:		RADIATOR . .	Cellular
FRONT . . .	35 x 4½ inches	IGNITION . . .	Jump spark
REAR	35 x 4½ inches	ELECTRIC SOURCE .	High-tension magneto and storage battery
BRAKE SYSTEMS .	Internal expanding on both rear wheels		
		DRIVE	Shaft
HORSE-POWER . .	N. A. C. C. (formerly A.L.A.M.) rating 33.7	TRANSMISSION . .	Selective sliding gear
		GEAR CHANGES .	Three forward, one reverse
CYLINDERS . . .	Six		
ARRANGED . . .	Vertically, under hood	POSITION OF DRIVER	Left-side drive and center control

Price includes top, top hood, electric lighting, electric self-
starter, windshield, speedometer and demountable rims

M E R C E R
A U T O M O B I L E
C O M P A N Y

T R E N T O N
N E W   J E R S E Y

Price	$3000
Six-Passenger Touring .	3000
Runabout	2900
Raceabout	2750

MERCER "22-70" SPORTING

COLOR	Brown, blue, green, gray or red	CAST	En bloc
SEATING CAPACITY	Four persons	BORE	3¾ inches
CLUTCH	Multiple disc dry plate	STROKE	6¾ inches
WHEELBASE . .	130 inches	COOLING . . .	Water
GAUGE	56 inches	RADIATOR . . .	Cellular
TIRE DIMENSIONS:		IGNITION . . .	Jump spark
FRONT . . .	34 x 4½ inches	ELECTRIC SOURCE .	High-tension magneto
REAR	34 x 4½ inches	DRIVE	Shaft
BRAKE SYSTEMS .	Expanding on drive shaft and both rear wheels	TRANSMISSION . .	Selective sliding gear
HORSE-POWER . .	N. A. C. C. (formerly A.L.A.M.) rating 22.5	GEAR CHANGES .	Four forward, one reverse
CYLINDERS . . .	Four	POSITION OF DRIVER	Left-side drive and center control
ARRANGED . . .	Vertically, under hood		

Price includes top, top hood, electric lighting, electric self-
starter, windshield, speedometer and demountable rims

REO MOTOR
CAR COMPANY

Price, $1050

L A N S I N G
M I C H I G A N

REO "FOUR" TOURING CAR

COLOR	Cobalt blue, trimmed with black
SEATING CAPACITY	Five persons
CLUTCH	Multiple disc dry plate
WHEELBASE . .	115 inches
GAUGE	56 or 60 inches
TIRE DIMENSIONS:	
FRONT . . .	34 x 4 inches
REAR	34 x 4 inches
BRAKE SYSTEMS .	Contracting and expanding on both rear wheels
HORSE-POWER . .	N. A. C. C. (formerly A.L.A.M.) rating 27.2
CYLINDERS . . .	Four
ARRANGED . . .	Vertically, under hood
CAST	In pairs
BORE	4⅛ inches
STROKE	4½ inches
COOLING . . .	Water
RADIATOR . . .	Tubular
IGNITION . . .	Jump spark
ELECTRIC SOURCE .	Generator, storage battery and dry cells
DRIVE	Shaft
TRANSMISSION . .	Selective sliding gear
GEAR CHANGES .	Three forward, one reverse
POSITION OF DRIVER	Left-side drive and center control

Price includes top, top hood, electric lighting, electric self-
starter, windshield, speedometer and demountable rim

REO MOTOR
CAR COMPANY

LANSING
MICHIGAN

Price, $1000

REO "FOUR" ROADSTER

COLOR	Black	BORE	4⅛ inches
SEATING CAPACITY	Two persons	STROKE	4½ inches
CLUTCH	Multiple disc dry plate	COOLING	Water
WHEELBASE	112 inches	RADIATOR	Tubular
GAUGE	56 or 60 inches	IGNITION	Jump spark
TIRE DIMENSIONS:		ELECTRIC SOURCE	Generator, storage battery and dry cells
FRONT	34 x 4 inches		
REAR	34 x 4 inches		
BRAKE SYSTEMS	Contracting and expanding on both rear wheels	DRIVE	Shaft
HORSE-POWER	N. A. C. C. (formerly A.L.A.M.) rating 27.2	TRANSMISSION	Selective sliding gear
CYLINDERS	Four	GEAR CHANGES	Three forward, one reverse
ARRANGED	Vertically, under hood	POSITION OF DRIVER	Left-side drive and center control
CAST	In pairs		

Price includes top, top hood, electric lighting, electric self-
starter, windshield, speedometer and demountable rims

REO MOTOR CAR COMPANY

Price, $1575

LANSING MICHIGAN

REO COUPE

COLOR	Cobalt blue, trimmed with black		ARRANGED . . .	Vertically, under hood
			CAST	In pairs
SEATING CAPACITY	Four persons		BORE	4⅛ inches
CLUTCH	Multiple disc dry plate		STROKE	4½ inches
			COOLING . . .	Water
WHEELBASE . .	112 inches		RADIATOR . . .	Tubular
GAUGE	56 or 60 inches		IGNITION . . .	Jump spark
TIRE DIMENSIONS:			ELECTRIC SOURCE .	Generator, storage battery and dry cells
FRONT . . .	34 x 4 inches			
REAR	34 x 4 inches		DRIVE	Shaft
BRAKE SYSTEMS .	Contracting and expanding on both rear wheels		TRANSMISSION . .	Selective sliding gear
			GEAR CHANGES .	Three forward, one reverse
HORSE-POWER . .	N. A. C. C. (formerly A.L.A.M.) rating 27.2		POSITION OF DRIVER	Left-side drive and center control
CYLINDERS . . .	Four			

Price includes electric starting, electric lighting, speedometer and demountable rim

REO MOTOR
CAR COMPANY

Price, $1385

L A N S I N G
M I C H I G A N

REO "SIX" TOURING CAR

COLOR	Cobalt blue, trimmed with black
SEATING CAPACITY	Five persons
CLUTCH	Multiple disc dry plate
WHEELBASE . .	122 inches
GAUGE	56 inches
TIRE DIMENSIONS:	
FRONT . . .	34 x 4 inches
REAR	34 x 4 inches
BRAKE SYSTEMS .	Contracting and expanding on both rear wheels
HORSE-POWER . .	N. A. C. C. (formerly A.L.A.M.) rating 30.4
CYLINDERS . . .	Six

ARRANGED . . .	Vertically, under hood
CAST	In blocks of three
BORE	3 9/16 inches
STROKE	5 1/8 inches
COOLING . . .	Water
RADIATOR . . .	Tubular
IGNITION . . .	Jump spark
ELECTRIC SOURCE .	Generator, storage battery and dry cells
DRIVE	Shaft
TRANSMISSION . .	Selective sliding gear
GEAR CHANGES .	Three forward, one reverse
POSITION OF DRIVER	Left-side drive and center control

Price includes top, top hood, electric lighting, electric self-
starter, windshield, speedometer and demountable rims

MITCHELL-
LEWIS MOTOR
COMPANY

R A C I N E
W I S C O N S I N

Price	$1250
Six-Passenger .	1300
Roadster . . .	1250

MITCHELL "LIGHT FOUR" TOURING CAR

COLOR	Imperial dark blue	CAST	In pairs
SEATING CAPACITY	Five persons	BORE	4 inches
CLUTCH	Cone	STROKE	5½ inches
WHEELBASE . .	116 inches	COOLING . . .	Water
GAUGE	56 inches	RADIATOR . . .	Tubular
TIRE DIMENSIONS:		IGNITION . . .	Jump spark
FRONT . . .	34 x 4 inches	ELECTRIC SOURCE .	Storage battery with igniter
REAR	34 x 4 inches		
BRAKE SYSTEMS .	Contracting and expanding on both rear wheels	DRIVE	Shaft
		TRANSMISSION . .	Selective sliding gear
HORSE-POWER . .	N. A. C. C. (formerly A.L.A.M.) rating 25.6	GEAR CHANGES .	Three forward, one reverse
CYLINDERS . . .	Four	POSITION OF DRIVER	Left-side drive and center control
ARRANGED . . .	Vertically, under hood		

Price includes top, top hood, electric lighting, electric self-
starter, windshield, speedometer and demountable rims

**MITCHELL-
LEWIS MOTOR
COMPANY**

**R A C I N E
W I S C O N S I N**

Price	$1585
Five-Passenger .	1585
Roadster . . .	1585

MITCHELL "LIGHT SIX" TOURING CAR

COLOR	Imperial dark blue	CAST	In pairs
SEATING CAPACITY	Six persons	BORE	4 inches
CLUTCH	Cone	STROKE	5½ inches
WHEELBASE . .	128 inches	COOLING . . .	Water
GAUGE	56 inches	RADIATOR . .	Cellular
TIRE DIMENSIONS:		IGNITION . . .	Jump spark
FRONT . . .	36 x 4 inches	ELECTRIC SOURCE .	Storage battery with igniter
REAR	36 x 4 inches		
BRAKE SYSTEMS .	Contracting and expanding on both rear wheels	DRIVE	Shaft
		TRANSMISSION . .	Selective sliding gear
HORSE-POWER . .	N. A. C. C. (formerly A.L.A.M.) rating 38.4	GEAR CHANGES .	Three forward, one reverse
CYLINDERS . . .	Six	POSITION OF DRIVER	Left-side drive and center control
ARRANGED . . .	Vertically, under hood		

Price includes top, top hood, electric lighting, electric self-
starter, windshield, speedometer and demountable rims

MITCHELL-
LEWIS MOTOR
COMPANY

R A C I N E
W I S C O N S I N

Price $1895
Six-Passenger . 1995

MITCHELL SPECIAL "SIX" TOURING CAR

COLOR	Imperial dark blue	CAST	In pairs
SEATING CAPACITY	Five persons	BORE	4¼ inches
CLUTCH	Cone	STROKE	6 inches
WHEELBASE . .	132 inches	COOLING . . .	Water
GAUGE	56 inches	RADIATOR . . .	Cellular
TIRE DIMENSIONS:		IGNITION . . .	Jump spark
FRONT . . .	36 x 4½ inches	ELECTRIC SOURCE .	Low-tension magneto
REAR	36 x 4½ inches		
BRAKE SYSTEMS .	Contracting and expanding on both rear wheels	DRIVE	Shaft
		TRANSMISSION . .	Selective sliding gear
HORSE-POWER . .	N. A. C. C. (formerly A.L.A.M.) rating 43.3	GEAR CHANGES .	Three forward, one reverse
CYLINDERS . . .	Six	POSITION OF DRIVER	Left-side drive and center control
ARRANGED . . .	Vertically, under hood		

Price includes top, top hood, electric lighting, electric self-
starter, windshield, speedometer and demountable rims

F. I. A. T.

POUGHKEEPSIE
NEW YORK

Price	. . . .	$5650
Roadster	. . . . . .	4650
Runabout	. . . . . .	4650
Five-Passenger Touring	. .	4650
Seven-Passenger Touring	. .	4650
Landaulet	. . . . . .	5750
Berline Limousine	. . .	5950

F. I. A. T. "55" LIMOUSINE

COLOR	Fiat blue, green or maroon
SEATING CAPACITY	Seven persons
CLUTCH	Multiple disc
WHEELBASE . .	128 inches
GAUGE	56 inches
TIRE DIMENSIONS:	
FRONT . . .	36 x 4½ inches
REAR	37 x 5 inches
BRAKE	Contracting and expanding on both rear wheels
HORSE-POWER . .	N. A. C. C. (formerly A.L.A.M.) rating 42
CYLINDERS . . .	Four
ARRANGED . . .	Vertically, under hood

CAST	En bloc
BORE	5⅛ inches
STROKE	6¾ inches
COOLING . . .	Water
RADIATOR . . .	Honeycomb
IGNITION . . .	Jump spark
ELECTRIC SOURCE .	High-tension magneto and storage battery
DRIVE	Shaft
TRANSMISSION . .	Selective sliding gear
GEAR CHANGES .	Four forward, one reverse
POSITION OF DRIVER	Right-side drive and right-hand control

Price includes electric lighting, electric self-starter, speedometer and demountable rims

COLE MOTOR
CAR COMPANY

INDIANAPOLIS
INDIANA

Price . . .	$2465
Roadster . .	2465
Coupe . .	2750
Limousine . .	3750

COLE BIG SIX "660"

COLOR	Body, Brewster green; running gear, black	ARRANGED . . .	Vertically, under hood
SEATING CAPACITY	Seven persons	CAST	In pairs
CLUTCH	Cone	BORE	4¼ inches
WHEELBASE . .	136 inches	STROKE	5¼ inches
GAUGE	56 inches	COOLING . . .	Water
TIRE DIMENSIONS:		RADIATOR . . .	Cellular
FRONT . . .	37 x 5 inches	IGNITION . . .	Jump spark
REAR	37 x 5 inches	ELECTRIC SOURCE .	Delco system
BRAKE SYSTEMS .	Contracting and expanding on both rear wheels	DRIVE	Shaft
		TRANSMISSION . .	Selective gear
		GEAR CHANGES .	Three forward, one reverse
HORSE-POWER . .	N. A. C. C. (formerly A.L.A.M.) rating 43.3	POSITION OF DRIVER	Left-side drive and center control
CYLINDERS . . .	Six		

Price includes top, top hood, electric lighting, electric self-
starter, windshield, speedometer and demountable rims

COLE MOTOR
CAR COMPANY

INDIANAPOLIS
INDIANA

Price . . $1485
Roadster . 1485
Coupe . . 1885

COLE STANDARD FOUR TOURING CAR "440"

COLOR	Body, Brewster green; running gear, black	CAST	In pairs
SEATING CAPACITY	Seven persons	BORE	4¼ inches
CLUTCH	Cone	STROKE	5¼ inches
WHEELBASE . .	120 inches	COOLING . . .	Water
GAUGE	56 inches	RADIATOR . . .	Cellular
TIRE DIMENSIONS:		IGNITION . . .	Jump spark
FRONT . . .	34 x 4 inches	ELECTRIC SOURCE .	Delco system
REAR	34 x 4 inches	DRIVE	Shaft
BRAKE SYSTEMS	Contracting and expanding on both rear wheels	TRANSMISSION . .	Selective gear
HORSE-POWER . .	N. A. C. C. (formerly A.L.A.M.) rating 28.9	GEAR CHANGES .	Three forward, one reverse
CYLINDERS . . .	Four	POSITION OF DRIVER	Left-side drive and center control
ARRANGED . . .	Vertically, under hood		

Price includes top, top hood, electric lighting, electric self-
starter, windshield, speedometer and demountable rims

**LOCOMOBILE
COMPANY
OF AMERICA**

**BRIDGEPORT
CONNECTICUT**

Price	$5400
Seven-Passenger Landaulet .	5500
Seven-Passenger Berline . .	5700
Five-Passenger Touring . .	4400
Four-Passenger Torpedo . .	4400
Two-Passenger Roadster . .	4400

LOCOMOBILE "38" LIMOUSINE "R-4"

COLOR	Optional	
SEATING CAPACITY	Seven persons	
CLUTCH	Multiple disc	
WHEELBASE . .	132 inches	
GAUGE	56 inches	
TIRE DIMENSIONS:		
FRONT . .	36 x 4½ inches	
REAR . . .	37 x 5 inches	
BRAKE SYSTEMS .	Contracting and expanding on both rear wheels	
HORSE-POWER . .	N. A. C. C. (formerly A.L.A.M.) rating 43.3	
CYLINDERS . . .	Six	
ARRANGED . . .	Vertically, under hood	

CAST	In pairs
BORE	4¼ inches
STROKE	5 inches
COOLING . . .	Water
RADIATOR . . .	Honeycomb
IGNITION . . .	Jump spark
ELECTRIC SOURCE .	High-tension magneto and storage battery
DRIVE	Shaft
TRANSMISSION . .	Selective sliding gear
GEAR CHANGES .	Four forward, one reverse
POSITION OF DRIVER	Left-side drive and center control

Price includes top, top hood, electric lighting, electric self-starter, windshield, speedometer and demountable rims

**LOCOMOBILE
COMPANY
OF AMERICA**

**BRIDGEPORT
CONNECTICUT**

Price	$4400
Two-Passenger Roadster . .	4400
Four-Passenger Torpedo . .	4400
Seven-Passenger Limousine .	5400
Seven-Passenger Landaulet .	5500
Seven-Passenger Berline . .	5700

LOCOMOBILE "38" TOURING CAR "R-5"

COLOR	Optional	CAST	In pairs
SEATING CAPACITY	Five persons	BORE	4¼ inches
CLUTCH	Multiple disc	STROKE	5 inches
WHEELBASE . .	132 inches	COOLING . . .	Water
GAUGE	56 inches	RADIATOR . . .	Honeycomb
TIRE DIMENSIONS:		IGNITION . . .	Jump spark
FRONT . . .	36 x 4½ inches	ELECTRIC SOURCE .	High-tension magneto and storage battery
REAR	37 x 5 inches		
BRAKE SYSTEMS .	Contracting and expanding on both rear wheels	DRIVE	Shaft
		TRANSMISSION . .	Selective sliding gear
HORSE-POWER . .	N. A. C. C. (formerly A.L.A.M.) rating 43.3	GEAR CHANGES .	Four forward, one reverse
CYLINDERS . . .	Six	POSITION OF DRIVER	Left-side drive and center control
ARRANGED . . .	Vertically, under hood		

Price includes top, top hood, electric lighting, electric self-
starter, windshield, speedometer and demountable rims

**LOCOMOBILE
COMPANY
OF AMERICA**
BRIDGEPORT
CONNECTICUT

Price	$5100
Two-Passenger Roadster . .	5100
Six-Passenger Torpedo . .	5100
Seven-Passenger Limousine .	6200
Seven-Passenger Landaulet .	6300
Seven-Passenger Berline . .	6500

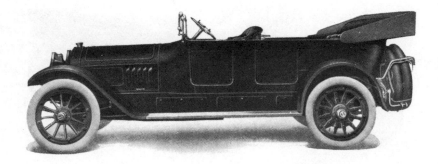

LOCOMOBILE "48" TOURING CAR "M-5"

COLOR	Optional	CAST	In pairs
SEATING CAPACITY	Seven persons	BORE	4½ inches
CLUTCH	Multiple disc	STROKE	5½ inches
WHEELBASE . .	140 inches	COOLING . . .	Water
GAUGE	56 inches	RADIATOR . . .	Honeycomb
TIRE DIMENSIONS:		IGNITION . . .	Jump spark
FRONT . . .	37 x 5 inches	ELECTRIC SOURCE .	High-tension magneto and storage battery
REAR	37 x 5 inches		
BRAKE SYSTEMS .	Contracting and expanding on both rear wheels	DRIVE	Shaft
		TRANSMISSION . .	Selective sliding gear
HORSE-POWER . .	N. A. C. C. (formerly A.L.A.M.) rating 48.6	GEAR CHANGES .	Four forward, one reverse
CYLINDERS . . .	Six	POSITION OF DRIVER	Left-side drive and center control
ARRANGED . . .	Vertically, under hood		

Price includes top, top hood, electric lighting, electric self-
starter, windshield, speedometer and demountable rims

J. I. CASE T. M. COMPANY, Inc.

Price, $1350

R A C I N E
W I S C O N S I N

CASE TOURING CAR "25"

COLOR	Dark Brewster green	CAST	In pairs
SEATING CAPACITY	Five persons	BORE	3¾ inches
CLUTCH	Multiple disc	STROKE	4¾ inches
WHEELBASE . .	115½ inches	COOLING . . .	Water
GAUGE	56 or 60 inches	RADIATOR . . .	Cellular
TIRE DIMENSIONS:		IGNITION . . .	Jump spark
FRONT . . .	34 x 4 inches	ELECTRIC SOURCE .	Storage battery and generator
REAR	34 x 4 inches		
BRAKE SYSTEMS .	Contracting and expanding on both rear wheels	DRIVE	Shaft
		TRANSMISSION . .	Selective sliding gear
HORSE-POWER . .	N. A. C. C. (formerly A.L.A.M.) rating 22.5	GEAR CHANGES .	Three forward, one reverse
CYLINDERS . . .	Four	POSITION OF DRIVER	Left-side drive and center control
ARRANGED . . .	Vertically, under hood		

Price includes top, top hood, electric lighting, electric self-
starter, windshield, speedometer and demountable rims

J. I. CASE T. M.
COMPANY, Inc.

Price, $1600

R A C I N E
W I S C O N S I N

CASE TOURING CAR " 35 "

COLOR	Blue and gray
SEATING CAPACITY	Five persons
CLUTCH	Multiple disc
WHEELBASE . .	120 inches
GAUGE	56 or 60 inches
TIRE DIMENSIONS:	
FRONT . . .	35 x 4½ inches
REAR	35 x 4½ inches
BRAKE SYSTEMS .	Contracting and expanding on both rear wheels
HORSE-POWER . .	N. A. C. C. (formerly A.L.A.M.) rating 28.9
CYLINDERS . . .	Four
ARRANGED . . .	Vertically, under hood

CAST	In pairs
BORE	4¼ inches
STROKE	5½ inches
COOLING . . .	Water
RADIATOR . . .	Cellular
IGNITION . . .	Jump spark
ELECTRIC SOURCE .	High-tension magneto and storage battery
DRIVE	Shaft
TRANSMISSION . .	Selective sliding gear
GEAR CHANGES .	Three forward, one reverse
POSITION OF DRIVER	Left-side drive and center control

Price includes top, top hood, electric lighting, electric self-starter, windshield, speedometer and demountable rims

**J. I. CASE T. M.
COMPANY, Inc.**

R A C I N E
W I S C O N S I N

Price	$1800
Seven-Passenger Touring .	2000

CASE TOURING CAR " 40 "

COLOR	Blue and gray	CAST	In pairs
SEATING CAPACITY	Five persons	BORE	4½ inches
CLUTCH	Single disc	STROKE	5¼ inches
WHEELBASE . .	124 inches	COOLING . . .	Water
GAUGE	56 or 60 inches	RADIATOR . . .	Cellular
TIRE DIMENSIONS:		IGNITION . . .	Jump spark
FRONT . . .	37 x 4½ inches	ELECTRIC SOURCE .	High-tension magneto and storage battery
REAR	37 x 4½ inches		
BRAKE SYSTEMS .	Contracting and expanding on both rear wheels	DRIVE	Shaft
		TRANSMISSION . .	Selective sliding gear
HORSE-POWER . .	N. A. C. C. (formerly A.L.A.M.) rating 32.4	GEAR CHANGES .	Three forward, one reverse
CYLINDERS . . .	Four	POSITION OF DRIVER	Right-side drive and right-hand control
ARRANGED . . .	Vertically, under hood		

Price includes top, top hood, electric lighting, electric self-starter, windshield, speedometer and demountable rims

S. G. V. COMPANY

R E A D I N G
P E N N S Y L V A N I A

Price	$3200
With Electric Starter . .	3300
Four-Passenger Touring .	3200
Roadster	3200
Closed Body Models . .	4000

S. G. V. LANDAULET-BROUGHAM "J"

COLOR	Optiona	
SEATING CAPACITY	Five persons	
CLUTCH	Multiple disc	
WHEELBASE . .	118 inches	
GAUGE	56 inches	
TIRE DIMENSIONS:		
FRONT . . .	34 x 4 inches	
REAR	34 x 4 inches	
BRAKE SYSTEMS .	Contracting on transmission and expanding on both rear wheels	
HORSE-POWER . .	N. A. C. C. (formerly A.L.A.M.) rating 24	
CYLINDERS . . .	Four	

ARRANGED . . .	Vertically, under hood
CAST	En bloc
BORE	3⅞ inches
STROKE	4⅜ inches
COOLING . . .	Water
RADIATOR . . .	Cellular
IGNITION . . .	Jump spark
ELECTRIC SOURCE .	High-tension magneto
DRIVE	Shaft
TRANSMISSION . .	Sliding gear
GEAR CHANGES .	Four forward, one reverse
POSITION OF DRIVER	Left-side drive and center control

Price includes electric lighting, windshield, speedometer and demountable rims

THE WHITE COMPANY
CLEVELAND, OHIO

Price . . .	$2700
Roadster . .	2650
Town Car .	4000
Sedan . .	4000

WHITE "30" FIVE-PASSENGER TOURING CAR

COLOR	White special maroon, White special gray, Cleveland gray, Brewster green, or cobalt blue	ARRANGED . . .	Vertically, under hood
		CAST	En bloc
		BORE	3¾ inches
		STROKE	5⅛ inches
SEATING CAPACITY	Five persons	COOLING . . .	Water
CLUTCH	Single plate	RADIATOR . . .	Honeycomb
WHEELBASE . .	115 inches	IGNITION . . .	Jump spark
GAUGE	56 inches	ELECTRIC SOURCE .	High-tension magneto
TIRE DIMENSIONS:			
FRONT . . .	32 x 4 inches	DRIVE	Shaft
REAR	32 x 4 inches	TRANSMISSION . .	Selective sliding gear
BRAKE SYSTEMS .	Contracting and expanding on both rear wheels	GEAR CHANGES .	Four forward, one reverse
HORSE-POWER . .	N. A. C. C. (formerly A.L.A.M.) rating 22.5	POSITION OF DRIVER	Left-side drive and center control
CYLINDERS . . .	Four		

Price includes top, top hood, electric lighting, electric self-starter, windshield, speedometer and demountable rims

THE WHITE
COMPANY

CLEVELAND, OHIO

Price	$3800
Semi-Touring	5300
Landaulet-Limousine .	5200
Limousine	5200

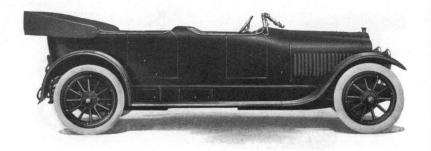

WHITE "45" SEVEN-PASSENGER TOURING CAR

COLOR	White special maroon, White special gray, Cleveland gray, Brewster green, or cobalt blue	CYLINDERS . . .	Four
		ARRANGED . . .	Vertically, under hood
		CAST	En bloc
SEATING CAPACITY	Seven persons	BORE	4¼ inches
CLUTCH	Single plate	STROKE . . .	6⅜ inches
WHEELBASE . .	133½ inches	COOLING . . .	Water
GAUGE	56 inches	RADIATOR . . .	Honeycomb
TIRE DIMENSIONS:		IGNITION . . .	Jump spark
FRONT . . .	36 x 4½ inches	ELECTRIC SOURCE .	High-tension magneto
REAR	36 x 4½ inches	DRIVE	Shaft
BRAKE SYSTEMS .	Contracting and expanding on both rear wheels	TRANSMISSION . .	Selective sliding gear
		GEAR CHANGES .	Four forward, one reverse
HORSE-POWER . .	N. A. C. C. (formerly A.L.A.M.) rating 28.9	POSITION OF DRIVER	Left-side drive and center control

Price includes top, top hood, electric lighting, electric self-
starter, windshield, speedometer and demountable rims

THE WHITE
COMPANY

CLEVELAND, OHIO

Price, $5500

WHITE "60" SEVEN-PASSENGER TOURING CAR

COLOR	White special maroon, White special gray, Cleveland gray, Brewster green, or cobalt blue	ARRANGED . . .	Vertically, under hood
		CAST	En bloc
		BORE	4¼ inches
		STROKE . . .	5¾ inches
SEATING CAPACITY	Seven persons	COOLING . . .	Water
CLUTCH	Single plate	RADIATOR . . .	Honeycomb
WHEELBASE . .	140¾ inches	IGNITION . . .	Jump spark
GAUGE	56 inches	ELECTRIC SOURCE .	High-tension magneto
TIRE DIMENSIONS:			
FRONT . . .	37 x 5 inches	DRIVE	Shaft
REAR . . .	37 x 5 inches	TRANSMISSION . .	Selective sliding gear
BRAKE SYSTEMS .	Contracting and expanding on both rear wheels		
		GEAR CHANGES .	Four forward, one reverse
HORSE-POWER . .	N. A. C. C. (formerly A.L.A.M.) rating 43.3	POSITION OF DRIVER	Left-side drive and center control
CYLINDERS . . .	Six		

Price includes top, top hood, electric lighting, electric self-starter, windshield, speedometer and demountable rims

A U S T I N
A U T O M O B I L E
C O M P A N Y

GRAND RAPIDS
M I C H I G A N

Price	. .	$3600
Runabout	. .	3600
Close Coupled	. .	3600
Five-Passenger Touring	. . .	3600
Six-Passenger Touring	. . .	3600
Enclosed Four-Passenger Limousine		4200
Enclosed Five-Passenger Limousine		4200
Seven-Passenger Limousine	. . .	4700

AUSTIN TOURING CAR "66"

COLOR	Special blue, gray or black	CAST	En bloc
SEATING CAPACITY	Four persons	BORE	4½ inches
CLUTCH	Multiple disc	STROKE	6 inches
WHEELBASE . .	141 inches	COOLING . . .	Water
GAUGE	56 inches	RADIATOR . . .	Honeycomb
TIRE DIMENSIONS:		IGNITION . . .	Jump spark
FRONT . . .	34 x 4½ inches	ELECTRIC SOURCE .	Generator and storage battery
REAR	34 x 4½ inches		
BRAKE SYSTEMS .	Contracting and expanding on both rear wheels	DRIVE	Shaft
		TRANSMISSION . .	Selective sliding gear
HORSE-POWER . .	N. A. C. C. (formerly A.L.A.M.) rating 48.6	GEAR CHANGES .	Six forward, two reverse (two-speed rear axle)
CYLINDERS . . .	Six		
ARRANGED . . .	Vertically, under hood	POSITION OF DRIVER	Left-side drive and center control

Price includes top, top hood, electric lighting, electric self-starter, double cantilever springs, windshield, speedometer and demountable rims

**ALLEN MOTOR
C O M P A N Y**

Price **$895**
Two-Passenger Roadster .   875

FOSTORIA - OHIO

ALLEN TOURING CAR " 34 "

COLOR	Black	CAST	En bloc
SEATING CAPACITY	Five persons	BORE	3⅝ inches
CLUTCH	Cone	STROKE	5 inches
WHEELBASE . .	110 inches	COOLING . . .	Water
GAUGE	56 inches	RADIATOR . . .	Vertical tube
TIRE DIMENSIONS:		IGNITION . . .	Jump spark
FRONT . . .	32 x 3½ inches	ELECTRIC SOURCE .	Generator and storage battery
REAR	32 x 3½ inches		
BRAKE SYSTEMS .	Contracting and expanding on both rear wheels	DRIVE	Shaft
		TRANSMISSION . .	Selective sliding gear
HORSE-POWER . .	N. A. C. C. (formerly A.L.A.M.) rating 21	GEAR CHANGES .	Three forward, one reverse
CYLINDERS . . .	Four	POSITION OF DRIVER	Left-side drive and center control
ARRANGED . . .	Vertically, under hood		

Price includes top, top hood, electric lighting, electric self-
starter, windshield, speedometer and demountable rims

ILLUSTRATIONS AND
SPECIFICATIONS
ELECTRIC
VEHICLES

THE WAVERLEY
C O M P A N Y

INDIANAPOLIS
I N D I A N A

Price	$2750
Five-Passenger Limousine .	3000
Front-Drive Four	2400
Rear-Drive Four	2300
Dual-Drive Four	2600
Roadster Coupe	2000

WAVERLEY CHAIR BROUGHAM "109"

COLOR	Black
SEATING CAPACITY	Four persons
BODY:	
LENGTH ALL OVER	131 inches
WIDTH ALL OVER	61 inches
WHEELBASE . .	106 inches
GAUGE	56 inches
TIRE DIMENSIONS:	
FRONT . . .	34 x 4 inches (pneumatic), or 34 x 2½ inches (cushion)
REAR . . .	34 x 4½ inches (pneumatic), or 34 x 2½ inches (cushion)

BRAKE SYSTEMS .	Dual internal expanding on both rear wheels, and motor brake
BATTERY . . .	42 cells; 11 or 13 plate
SPEED	20 miles per hour
No. FORWARD SPEEDS	Four
No. REVERSE SPEEDS	Four
CONTROL . . .	Lever operated
STEERING . . .	Lever

WOODS MOTOR VEHICLE CO.

C H I C A G O
I L L I N O I S

Price	. $3100
Five-Passenger Front Control	. 3000
Five-Passenger Rear Control	. 3000
Four-Passenger Rear Control	. 2850

WOODS DUAL CONTROL ELECTRIC " 1501 "

COLOR . . . . Body, blue,
green or maroon;
running gear,
black

SEATING CAPACITY Five persons

BODY:
  LENGTH ALL OVER 150 inches
  WIDTH ALL OVER 64½ inches

WHEELBASE . . 110 inches

GAUGE . . . . 56 inches

TIRE DIMENSIONS:
  FRONT . . . 34 x 4 inches
  (cushion)
  REAR . . . . 38 x 4½ inches
  (cushion)

BRAKE SYSTEMS . Contracting on
armature shaft
and expanding on
both rear wheels

BATTERY . . . 42 cells, 13 plates

SPEED . . . . 20 miles per hour

No. FORWARD SPEEDS Five

No. REVERSE SPEEDS Five

CONTROL . . . Lever operated

STEERING . . . Lever

OHIO ELECTRIC CAR COMPANY

T O L E D O
O H I O

Price	. . . .	$2900
Model 21 Roadster	. . . . . .	2650
Model 51 Double-Drive Brougham	.	3000
Model 11 Single-Drive Coupe	. .	2400

OHIO BROUGHAM "41"

COLOR	Coach blue	
SEATING CAPACITY	Four persons	
BODY:		
LENGTH ALL OVER	117 inches	
WIDTH ALL OVER	52 inches	
WHEELBASE . .	98½ inches	
GAUGE	56 inches	
TIRE DIMENSIONS:		
FRONT . . .	34 x 4½ inches (pneumatic), or 36 x 4 inches (cushion)	
REAR	34 x 4½ inches (pneumatic), or 36 x 4 inches (cushion)	

BRAKE SYSTEMS .	Contracting on both rear wheels, with magnetic brake operating on motor
BATTERY . . .	42 cells, 11 plate
SPEED	20 miles per hour
NO. FORWARD SPEEDS	Five
NO. REVERSE SPEEDS	Three
CONTROL . . .	Magnetic
STEERING . . .	Lever operated

**OHIO ELECTRIC
CAR COMPANY**

TOLEDO, OHIO

Price	$3250
Two-Passenger Roadster	2650
Four-Passenger Single-Drive Brougham	2600
Five-Passenger Single-Drive Brougham	2900
Five-Passenger Double-Drive Brougham	3000

OHIO ELECTRIC "61"

COLOR . . . . Ohio blue, green or maroon

SEATING CAPACITY Five persons

BODY:
  LENGTH ALL OVER 117 inches
  WIDTH ALL OVER 53 inches

WHEELBASE . . 98½ inches

GAUGE . . . . 56 inches

TIRE DIMENSIONS:
  FRONT . . . 34 x 4½ inches (pneumatic), or 36 x 4½ inches (cushion)

  REAR . . . . 34 x 4½ inches (pneumatic), or 36 x 4½ inches (cushion)

BRAKE SYSTEMS . Double external contracting on both rear wheels and magnetic brake operated by button

BATTERY . . . 44 cells, 11 plate

SPEED . . . . 20 miles per hour

NO. FORWARD SPEEDS Five

NO. REVERSE SPEEDS Three

CONTROL . . . Magnetic, operated by disc

STEERING . . . Lever

**A N D E R S O N
E L E C T R I C
CAR COMPANY**

**D E T R O I T
M I C H I G A N**

Price	**$2950**
Model 50 Cabriolet	2650
Model 51 Small Brougham . . .	2850
Model 52 Duplex-Drive Brougham .	3000
Model 53 Front-Drive Brougham .	2950
Model 55 Small Brougham . . .	2600

DETROIT REAR-SEAT BROUGHAM "54"

COLOR	Blue		BRAKE SYSTEMS .	Internal expanding on both rear wheels; also magnetic controller brake
SEATING CAPACITY	Five persons			
BODY:				
LENGTH ALL OVER	142 inches			
WIDTH ALL OVER	67 inches		BATTERY . . .	42 cells, 15 WTX
WHEELBASE . .	100 inches			
GAUGE	56 inches		SPEED	22 miles per hour
TIRE DIMENSIONS:				
FRONT . . .	34 x 4½ inches (pneumatic), or 36 x 4½ inches (cushion)		No. FORWARD SPEEDS	Five
			No. REVERSE SPEEDS	Five
REAR	34 x 4½ inches (pneumatic), or 36 x 4½ inches (cushion)		CONTROL . . .	Lever operated
			STEERING . . .	Lever

**RAUCH & LANG
C A R R I A G E
C O M P A N Y**

CLEVELAND, OHIO

Price, Coach J-5 Double Control . $3200
Coach J-5 Front Control 3100
Coach J-5 Rear Control 3100

RAUCH & LANG COACH "J-5"

Color	Optional	Brake Systems .	Contracting on motor and expanding on both rear wheels, also electric brake
Seating Capacity	Five persons		
Body:			
Length All Over	144 inches	Battery . . .	42 cells, 11 MV Hycap
Width All Over	64 inches		
Wheelbase . .	102 inches	Speed	21 miles per hour
Gauge	56 inches	No. Forward Speeds Six	
Tire Dimensions:		No. Reverse Speeds Three	
Front . . .	33 x 4½ inches (pneumatic), or 36 x 4 inches (cushion)	Control . . .	Lever operated
		Steering . . .	Lever
Rear	33 x 4½ inches (pneumatic), or 36 x 4 inches (cushion)		

**BROC ELECTRIC
V E H I C L E
C O M P A N Y**

S A G I N A W
M I C H I G A N

Price	$3200
Model 33 Rear-Drive Brougham .	3100
Model 34 Rear-Drive Brougham .	3150

AMERICAN-BROC DOUBLE-DRIVE BROUGHAM "36"

COLOR	Optional
SEATING CAPACITY	Five persons
BODY:	
LENGTH ALL OVER	123 inches
WIDTH ALL OVER	68 inches
WHEELBASE . .	96 inches
GAUGE	56 inches
TIRE DIMENSIONS:	
FRONT . . .	34 x 4 inches (pneumatic), or 36 x 4 inches (cushion)
REAR	34 x 4 inches (pneumatic), or 36 x 4 inches (cushion)

BRAKE SYSTEMS .	Contracting on drive shaft and expanding on both rear wheels
BATTERY . . .	40 cells, 11 plate MV Hycap Exide
SPEED	24 miles per hour
NO. FORWARD SPEEDS	Five
NO. REVERSE SPEEDS	Five
CONTROL . . .	Lever operated
STEERING . . .	Lever

ARGO ELECTRIC
V E H I C L E
C O M P A N Y
S A G I N A W
M I C H I G A N

Price, Chassis $1200

AMERICAN-ARGO "K-10"

Color	Optional
Carrying Capacity	1,000 pounds
Body:	
Length All Over	129½ inches
Width All Over	68 inches
Wheelbase . .	86 inches
Gauge	54 inches
Tire Dimensions:	
Front . . .	34 x 3 inches (cushion or solid)
Rear	34 x 3 inches (cushion or solid)

Brake Systems .	Double expanding on both rear wheels
Battery . . .	40 cells, 11 plate MV Hycap Exide
Speed	16 miles per hour
No. Forward Speeds	Four
No. Reverse Speeds	Two
Control . . .	Lever operated
Steering . . .	Wheel

**THE
BAKER MOTOR
VEHICLE
COMPANY**

CLEVELAND, OHIO

Price, $2800

BAKER D. A. COUPE

COLOR	Black, with blue, green or maroon panels
SEATING CAPACITY	Four persons
BODY:	
LENGTH ALL OVER	120 inches
WIDTH ALL OVER	65¼ inches
WHEELBASE . .	90 inches
GAUGE	56 inches
TIRE DIMENSIONS:	
FRONT . . .	32 x 4 inches (pneumatic), or 34 x 4 inches (cushion)
REAR	32 x 4 inches (pneumatic), or 34 x 4 inches (cushion)
BRAKE SYSTEMS .	Internal expanding on both rear wheels
BATTERY . . .	32 cells, 11 MV Hycap Exide
SPEED	23 miles per hour
No. FORWARD SPEEDS	Seven
No. REVERSE SPEEDS	Three
CONTROL . . .	Horizontal lever operated
STEERING . . .	Wheel or lever

**BORLAND-
GRANNIS
COMPANY**

S A G I N A W
M I C H I G A N

Price . . .	$2550
Roadster . .	2250
Limousine .	5500

AMERICAN-BORLAND "50"

COLOR	Optional
SEATING CAPACITY	Four persons
BODY:	
LENGTH ALL OVER	120¾ inches
WIDTH ALL OVER	67½ inches
WHEELBASE . .	96 inches
GAUGE	56 inches
TIRE DIMENSIONS:	
FRONT . . .	34 x 4 inches (pneumatic or cushion)
REAR	34 x 4 inches (pneumatic or cushion)

BRAKE SYSTEMS .	Internal expanding on both rear wheels
BATTERY . . .	40 cells, 11 plate MV Hycap Exide
SPEED	22 miles per hour
NO. FORWARD SPEEDS	Six
NO. REVERSE SPEEDS	Three
CONTROL . . .	Lever operated
STEERING . . .	Lever

ILLUSTRATIONS AND
SPECIFICATIONS
GASOLINE
COMMERCIAL
VEHICLES

KELLY-SPRINGFIELD MOTOR TRUCK COMPANY

SPRINGFIELD
O   H   I   O

Price, $2060

KELLY 3,000-POUND TRUCK "K-31"

COLOR	Optional	
CARRYING CAPACITY	3,000 pounds	
CLUTCH	Cone	
WHEELBASE . .	120 or 144 inches	
GAUGE	Front, 56 inches; rear, 60 inches	
TIRE DIMENSIONS:		
FRONT . . .	36 x 3½ inches (single solid)	
REAR	36 x 3 inches (dual solid)	
BRAKE SYSTEMS .	Expanding on both rear wheels	
HORSE-POWER . .	N. A. C. C. (formerly A.L.A.M.) rating 22.5	
CYLINDERS . . .	Four	
ARRANGED . . .	Vertically, under hood	

CAST	En bloc
BORE	3¾ inches
STROKE	5¼ inches
COOLING . . .	Water
RADIATOR . . .	Cellular
IGNITION . . .	Jump spark
ELECTRIC SOURCE .	High-tension magneto
DRIVE	Side chain
TRANSMISSION . .	Selective sliding gear
GEAR CHANGES .	Three forward, one reverse
POSITION OF DRIVER	Left-side drive and center control

**REO MOTOR
CAR COMPANY**

LANSING
MICHIGAN

Price, Chassis, $1650

REO TWO-TON TRUCK "J"

COLOR	Optional	ARRANGED . . .	Vertically, under hood
CARRYING CAPACITY	Two tons	CAST	In pairs
CLUTCH	Multiple disc	BORE	4⅛ inches
WHEELBASE . .	130 or 146 inches	STROKE	4½ inches
GAUGE	60 inches	COOLING . . .	Water
TIRE DIMENSIONS:		RADIATOR . . .	Sectional tubular
FRONT . . .	36 x 4 inches (single solid)	IGNITION . . .	Jump spark
REAR	36 x 3½ inches (dual solid)	ELECTRIC SOURCE .	Low-tension magneto and dry batteries
BRAKE SYSTEMS .	Contracting on jack shaft and expanding on both rear wheels	DRIVE	Double side chain
		TRANSMISSION . .	Selective sliding gear
HORSE-POWER . .	N. A. C. C. (formerly A.L.A.M.) rating 27.2	GEAR CHANGES .	Three forward, one reverse
		POSITION OF DRIVER	Left-side drive and center control
CYLINDERS . . .	Four		

Price includes detachable driver's cab

**G R A M M
MOTOR TRUCK
C O M P A N Y**

L I M A ,   O H I O

Price, Chassis $1350
With Standard Express Body . 1500

WILLYS UTILITY 1500-POUND TRUCK

COLOR	Lead
CARRYING CAPACITY	1500 pounds
CLUTCH	Cone
WHEELBASE . .	120 inches
GAUGE	Front, 56 inches; rear, 58 inches
TIRE DIMENSIONS:	
FRONT . . .	34 x 4½ inches (pneumatic)
REAR	36 x 3½ inches (solid)
BRAKE SYSTEMS .	Contracting on jack shaft and expanding on both rear wheels
HORSE-POWER . .	N. A. C. C. (formerly A.L.A.M.) rating 27.2
CYLINDERS . . .	Four

ARRANGED . . .	Vertically, under hood
CAST	Separately
BORE	4⅛ inches
STROKE	4½ inches
COOLING . . .	Water
RADIATOR . . .	Cellular
IGNITION . . .	Jump spark
ELECTRIC SOURCE .	Magneto and dry batteries
DRIVE	Double side chain
TRANSMISSION . .	Selective sliding gear
GEAR CHANGES	Three forward, one reverse
POSITION OF DRIVER	Right-side drive and center control

WALTER
MOTOR TRUCK
COMPANY

49 WEST 66th ST.
NEW YORK

Price, Chassis	. . . .	$4500
Six-Ton	. . . . . .	4750
Seven and One-half Ton	.	5000

WALTER FOUR-WHEEL DRIVE FIVE-TON TRUCK

COLOR	. . . .	Lead	CAST	En bloc
CARRYING CAPACITY	Five tons	BORE	4⅜ inches
CLUTCH	. . . .	Cone	STROKE	6 inches
WHEELBASE	. .	96 to 168 inches	COOLING . . .	Water
GAUGE	. . . .	Front, 64 inches; rear, 66 inches	RADIATOR . . .	Tubular
TIRE DIMENSIONS:			IGNITION . . .	Jump spark
FRONT	. . .	40 x 4 inches (dual solid)	ELECTRIC SOURCE .	High-tension magneto and storage battery
REAR	. . . .	40 x 5 inches (dual solid)		
BRAKE SYSTEMS	.	Contracting on transmission shaft and both rear wheels	DRIVE	Spur gear to wheels
			TRANSMISSION . .	Selective gear
HORSE-POWER	. .	N. A. C. C. (formerly A.L.A.M.) rating 30.6	GEAR CHANGES .	Four forward, one reverse
CYLINDERS	. . .	Four	POSITION OF DRIVER	Left-side drive and center control
ARRANGED	. . .	Vertically, under hood		

Price includes cab

VELIE MOTOR   Price, $2250
VEHICLE
COMPANY
MOLINE
ILLINOIS

VELIE ONE AND ONE-HALF TON TRUCK

COLOR	Lead	CAST	In pairs
CARRYING CAPACITY	3,000 pounds	BORE	4⅝ inches
CLUTCH	Multiple disc	STROKE	5¼ inches
WHEELBASE . .	140 inches	COOLING . . .	Water
GAUGE	56 inches	RADIATOR . . .	Honeycomb
TIRE DIMENSIONS:		IGNITION . . .	Jump spark
FRONT . . .	36 x 5½ inches (pneumatic)	ELECTRIC SOURCE .	High-tension magneto
REAR	36 x 5 inches (single solid)	DRIVE	Worm
BRAKE SYSTEMS .	Contracting and expanding on both rear wheels	TRANSMISSION . .	Selective sliding gear
HORSE-POWER . .	N. A. C. C. (formerly A.L.A.M.) rating 34.2	GEAR CHANGES .	Three forward, one reverse
CYLINDERS . . .	Four	POSITION OF DRIVER	Left-side drive and center control
ARRANGED . . .	Vertically, under hood		

Price includes top, prestolite tank and demountable rims

**THE AUTOCAR
COMPANY**

**A R D M O R E
P E N N S Y L V A N I A**

Price, Chassis			$1850
With Coal Dump Body			2200
With Contracting Dump Body			2100
With Hotel Bus Body			2600
With Tourer Body			2650

AUTOCAR TYPE "XXI-F"

COLOR	Body, optional; running gear, Autocar red	CAST	Separately
CARRYING CAPACITY	3,000 pounds	BORE	4¾ inches
CLUTCH	Multiple disc	STROKE	4½ inches
WHEELBASE	97 inches	COOLING	Water
GAUGE	58 inches	RADIATOR	Vertical tube
TIRE DIMENSIONS:			
FRONT	34 x 4½ inches	IGNITION	Jump spark
REAR	34 x 5 inches	ELECTRIC SOURCE	High-tension magneto
BRAKE SYSTEMS	Contracting and expanding on both rear wheels	DRIVE	Shaft
HORSE-POWER	N. A. C. C. (formerly A.L.A.M.) rating 18	TRANSMISSION	Progressive gear
		GEAR CHANGES	Three forward, one reverse
CYLINDERS	Two		
ARRANGED	Horizontally, under driver's seat	POSITION OF DRIVER	Right-side drive and right-hand control

Price includes prestolite tank

THE AUTOCAR COMPANY

ARDMORE
PENNSYLVANIA

Price, Chassis	$1850
With Single Curved Closed Body	2050
With Open Express Body	2000
With Furniture Body	2075
With Piano Body	2100

AUTOCAR TYPE "XXI-UF"

COLOR	Body, optional; running gear, Autocar red
CARRYING CAPACITY	3,000 pounds
CLUTCH	Multiple disc
WHEELBASE	97 inches
GAUGE	58 inches
TIRE DIMENSIONS:	
FRONT	34 x 4½ inches
REAR	34 x 5 inches
BRAKE SYSTEMS	Horizontally and expanding on both rear wheels
HORSE-POWER	N. A. C. C. (formerly A.L.A.M.) rating 18
CYLINDERS	Two

ARRANGED	Vertically, under driver's seat
CAST	Separately
BORE	4¾ inches
STROKE	4½ inches
COOLING	Water
RADIATOR	Vertical tube
IGNITION	Jump spark
ELECTRIC SOURCE	High-tension magneto
DRIVE	Shaft
TRANSMISSION	Progressive gear
GEAR CHANGES	Three forward, one reverse
POSITION OF DRIVER	Right-side drive and right-hand control

Price includes prestolite tank

HEWITT MOTOR COMPANY

WEST END AVE. &
64th STREET
NEW YORK, N. Y.

Price, Chassis, $5500

HEWITT TEN-TON TRUCK

COLOR	Optional
CARRYING CAPACITY	Ten tons
CLUTCH	Cone
WHEELBASE	138 to 164 inches
GAUGE	68 inches
TIRE DIMENSIONS:	
FRONT	36 x 5 inches (single)
REAR	44½ x 7 inches (dual)
BRAKE SYSTEMS	Service brake on gear box and expanding on both rear wheels
HORSE-POWER	N. A. C. C. (formerly A.L.A.M.) rating 28.9
CYLINDERS	Four

ARRANGED	Vertically, between driver's seats
CAST	In pairs
BORE	4¼ inches
STROKE	6 inches
COOLING	Water
RADIATOR	Cellular
IGNITION	Jump spark
ELECTRIC SOURCE	High-tension magneto
DRIVE	Double side chain
TRANSMISSION	Planetary
GEAR CHANGES	Two forward, one reverse
POSITION OF DRIVER	Left-side drive and left-hand control

MACK BROS.
MOTOR CAR
COMPANY

Price, Chassis, $2700

WEST END AVE. &
64th STREET
NEW YORK, N. Y.

MACK TWO-TON TRUCK

Color	Optional		Arranged . . .	Vertically, under hood
Carrying Capacity	Two tons		Cast	In pairs
Clutch	Multiple disc		Bore	4½ inches
Wheelbase . .	126, 138, 150 or 162 inches		Stroke	5½ inches
Gauge	59 inches		Cooling . .	Water
Tire Dimensions:			Radiator . . .	Honeycomb
Front . . .	36 x 4 inches (single solid)		Ignition . . .	Jump spark
			Electric Source .	High-tension magneto
Rear	36 x 3½ inches (dual solid)		Drive	Double side chain
Brake Systems	Contracting on differential and expanding on both rear wheels		Transmission . .	Mack patent non-sliding gear
			Gear Changes .	Three forward, one reverse
Horse-power . .	N. A. C. C. (formerly A.L.A.M.) rating 32.4		Position of Driver	Left-side drive and center control
Cylinders . . .	Four			

S A U R E R
M O T O R
C O M P A N Y

WEST END AVE. &
64th   STREET
NEW YORK, N. Y.

Price, Chassis, $4800

SAURER FIVE-TON TRUCK

COLOR	Optional
CARRYING CAPACITY	Five tons
CLUTCH	Cone
WHEELBASE . .	153½ or 177½ inches
GAUGE	66¼ inches
TIRE DIMENSIONS:	
FRONT . . .	36 x 5 inches (single solid)
REAR	42 x 5 inches (dual solid)
BRAKE SYSTEMS .	Air brake, and contracting on differential and expanding on both rear wheels
HORSE-POWER . .	N. A. C. C. (formerly A.L.A.M.) rating 30.6
CYLINDERS . . .	Four

ARRANGED . . .	Vertically, under hood
CAST	In pairs
BORE	4⅜ inches
STROKE	5½ inches
COOLING . . .	Water
RADIATOR . . .	Honeycomb
IGNITION . . .	Jump spark
ELECTRIC SOURCE .	High-tension magneto
DRIVE	Double side chain
TRANSMISSION . .	Selective sliding gear
GEAR CHANGES .	Four forward, one reverse
POSITION OF DRIVER	Right-side drive and right-hand control

PEERLESS MOTOR CAR COMPANY

CLEVELAND, OHIO

Price, Chassis	.	$4500
Three-Ton	. .	3700
Four-Ton .	. .	4000
Six-Ton .	. .	5000

PEERLESS FIVE-TON TRUCK

COLOR	Lead	
CARRYING CAPACITY	Five tons	
CLUTCH	Cone	
WHEELBASE . .	151 or 174 inches	
GAUGE	Front, 68 inches, rear, 73½ inches	
TIRE DIMENSIONS:		
FRONT . . .	38 x 6 inches (single solid)	
REAR	42 x 6 inches (dual solid)	
BRAKE SYSTEMS .	Contracting on jack shaft and expanding on both rear wheels	
HORSE-POWER . .	N. A. C. C. (formerly A.L.A.M.) rating 32.4	
CYLINDERS . . .	Four	

ARRANGED . . .	Vertically, under hood
CAST	In pairs
BORE	4½ inches
STROKE	6½ inches
COOLING . . .	Water
RADIATOR . . .	Tube and fin
IGNITION . . .	Jump spark
ELECTRIC SOURCE .	High-tension magneto
DRIVE	Double side chain
TRANSMISSION . .	Selective sliding gear
GEAR CHANGES .	Four forward, one reverse
POSITION OF DRIVER	Right-side drive and right-hand control

AMERICAN-
LA FRANCE
FIRE ENGINE
COMPANY, Inc.

E L M I R A
N E W   Y O R K

Price, $9000

AMERICAN-LA FRANCE PUMPING ENGINE—TYPE 12

COLOR	Optional	
CLUTCH	Multiple disc	
WHEELBASE . .	156¾ inches	
GAUGE	Front, 62 inches; rear, 65⅝ inches	
TIRE DIMENSIONS:		
FRONT . . .	38 x 4½ inches (single cushion)	
REAR	38 x 4½ inches (dual cushion)	
BRAKE SYSTEMS .	Expanding on both rear wheels	
HORSE-POWER . .	N. A. C. C. (formerly A.L.A.M.) rating 72.6	
CYLINDERS . .	Six	
ARRANGED . . .	Vertically, under hood	
CAST	In pairs	
BORE	5½ inches	
STROKE	6 inches	
COOLING . . .	Water	
RADIATOR . . .	Honeycomb	
IGNITION . . .	Jump spark	
ELECTRIC SOURCE .	High-tension magneto	
DRIVE	Double side chain	
TRANSMISSION . .	Selective sliding gear	
GEAR CHANGES .	Three forward, one reverse	
POSITION OF DRIVER	Right-side drive and right-hand control	

Price includes electric lighting, speedometer and demountable rims

AMERICAN-
LA FRANCE
FIRE ENGINE
COMPANY, Inc.

Price, $10,000

E L M I R A
N E W   Y O R K

AMERICAN-LA FRANCE PUMPING ENGINE—TYPE 15

COLOR	Optional
CLUTCH . .	Multiple disc
WHEELBASE . .	172¾ inches
GAUGE	Front, 62 inches; rear, 67 inches
TIRE DIMENSIONS:	
FRONT . . .	38 x 5 inches (single solid)
REAR	38 x 4 inches (dual solid)
BRAKE SYSTEMS .	Expanding on both rear wheels
HORSE-POWER . .	N. A. C. C. (formerly A.L.A.M.) rating 121.8
CYLINDERS . . .	Six
ARRANGED . . .	Vertically, under hood

CAST	In pairs
BORE	7⅛ inches
STROKE	8 inches
COOLING . . .	Water
RADIATOR . . .	Honeycomb
IGNITION . . .	Jump spark
ELECTRIC SOURCE .	High-tension magneto
DRIVE	Double side chain
TRANSMISSION . .	Selective sliding gear
GEAR CHANGES .	Three forward, one reverse
POSITION OF DRIVER	Right-side drive and right-hand control

Price includes electric lighting, electric self-
starter, speedometer and demountable rims

AMERICAN-
LA FRANCE
FIRE   ENGINE
COMPANY, Inc.

E L M I R A
N E W   Y O R K

Price, $5500

AMERICAN-LA FRANCE CHEMICAL ENGINE AND HOSE CAR—TYPE 10

COLOR	Optional
CLUTCH	Multiple disc
WHEELBASE . .	140¾ inches
GAUGE	Front, 62 inches; rear, 65⅝ inches
TIRE DIMENSIONS:	
FRONT . . .	38 x 4½ inches (single cushion)
REAR	38 x 4½ inches (dual cushion)
BRAKE SYSTEMS .	Expanding on both rear wheels
HORSE-POWER . .	N. A. C. C. (formerly A.L.A.M.) rating 48.4
CYLINDERS . . .	Four
ARRANGED . . .	Vertically, under hood

CAST	In pairs
BORE	5½ inches
STROKE	6 inches
COOLING . . .	Water
RADIATOR . . .	Honeycomb
IGNITION . . .	Jump spark
ELECTRIC SOURCE .	High-tension magneto
DRIVE	Double side chain
TRANSMISSION . .	Selective sliding gear
GEAR CHANGES .	Three forward, one reverse
POSITION OF DRIVER	Right-side drive and right-hand control

Price includes electric lighting, speedometer and demountable rims

AMERICAN-
LA FRANCE
FIRE ENGINE
COMPANY, Inc.

Price, $4500

E   L   M   I   R   A
N E W   Y O R K

AMERICAN-LA FRANCE COMBINATION CHEMICAL AND HOSE CAR—TYPE 20

COLOR	Optional	
CLUTCH	Multiple disc	
WHEELBASE . .	140¾ inches	
GAUGE	66¾ inches	
TIRE DIMENSIONS:		
FRONT . . .	38 x 4 inches (single solid cushion)	
REAR	38 x 3½ inches (dual solid cushion)	
BRAKE SYSTEMS .	Contracting and expanding on both rear wheels	
HORSE-POWER . .	N. A. C. C. (formerly A.L.A.M.) rating 38.4	
CYLINDERS . . .	Six	

ARRANGED . . .	Vertically, under hood
CAST	In blocks of three
BORE	4 inches
STROKE	5½ inches
COOLING . . .	Water
RADIATOR . . .	Honeycomb
IGNITION . . .	Jump spark
ELECTRIC SOURCE .	High-tension magneto
DRIVE	Double side chain
TRANSMISSION . .	Selective sliding gear
GEAR CHANGES .	Three forward, one reverse
POSITION OF DRIVER	Right-side drive and right-hand control

Price includes electric lighting, speedometer and demountable rims

AMERICAN -
LA FRANCE
FIRE ENGINE
COMPANY, Inc.
▊▊▊▊▊▊▊▊▊▊▊▊▊▊▊▊▊▊▊▊▊▊▊▊▊▊▊
E L M I R A
N E W   Y O R K

Price, $6000

AMERICAN-LA FRANCE SERVICE HOOK AND LADDER TRUCK—TYPE 14

COLOR	Optional
CLUTCH	Multiple disc
WHEELBASE . .	242 inches
GAUGE	Front, 62 inches; rear 65⅝ inches
TIRE DIMENSIONS:	
FRONT . . .	38 x 4½ inches (single cushion)
REAR	38 x 4½ inches (dual cushion)
BRAKE SYSTEMS .	Expanding on both rear wheels
HORSE-POWER . .	N. A. C. C. (formerly A.L.A.M.) rating 48.4
CYLINDERS . . .	Four
ARRANGED . . .	Vertically, under hood

CAST	In pairs
BORE	5½ inches
STROKE	6 inches
COOLING . . .	Water
RADIATOR . . .	Honeycomb
IGNITION . . .	Jump spark
ELECTRIC SOURCE .	High-tension magneto
DRIVE	Double side chain
TRANSMISSION . .	Selective sliding gear
GEAR CHANGES .	Three forward, one reverse
POSITION OF DRIVER	Right-side drive and right-hand control

Price includes electric lighting, speedometer and demountable rims

AMERICAN- LA FRANCE FIRE ENGINE COMPANY, Inc.

**E L M I R A
N E W   Y O R K**

Price, $10,000 to $11,500

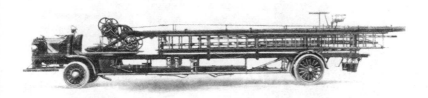

AMERICAN-LA FRANCE AERIAL HOOK AND LADDER TRUCK—TYPE 25

COLOR	Optional
CLUTCH	Multiple disc
WHEELBASE . .	333 inches
GAUGE	66 inches
TIRE DIMENSIONS:	
FRONT . . .	38 x 5 inches (dual solid)
REAR	38 x 4 inches (single solid)
BRAKE SYSTEMS .	Contracting on transmission and expanding on both rear wheels
HORSE-POWER . .	N. A. C. C. (formerly A.L.A.M.) rating 72.6
CYLINDERS . . .	Six
ARRANGED . . .	Vertically, under hood

CAST	In pairs
BORE	5½ inches
STROKE	6 inches
COOLING . . .	Water
RADIATOR . . .	Honeycomb
IGNITION . . .	Jump spark
ELECTRIC SOURCE .	High-tension magneto
DRIVE	Double side chain
TRANSMISSION . .	Selective sliding gear
GEAR CHANGES .	Three forward, one reverse
POSITION OF DRIVER	Right-side drive and right-hand control

Price includes electric lighting, speedometer and demountable rims

**AMERICAN-
LA FRANCE
FIRE ENGINE
COMPANY, Inc.**

E   L   M   I   R   A
N E W   Y O R K

AMERICAN-LA FRANCE MOTOR STEAM FIRE ENGINE—TYPE 29

COLOR	Optional	
CLUTCH	Multiple disc	
WHEELBASE . .	142 inches	
GAUGE	68½ inches	
TIRE DIMENSIONS:		
FRONT . . .	38 x 4 inches (dual solid)	
REAR	38 x 4 inches (single solid)	
BRAKE SYSTEMS .	Contracting on transmission and expanding on both front wheels	
HORSE-POWER . .	N. A. C. C. (formerly A.L.A.M.) rating 48.4	
CYLINDERS . . .	Four	
ARRANGED . . .	Vertically, under hood	

CAST	In pairs
BORE	5½ inches
STROKE	6 inches
COOLING . . .	Water
RADIATOR . . .	Honeycomb
IGNITION . . .	Jump spark
ELECTRIC SOURCE .	High-tension magneto
DRIVE	Double side chain
TRANSMISSION . .	Selective sliding gear
GEAR CHANGES .	Three forward, one reverse
POSITION OF DRIVER	Right-side drive and right-hand control

Price includes electric lighting, speedometer and demountable rims

**AMERICAN-
LA FRANCE
FIRE ENGINE
COMPANY, Inc.**

E L M I R A
N E W   Y O R K

Price, $5500

AMERICAN-LA FRANCE SIX-TON TRUCK—TYPE 6

COLOR	Gray	BORE	5½ inches
CARRYING CAPACITY	Six tons	STROKE	6 inches
WHEELBASE . .	129 inches	COOLING . . .	Water
GAUGE	68 inches	RADIATOR . . .	Honeycomb
TIRE DIMENSIONS:		IGNITION . . .	Jump spark
FRONT . . .	36 x 5 inches (single solid)	ELECTRIC SOURCE .	High-tension magneto—dual system
REAR	38 x 6 inches (dual solid)	DRIVE	Double side chain
BRAKE SYSTEMS .	Expanding on both rear wheels	TRANSMISSION . .	Hydraulic
HORSE-POWER . .	N. A. C. C. (formerly A.L.A.M.) rating 48.4	SPEED CHANGES .	Forward, 0 to maximum; reverse, 0 to maximum
CYLINDERS . . .	Four		
ARRANGED . . .	Vertically, under hood	POSITION OF DRIVER	Right-side drive and right-hand control
CAST	In pairs		

S E L D E N
M O T O R
V E H I C L E
C O M P A N Y

R O C H E S T E R
N E W   Y O R K

Price, Chassis, $2000

SELDEN ONE AND ONE-HALF TON TRUCK "JB"

COLOR	Body, green; running gear, red	
CARRYING CAPACITY	1½ tons	
CLUTCH	Multiple disc	
WHEELBASE . .	150 inches	
GAUGE	Front, 56 inches; rear, 60 inches	
TIRE DIMENSIONS:		
FRONT . . .	36 x 3½ inches	
REAR . . .	36 x 5 inches	
BRAKE SYSTEMS .	Contracting on jack shaft and expanding on both rear wheels	
HORSE-POWER . .	30	
CYLINDERS . . .	Four	
ARRANGED . . .	Vertically, under hood	

CAST	En bloc
BORE	3¾ inches
STROKE	5¼ inches
COOLING . . .	Water
RADIATOR . . .	Vertical tube
IGNITION . . .	Jump spark
ELECTRIC SOURCE .	High-tension magneto
DRIVE	Double chain
TRANSMISSION . .	Selective sliding gear
GEAR CHANGES .	Three forward, one reverse
POSITION OF DRIVER	Left-side drive and center control

SELDEN
MOTOR
VEHICLE
COMPANY

ROCHESTER
NEW YORK

Price, Chassis, $2000

SELDEN ONE AND ONE-HALF TON TRUCK "JB"

COLOR	Body, red; running gear, green
CARRYING CAPACITY	1½ tons
CLUTCH	Multiple disc
WHEELBASE . .	150 inches
GAUGE	Front, 56 inches; rear, 60 inches
TIRE DIMENSIONS:	
FRONT . . .	36 x 3½ inches
REAR	36 x 5 inches
BRAKE SYSTEMS .	Contracting on jack shaft and expanding on both rear wheels
HORSE-POWER . .	30
CYLINDERS . . .	Four
ARRANGED . . .	Vertically, under hood

CAST	En bloc
BORE	3¾ inches
STROKE	5¼ inches
COOLING . . .	Water
RADIATOR . . .	Vertical tube
IGNITION . . .	Jump spark
ELECTRIC SOURCE .	High-tension magneto
DRIVE	Double chain
TRANSMISSION . .	Selective sliding gear
GEAR CHANGES .	Three forward, one reverse
POSITION OF DRIVER	Left-side drive and center control

THE WHITE
COMPANY

CLEVELAND
O   H   I   O

Price, Chassis   .   .   . $2100
With Standard Body   .   2250

WHITE "GBBE" THREE-QUARTER TON TRUCK

COLOR	Chassis, red; body, dark green		ARRANGED . . .	Vertically, under hood	
CARRYING CAPACITY	1500 pounds		CAST	En bloc	
CLUTCH	Single plate		BORE	3¾ inches	
WHEELBASE . .	133½ inches		STROKE	5⅛ inches	
GAUGE	56 inches		COOLING . . .	Water	
TIRE DIMENSIONS:			RADIATOR . . .	Honeycomb	
FRONT . . .	34 x 4½ inches (pneumatic)		IGNITION . . .	Jump spark	
			ELECTRIC SOURCE .	High-tension magneto	
REAR	34 x 4½ inches (pneumatic)		DRIVE	Shaft	
BRAKE SYSTEMS .	Contracting and expanding on both rear wheels		TRANSMISSION . .	Selective sliding gear	
			GEAR CHANGES .	Four forward, one reverse	
HORSE-POWER . .	N. A. C. C. (formerly A.L.A.M.) rating 22.5		POSITION OF DRIVER	Left-side drive and center control	
CYLINDERS . . .	Four				

Price includes prestolite tank and demountable rims

THE WHITE
COMPANY

CLEVELAND
O   H   I   O

Price, Chassis . . . $3000
With Standard Body . 3150

WHITE "TBC" ONE AND ONE-HALF TON TRUCK

COLOR	Red
CARRYING CAPACITY	1½ tons
CLUTCH	Single plate
WHEELBASE . .	145½ inches
GAUGE	56 inches
TIRE DIMENSIONS:	
FRONT . . .	36 x 4½ inches (pneumatic)
REAR	36 x 4½ inches (pneumatic)
BRAKE SYSTEMS .	Contracting and expanding on both rear wheels
HORSE-POWER . .	N. A. C. C. (formerly A.L.A.M.) rating 22.5
CYLINDERS . . .	Four

ARRANGED . . .	Vertically, under hood
CAST	En bloc
BORE	3¾ inches
STROKE	5⅛ inches
COOLING . . .	Water
RADIATOR . . .	Honeycomb
IGNITION . . .	Jump spark
ELECTRIC SOURCE .	High-tension magneto
DRIVE	Shaft
TRANSMISSION . .	Selective sliding gear
GEAR CHANGES .	Four forward, one reverse
POSITION OF DRIVER	Left-side drive and center control

Price includes demountable rims

THE WHITE
COMPANY

CLEVELAND
O   H   I   O

Price, Chassis . . . **$3700**
With Standard Body . 3850

WHITE "TAD" THREE-TON TRUCK

COLOR	Red
CARRYING CAPACITY	Three tons
CLUTCH	Single plate
WHEELBASE . .	163 inches
GAUGE	Front, 64 inches
TIRE DIMENSIONS:	
FRONT . . .	36 x 5 inches (single solid)
REAR	40 x 5 inches (dual solid)
BRAKE SYSTEMS .	Contracting on jack shaft and expanding on both rear wheels
HORSE-POWER .	N. A. C. C. (formerly A.L.A.M.) rating 22.5
CYLINDERS . . .	Four

ARRANGED	Vertically, under hood
CAST	En bloc
BORE	3¾ inches
STROKE	5⅛ inches
COOLING . . .	Water
RADIATOR . . .	Honeycomb
IGNITION . . .	Jump spark
ELECTRIC SOURCE .	High-tension magneto
DRIVE	Double side chain
TRANSMISSION . .	Selective sliding gear
GEAR CHANGES .	Four forward, one reverse
POSITION OF DRIVER	Left-side drive and center control

THE WHITE
COMPANY

CLEVELAND
O H I O

Price, with Standard Body, $5200

WHITE "ATC" FIVE-TON POWER DUMPING TRUCK

COLOR	Red
CARRYING CAPACITY	Five tons
CLUTCH	Single plate
WHEELBASE . .	149 inches
GAUGE	64 inches
TIRE DIMENSIONS:	
FRONT . . .	36 x 5 inches (single solid)
REAR	40 x 6 inches (dual solid)
BRAKE SYSTEMS .	Contracting on jack shaft and expanding on both rear wheels
HORSE-POWER . .	N. A. C. C. (formerly A.L.A.M.) rating 28.9
CYLINDERS . . .	Four

ARRANGED . . .	Vertically, under hood
CAST	En bloc
BORE	4¼ inches
STROKE	6⅜ inches
COOLING . . .	Water
RADIATOR . . .	Honeycomb
IGNITION . . .	Jump spark
ELECTRIC SOURCE .	High-tension magneto
DRIVE	Double side chain
TRANSMISSION . .	Selective sliding gear
GEAR CHANGES .	Four forward, one reverse
POSITION OF DRIVER	Left-side drive and center control

STUDEBAKER
CORPORATION
OF AMERICA

DETROIT
MICHIGAN

Price, $1085

STUDEBAKER LIGHT DELIVERY "5"

COLOR	Optional	
CARRYING CAPACITY	1500 pounds	
CLUTCH	Cone	
WHEELBASE . .	108 inches	
GAUGE	56 inches	
TIRE DIMENSIONS:		
FRONT . . .	34 x 4½ inches (pneumatic)	
REAR	34 x 4½ inches (pneumatic)	
BRAKE SYSTEMS .	Contracting and expanding on both rear wheels	
HORSE-POWER . .	N. A. C. C. (formerly A.L.A.M.) rating 19.6	
CYLINDERS . . .	Four	
ARRANGED . . .	Vertically, under hood	

CAST	En bloc
BORE	3½ inches
STROKE	5 inches
COOLING . . .	Water
RADIATOR . . .	Tubular
IGNITION . . .	Jump spark
ELECTRIC SOURCE .	Storage battery
DRIVE	Shaft
TRANSMISSION . .	Selective sliding gear
GEAR CHANGES .	Three forward, one reverse
POSITION OF DRIVER	Left-side drive and center control

Price includes electric lighting, electric self-starter,
windshield, speedometer and demountable rims

PIERCE-ARROW MOTOR CAR CO.

B U F F A L O
N E W   Y O R K

Price, Chassis, $4500

PIERCE-ARROW FIVE-TON TRUCK "R-5"

COLOR	Optional
CARRYING CAPACITY	Five tons
CLUTCH	Cone
WHEELBASE . .	168 or 204 inches
GAUGE	64 inches
TIRE DIMENSIONS:	
FRONT . . .	36 x 5 inches (single solid)
REAR	40 x 6 inches (dual solid)
BRAKE SYSTEMS .	Contracting on transmission and expanding on both rear wheels
HORSE-POWER . .	N. A. C. C. (formerly A.L.A.M.) rating 38
CYLINDERS . . .	Four

ARRANGED . . .	Vertically, under hood
CAST	In pairs
BORE	4⅞ inches
STROKE	6 inches
COOLING . . .	Water
RADIATOR . . .	Vertical tube
IGNITION . . .	Jump spark
ELECTRIC SOURCE .	High-tension magneto and dry battery
DRIVE	Worm
TRANSMISSION . .	Selective sliding gear
GEAR CHANGES .	Three forward, one reverse
POSITION OF DRIVER	Right-side drive and right-hand control

PIERCE-ARROW
MOTOR CAR CO.

Price, Chassis, $3000

B U F F A L O
N E W   Y O R K

PIERCE-ARROW TWO-TON TRUCK "X-2"

COLOR	Optional
CARRYING CAPACITY	Two tons
CLUTCH	Cone
WHEELBASE . .	150 or 180 inches
GAUGE	56 inches
TIRE DIMENSIONS:	
FRONT . . .	36 x 4 inches (single solid)
REAR	36 x 4 inches (dual solid)
BRAKE SYSTEMS .	Contracting on transmission and expanding on both rear wheels
HORSE-POWER . .	N. A. C. C. (formerly A.L.A.M.) rating 25.6
CYLINDERS . . .	Four

ARRANGED . . .	Vertically, under hood
CAST	In pairs
BORE	4 inches
STROKE	5½ inches
COOLING . . .	Water
RADIATOR	Vertical tube
IGNITION . . .	Jump spark
ELECTRIC SOURCE .	High-tension magneto
DRIVE	Worm
TRANSMISSION . .	Selective sliding gear
GEAR CHANGES .	Three forward, one reverse
POSITION OF DRIVER	Right-side drive and right-hand control

**F E D E R A L
MOTOR TRUCK
C O M P A N Y**

**D E T R O I T
M I C H I G A N**

Price, Chassis	$1800
With Stake Body H 150	1970
With Stake Body G 151	1945
With Express Body with Top . .	2020
With Express Body without Top .	1945
Chassis with Worm Drive . . .	1900

FEDERAL 3,000-POUND TRUCK

COLOR	Lead	ARRANGED . . .	Vertically, under driver's seat	
CARRYING CAPACITY	3,000 pounds			
CLUTCH	Cone	CAST	En bloc	
WHEELBASE . .	120 or 144 inches	BORE	4⅛ inches	
GAUGE	Front, 56 inches; rear, 59½ inches	STROKE	5¼ inches	
		COOLING . . .	Water	
TIRE DIMENSIONS:		RADIATOR . . .	Cellular	
FRONT . . .	36 x 3½ inches (solid)	IGNITION . . .	High-tension magneto	
REAR	36 x 5 inches (solid)	DRIVE	Double side chain or worm gear	
BRAKE SYSTEMS .	Expanding on jack shaft and both rear wheels	TRANSMISSION . .	Selective sliding gear	
		GEAR CHANGES .	Three forward, one reverse	
HORSE-POWER . .	N. A. C. C. (formerly A.L.A.M.) rating 27.2	POSITION OF DRIVER	Left-side drive and center control	
CYLINDERS . . .	Four			

GENERAL
MOTORS
TRUCK CO.
PONTIAC
MICHIGAN

Price, Chassis $1090
Flare Board Open Express . 1215

G M C 1500-POUND TRUCK "15"

COLOR	"G M C" gray	ARRANGED . . .	Vertically, under hood
CARRYING CAPACITY	1500 pounds	CAST	En bloc
CLUTCH	Cone	BORE	3½ inches
WHEELBASE . .	122 inches	STROKE	5 inches
GAUGE	56 inches	COOLING . . .	Water
TIRE DIMENSIONS:		RADIATOR . . .	Tubular
FRONT . . .	35 x 5 inches (pneumatic)	IGNITION . . .	Jump spark
		ELECTRIC SOURCE .	High-tension magneto
REAR	35 x 5 inches (pneumatic)	DRIVE	Shaft
BRAKE SYSTEMS .	Contracting and expanding on both rear wheels	TRANSMISSION . .	Selective sliding gear
		GEAR CHANGES .	Three forward, one reverse
HORSE-POWER . .	N. A. C. C. (formerly A.L.A.M.) rating 19.6	POSITION OF DRIVER	Left-side drive and center control
CYLINDERS . . .	Four		

K I S S E L
M O T O R   C A R
C O M P A N Y

H A R T F O R D
W I S C O N S I N

Price, Chassis . . .	**$1500**
With Express Body .	1625
With Stake Body . .	1625

KISSEL KAR 1500-POUND   TRUCK

COLOR	Optional	CAST	In pairs
CARRYING CAPACITY	1500 pounds	BORE	4¼ inches
CLUTCH	Cone	STROKE	5¼ inches
WHEELBASE . .	125 inches	COOLING . . .	Water
GAUGE	56 inches	RADIATOR . . .	Square tube
TIRE DIMENSIONS:		IGNITION . . .	Jump spark
FRONT . .	35 x 4½ inches	ELECTRIC SOURCE .	High-tension magneto
REAR . . .	35 x 4½ inches		
BRAKE SYSTEMS .	Contracting and expanding on both rear wheels	DRIVE	Shaft
		TRANSMISSION . .	Selective sliding gear
HORSE-POWER . .	N. A. C. C. (formerly A.L.A.M.) rating 28.9	GEAR CHANGES .	Three forward, one reverse
CYLINDERS . . .	Four	POSITION OF DRIVER	Left-side drive and center control
ARRANGED . . .	Vertically, under hood		

KISSEL
MOTOR CAR
COMPANY
HARTFORD
WISCONSIN

Price, Chassis . . .	$2750
With Stake Body . .	2900
With Express Body .	2900

KISSEL KAR TWO AND ONE-HALF TON TRUCK

COLOR	Optional	ARRANGED . . .	Vertically, under hood
CARRYING CAPACITY	Two and one-half tons	CAST	In pairs
CLUTCH	Cone	BORE	4½ inches
WHEELBASE . .	144 inches	STROKE	5¼ inches
GAUGE	62 inches	COOLING . . .	Water
TIRE DIMENSIONS:		RADIATOR . . .	Square tube
FRONT . . .	36 x 4 inches (single solid)	IGNITION . . .	Jump spark
REAR	38 x 4 inches (dual solid)	ELECTRIC SOURCE .	High-tension magneto
BRAKE SYSTEMS .	Contracting on jack shaft and expanding on both rear wheels	DRIVE	Double side chain
		TRANSMISSION . .	Selective sliding gear
HORSE-POWER . .	N. A. C. C. (formerly A.L.A.M.) rating 32.4	GEAR CHANGES .	Four forward, one reverse
		POSITION OF DRIVER	Left-side drive and center control
CYLINDERS . . .	Four		

K I S S E L
MOTOR CAR
C O M P A N Y
H A R T F O R D
W I S C O N S I N

Price, Chassis . . .	$4350
With Express Body .	4500
With Stake Body .	4500

KISSEL KAR SIX-TON TRUCK

COLOR	Optional	ARRANGED . . .	Vertically, under hood
CARRYING CAPACITY	Six tons	CAST	In pairs
CLUTCH	Cone	BORE	4⅞ inches
WHEELBASE . .	168 inches	STROKE	5 inches
GAUGE	72½ inches	COOLING . . .	Water
TIRE DIMENSIONS:		RADIATOR . . .	Square tube
FRONT . . .	36 x 6 inches (single solid)	IGNITION . . .	Jump spark
REAR	40 x 6 inches (dual solid)	ELECTRIC SOURCE .	High-tension magneto
BRAKE SYSTEMS .	Contracting on jack shaft and expanding on both rear wheels	DRIVE	Double side chain
		TRANSMISSION . .	Selective sliding gear
		GEAR CHANGES .	Four forward, one reverse
HORSE-POWER . .	N. A. C. C. (formerly A.L.A.M.) rating 38	POSITION OF DRIVER	Left-side drive and center control
CYLINDERS . . .	Four		

THE THOMAS B.
J E F F E R Y
C O M P A N Y

K E N O S H A
W I S C O N S I N

Price, Chassis	$2750
With Platform Stake Body .	3050
With U. S. Army Box Body .	3000

JEFFERY QUAD TWO-TON TRUCK AND TRACTOR

COLOR	Orange yellow
CARRYING CAPACITY	4,000 pounds
CLUTCH	Single disc
WHEELBASE . .	124 inches
GAUGE	56 inches
TIRE DIMENSIONS:	
FRONT . . .	36 x 5 inches
REAR	36 x 5 inches
BRAKE SYSTEMS .	Four-wheel brake (internal expanding in each wheel drum) and one external contracting brake on drive shaft
HORSE-POWER . .	N. A. C. C. (formerly A.L.A.M.) rating 22.5
CYLINDERS . . .	Four

ARRANGED . . .	Vertically, under hood
CAST	En bloc
BORE	3¾ inches
STROKE	5¼ inches
COOLING . . .	Water
RADIATOR . . .	Honeycomb
IGNITION . . .	Jump spark
ELECTRIC SOURCE .	Magneto and dry cells
DRIVE	Internal gear in each of the four wheels
TRANSMISSION . .	Selective gear
GEAR CHANGES .	Four forward, one reverse
POSITION OF DRIVER	Left-side drive and center control

Price includes prestolite tank

GENERAL VEHICLE COMPANY, Inc.

LONG ISLAND CITY NEW YORK

AMERICAN DAIMLER "FV"

COLOR	Lead
CARRYING CAPACITY	12,000 pounds
CLUTCH	Cone
WHEELBASE . .	169¼ inches
GAUGE	60⅝ inches
TIRE DIMENSIONS:	
FRONT . . .	34 x 5 inches (single solid)
REAR . . .	40 x 6 inches (dual solid)
BRAKE SYSTEMS .	Contracting on transmission and both rear wheels
HORSE-POWER . .	N. A. C. C. (formerly A.L.A.M.) rating 28.9

CYLINDERS . . .	Four
ARRANGED . . .	Vertically, under hood
CAST	In pairs
BORE	4¼ inches
STROKE	5 ⁹/₁₀ inches
COOLING . . .	Water
RADIATOR . . .	Cellular
IGNITION . . .	Jump spark
ELECTRIC SOURCE .	High-tension magneto
DRIVE	Shaft
TRANSMISSION . .	Selective sliding gear
GEAR CHANGES .	Four forward, one reverse
POSITION OF DRIVER	Right-side drive and right-hand control

HAND BOOK
OF
AUTOMOBILES

HAND BOOK
OF
AUTOMOBILES

1916

NATIONAL AUTOMOBILE
CHAMBER OF COMMERCE
INCORPORATED

THIRTEENTH ANNUAL ANNOUNCEMENT

WITH illustrations and specifications describing in detail the products of the principal manufacturers of automobiles in the United States, it is believed that this issue of the annual Hand Book, now the standard authority in the industry, will prove as useful as previous issues.

That comparison may be easy and accurate, all cars herein have been subjected to a uniform investigation as to the equipment and details of construction.

Individual manufacturers listed in this Hand Book will be glad, upon request, to send complete catalogs descriptive of their product, and catalogs may also be obtained from dealers in the principal cities and towns.

January, 1916.

ORGANIZATION OF

NATIONAL AUTOMOBILE
CHAMBER OF COMMERCE
(INCORPORATED)

OFFICERS

Charles Clifton, *President* . . . . Pierce-Arrow Motor Car Company

Wilfred C. Leland, *Vice-President* . . . Cadillac Motor Car Company

Hugh Chalmers, *Second Vice-President* . . Chalmers Motor Company
Gasoline Passenger Division

Windsor T. White, *Second Vice-President* . . . The White Company
Commerical Vehicle Division

H. H. Rice, *Second Vice-President* . . . . . The Waverley Company
Electric Vehicle Division

R. D. Chapin, *Secretary* . . . . . . Hudson Motor Car Company

George Pope, *Treasurer* . . . . . . Pope Manufacturing Company

Alfred Reeves, *General Manager*

National Automobile Chamber of Commerce

S. A. Miles, *Show Manager* . National Automobile Chamber of Commerce

BOARD OF DIRECTORS

Charles Clifton . . . . Pierce-Arrow Motor Car Company

Wilfred C. Leland . . . . . . Cadillac Motor Car Company

C. C. Hanch . . . . Studebaker Corporation

Hugh Chalmers . . . . Chalmers Motor Company

Alvan Macauley . . . . . . Packard Motor Car Company

Windsor T. White . . . . The White Company

Wm. E. Metzger . . . . Argo Electric Vehicle Company

J. Walter Drake . . . . Hupp Motor Car Company

Carl H. Pelton . . . . . . Maxwell Motor Company, Inc.

R. E. Olds . . . . Reo Motor Car Company

H. H. Rice . . . . The Waverley Company

John N. Willys . . . . Willys-Overland Company

R. D. Chapin . . . . Hudson Motor Car Company

C. W. Churchill . . . . The Winton Company

PATENTS COMMITTEE

C. C. Hanch, *Chairman* . . . .   Studebaker Corporation
Wm. H. VanDervoort . . . . . .   Moline Automobile Company
Windsor T. White . . . . The White Company
Wilfred C. Leland . . . . . .   Cadillac Motor Car Company
Howard E. Coffin . . . . Hudson Motor Car Company

TRAFFIC COMMITTEE

Wm. E. Metzger, *Chairman* . . . . Argo Electric Vehicle Company
R. E. Olds . . . .   Reo Motor Car Company
A. I. Philp . . . .   Dodge Brothers

SHOW COMMITTEE

George Pope, *Chairman* . . . . . .   Pope Manufacturing Company
Wilfred C. Leland . . . .   Cadillac Motor Car Company

LEGISLATIVE COMMITTEE

H. H. Rice, *Chairman* . . . .   The Waverley Company
J. Walter Drake . . . .   Hupp Motor Car Company
J. I. Farley . . . .   Auburn Automobile Company

ELECTRIC VEHICLE COMMITTEE

H. H. Rice, *Chairman* . . . .   The Waverley Company
Fred R. White . . . .   The Baker R. & L. Company
W. C. Anderson . . . .   Anderson Electric Car Company

COMMERCIAL VEHICLE COMMITTEE

Windsor T. White, *Chairman* . . . . . .   The White Company
Alvan Macauley . . . .   Packard Motor Car Company
H. Kerr Thomas . . . .   Pierce-Arrow Motor Car Company
P. D. Wagoner . . . .   General Vehicle Company
M. L. Pulcher . . . .   Federal Motor Truck Company

GOOD ROADS COMMITTEE

R. D. Chapin, *Chairman* . . . . .   Hudson Motor Car Company
S. D. Waldon . . . .   Cadillac Motor Car Company
Wm. E. Metzger . . . .   Argo Electric Vehicle Company

HAND BOOK COMMITTEE

Carl H. Pelton, *Chairman* . . . . .   Maxwell Motor Company, Inc.
A. I. Philp . . . .   Dodge Brothers
A. L. Riker . . . .   Locomobile Co. of America

ALPHABETICAL INDEX

GASOLINE PASSENGER VEHICLES

ALPHABETICAL INDEX—Continued

INDEX OF TRADE NAMES

GASOLINE PASSENGER VEHICLES

INDEX OF TRADE NAMES—Continued

ELECTRIC VEHICLES

GASOLINE COMMERCIAL VEHICLES

N. A. C. C. HORSE-POWER RATING

The standard horse-power rating, formerly known as the A. L. A. M. Rating, has been officially adopted by the National Automobile Chamber of Commerce, Inc.

The formula adopted is $\frac{D^2 \times N}{2.5}$. D is the cylinder bore in inches, N the number of cylinders, and 2.5 a constant, based on the average view of eminent engineers as to a fair, conservative rating for a four-cycle motor at one thousand feet per minute piston speed.

TABLE OF HORSE-POWER FOR USUAL SIZES OF MOTORS

Ins.	2 CYLS.	4 CYLS.	6 CYLS.	8 CYLS.	12 CYLS.
2½	5.00	10.00	15.00	20.00	30.00
2⅝	5.50	11.03	16.54	22.05	33.08
2¾	6.00	12.10	18.15	24.20	36.30
2⅞	6.62	13.23	19.84	26.45	39.68
3	7.20	14.40	21.60	28.80	43.20
3⅛	7.81	15.63	23.44	31.25	46.88
3¼	8.50	16.90	25.35	33.80	50.70
3⅜	9.12	18.23	27.34	36.45	54.68
3½	9.80	19.60	29.40	39.20	58.80
3⅝	10.50	21.03	31.54	42.05	63.08
3¾	11.25	22.50	33.75	45.00	67.50
3⅞	12.00	24.03	36.04	48.05	72.08
4	12.80	25.60	38.40	51.20	76.80
4⅛	13.62	27.23	40.84	54.45	81.68
4¼	14.50	28.90	43.35	57.80	86.70
4⅜	15.31	30.63	45.94	61.25	91.88
4½	16.20	32.40	48.60	64.80	97.20
4⅝	17.12	34.23	51.34	68.45	102.68
4¾	18.00	36.10	54.15	72.20	108.30
4⅞	19.00	38.03	57.04	76.05	114.08
5	20.00	40.00	60.00	80.00	120.00
5⅛	21.00	42.03	63.04	84.05	126.08
5¼	22.00	44.10	66.15	88.20	132.30
5⅜	23.00	46.23	69.34	92.45	138.68
5½	24.20	48.40	72.60	96.80	145.20
5⅝	25.31	50.63	75.94	101.25	151.88
5¾	26.50	52.90	79.35	105.80	158.70
5⅞	27.62	55.23	82.84	110.45	165.68
6	28.80	57.60	86.40	115.20	172.80

ILLUSTRATIONS AND SPECIFICATIONS GASOLINE PASSENGER VEHICLES

D O D G E
B R O T H E R S

D E T R O I T
M I C H I G A N

Price	$785
Winter Touring Car . .	950
Winter Roadster . . .	950
Standard Roadster . .	785

DODGE BROTHERS MOTOR CAR

COLOR	Ebony black		RADIATOR	Tubular
SEATING CAPACITY .	Five persons		COOLING	Water pump
POSITION OF DRIVER	Left side		IGNITION	High-tension magneto
WHEELBASE	110 inches			
GAUGE	56 or 60 inches		STARTING SYSTEM . .	Single unit
WHEELS	Wood		STARTER OPERATED .	Chain to crank shaft
FRONT TIRES	32 x 3½ inches			
REAR TIRES	32 x 3½ inches, anti-skid		LIGHTING SYSTEM . .	Electric
			VOLTAGES	Starting, twelve; lighting, fourteen
SERVICE BRAKE . . .	Contracting on rear wheels		WIRING SYSTEM . . .	Starting, double; lighting, single
EMERGENCY BRAKE .	Expanding on rear wheels		GASOLINE SYSTEM . .	Vacuum
CYLINDERS	Four		CLUTCH	Cone
ARRANGED	Vertically		TRANSMISSION . . .	Selective sliding
CAST	En bloc		GEAR CHANGES . . .	Three forward, one reverse
HORSEPOWER	24.03 (N. A. C. C. Rating)			
			DRIVE	Plain bevel
BORE AND STROKE .	3⅞ x 4½ inches		REAR AXLE	Full floating
LUBRICATION	Splash with circulating pump		STEERING GEAR . . .	Worm and worm wheel

In addition to above specifications, price includes top, top hood,
windshield, speedometer, battery indicator and demountable rim

**H. H. FRANKLIN
MANUFACTUR-
ING COMPANY**

SYRACUSE
NEW YORK

Price	$1950
Three-Passenger Roadster .	1900
Five-Passenger Sedan . . .	2850
Four - Passenger Doctor's Car	2800
Seven-Passenger Berlin . .	3100

FRANKLIN TOURING CAR

COLOR	Brewster green with russet brown wheels	BORE AND STROKE . .	3⅝ x 4 inches
		LUBRICATION	Force feed
		COOLING	Air
SEATING CAPACITY .	Five persons	IGNITION	High-tension magneto
POSITION OF DRIVER	Left side		
WHEELBASE	120 inches	STARTING SYSTEM . .	Single unit
GAUGE	56 inches	STARTER OPERATED .	Chain to crankshaft
WHEELS	Wood	LIGHTING SYSTEM . .	Electric
FRONT TIRES	34 x 4½ inches	VOLTAGES	Twelve
REAR TIRES	34 x 4½ inches, anti-skid	WIRING SYSTEM . . .	Double
		GASOLINE SYSTEM . .	Gravity
SERVICE BRAKE . . .	Contracting on transmission	CLUTCH	Multiple disc in oil
EMERGENCY BRAKE .	Contracting on rear wheels	TRANSMISSION . . .	Selective sliding
		GEAR CHANGES . . .	Three forward, one reverse
CYLINDERS	Six		
ARRANGED	Vertically	DRIVE	Spiral bevel
CAST	Separately	REAR AXLE	Semi-floating
HORSEPOWER	31.54	STEERING GEAR . . .	Worm and gear
(N. A. C. C. Rating)			

In addition to above specifications, price includes
top, top hood, windshield and speedometer

**LOZIER MOTOR
C O M P A N Y**
|||||||||||||||||||||||||||||||||||||||||||||||
**D E T R O I T
M I C H I G A N**

Price, $3250

LOZIER TOURING CAR—TYPE 82

COLOR	Lozier blue
SEATING CAPACITY .	Seven persons
POSITION OF DRIVER .	Left side
WHEELBASE	132 inches
GAUGE	56 inches
WHEELS	Wood
FRONT TIRES	36 x 4½ inches
REAR TIRES	36 x 4½ inches, anti-skid
SERVICE BRAKE . . .	Internal on rear wheels
EMERGENCY BRAKE .	Internal on rear wheels
CYLINDERS	Six
ARRANGED	Vertically
CAST	In threes
HORSEPOWER	36.04
(N. A. C. C. Rating)	
BORE AND STROKE .	3⅞ x 6 inches
LUBRICATION	Splash with circulating pump

RADIATOR	Cellular
COOLING	Water pump
IGNITION	High tension magneto and storage battery
STARTING SYSTEM . .	Two unit
STARTER OPERATED .	Gear to fly wheel
LIGHTING SYSTEM . .	Electric
VOLTAGES	Six
WIRING SYSTEM . . .	Single
GASOLINE SYSTEM . .	Pressure
CLUTCH	Multiple disc in oil
TRANSMISSION . . .	Selective sliding
GEAR CHANGES . . .	Three forward, one reverse
DRIVE	Spiral bevel
REAR AXLE	Full floating
STEERING GEAR . . .	Worm

In addition to above specifications, price includes top, top hood, windshield, speedometer, ammeter, voltmeter, clock and demountable rims

**HUPP   MOTOR
CAR   COMPANY**

DETROIT
MICHIGAN

Price $1085
Two-Passenger Roadster . .   1085

HUPMOBILE FIVE-PASSENGER TOURING CAR

COLOR . . . . . . Body, Brewster green; chassis, black.
SEATING CAPACITY . Five persons
POSITION OF DRIVER Left side
WHEELBASE . . . . 119 inches
GAUGE . . . . . . 56 or 60 inches
WHEELS . . . . . . Wood
FRONT TIRES . . . . 34 x 4 inches
REAR TIRES . . . . 34 x 4 inches, anti-skid
SERVICE BRAKE . . . Contracting on rear wheels
EMERGENCY BRAKE . Expanding on rear wheels
CYLINDERS . . . . . Four
ARRANGED . . . . . Vertically, under hood
CAST . . . . En bloc
HORSEPOWER 22.5
(N. A. C. C. Rating)

BORE AND STROKE . 3¾ x 5½ inches
LUBRICATION . . . . Force feed and splash
RADIATOR . . . . . Cellular
COOLING . . . . . . Thermo-syphon
IGNITION . . . . . . Storage battery
STARTING SYSTEM . . Two unit
STARTER OPERATED . Gear to fly wheel
LIGHTING SYSTEM . . Electric
VOLTAGES . . . . . Six
WIRING SYSTEM . . . Single
GASOLINE SYSTEM . . Gravity
CLUTCH . . . . . . Multiple disc in oil
TRANSMISSION . . . Selective sliding
GEAR CHANGES . . . Three forward, one reverse
DRIVE . . . . Spiral bevel
REAR AXLE . . . . Three-quarters floating
STEERING GEAR . . . Split nut

In addition to above specifications, price includes top,
top hood, windshield, speedometer and demountable rims

HUPP   MOTOR
CAR COMPANY

D E T R O I T
M I C H I G A N

Price $1185
Two-Passenger Year-'round Coupe   .   1165

HUPMOBILE YEAR-'ROUND TOURING CAR

COLOR	Body, Brewster green; chassis, black
SEATING CAPACITY .	Five persons
POSITION OF DRIVER	Left side
WHEELBASE	119 inches
GAUGE	56 or 60 inches
WHEELS	Wood
FRONT TIRES	34 x 4 inches
REAR TIRES	34 x 4 inches, anti-skid
SERVICE BRAKE. . .	Contracting on rear wheels
EMERGENCY BRAKE .	Expanding on rear wheels
CYLINDERS	Four
ARRANGED	Vertically
CAST	En bloc
HORSEPOWER	22.5
(N. A. C. C. Rating)	
BORE AND STROKE. .	3¾ x 5½ inches

LUBRICATION	Force feed and splash
RADIATOR	Cellular
COOLING	Thermo-syphon
IGNITION	Storage battery
STARTING SYSTEM . .	Two unit
STARTER OPERATED .	Gear to fly wheel
LIGHTING SYSTEM . .	Electric
VOLTAGES	Six
WIRING SYSTEM. . .	Single
GASOLINE SYSTEM . .	Gravity
CLUTCH	Multiple disc in oil
TRANSMISSION . . .	Selective sliding
GEAR CHANGES . . .	Three forward, one reverse
DRIVE	Spiral bevel
REAR AXLE	Three-quarters floating
STEERING GEAR. . .	Split nut

HUPP MOTOR CAR COMPANY

DETROIT MICHIGAN

Price $1225
Seven-Passenger Limousine . 2365

HUPMOBILE SEVEN-PASSENGER TOURING CAR

COLOR	Body, Brewster green; chassis, black
SEATING CAPACITY .	Seven persons
POSITION OF DRIVER	Left side
WHEELBASE	134 inches
GAUGE	56 or 60 inches
WHEELS	Wood
FRONT TIRES	35 x 4½ inches
REAR TIRES	35 x 4½ inches, anti-skid
SERVICE BRAKE . . .	Contracting on rear wheels
EMERGENCY BRAKE .	Expanding on rear wheels
CYLINDERS	Four
ARRANGED	Vertically
CAST	En bloc
HORSEPOWER	22.5 (N. A. C. C. Rating)
BORE AND STROKE .	3¾ x 5½ inches

LUBRICATION	Force feed and splash
RADIATOR	Cellular
COOLING	Thermo-syphon
IGNITION	Storage battery
STARTING SYSTEM . .	Two unit
STARTER OPERATED .	Gear to fly wheel
LIGHTING SYSTEM . .	Electric
VOLTAGES	Six
WIRING SYSTEM . . .	Single
GASOLINE SYSTEM . .	Gravity
CLUTCH	Multiple disc in oil
TRANSMISSION . . .	Selective sliding
GEAR CHANGES . . .	Three forward, one reverse
DRIVE	Spiral bevel
REAR AXLE	Three-quarters floating
STEERING GEAR . . .	Split nut

In addition to above specifications, price includes top, top hood, windshield, speedometer and demountable rims

HUPP MOTOR CAR COMPANY

Price, $1365

D E T R O I T
M I C H I G A N

HUPMOBILE SEDAN

COLOR	Body, Hupmobile blue; chassis, black	LUBRICATION	Force feed and splash	
SEATING CAPACITY .	Five persons	RADIATOR	Cellular	
POSITION OF DRIVER.	Left side	COOLING	Thermo-syphon	
WHEELBASE	119 inches	IGNITION	Storage battery	
GAUGE	56 or 60 inches	STARTING SYSTEM . .	Two unit	
WHEELS	Wood	STARTER OPERATED .	Gear to fly wheel	
FRONT TIRES	34 x 4 inches	LIGHTING SYSTEM . .	Electric	
REAR TIRES	34 x 4 inches, anti-skid	VOLTAGES	Six	
SERVICE BRAKE . . .	Contracting on rear wheels	WIRING SYSTEM. . .	Single	
EMERGENCY BRAKE .	Expanding on rear wheels	GASOLINE SYSTEM .	Gravity	
		CLUTCH	Multiple disc in oil	
CYLINDERS	Four	TRANSMISSION . . .	Selective sliding	
ARRANGED	Vertically	GEAR CHANGES . . .	Three forward, one reverse	
CAST	En bloc	DRIVE	Spiral bevel	
HORSEPOWER	22.5 (N. A. C. C. Rating)	REAR AXLE	Three-quarters floating	
BORE AND STROKE .	3¾ x 5½ inches	STEERING GEAR . .	Split nut	

**McFARLAN
MOTOR
COMPANY**

**CONNERSVILLE
INDIANA**

Price	$2990
Touring Roadster	2990
Four-Passenger Submarine .	3140
Six-Passenger Touring . . .	2990
Semi-Touring	4400
Six-Passenger Sedan	4000
Town Car	4000
Coupe	3600
Berline	4300
Limousine	4200
Landaulet	4200

McFARLAN SIX—SERIES X-107

COLOR	Optional	BORE AND STROKE .	4½ x 6 inches
SEATING CAPACITY .	Seven persons	LUBRICATION	Force feed and splash
POSITION OF DRIVER	Left side	RADIATOR	Honeycomb
WHEELBASE	132 inches	COOLING	Water pump
GAUGE	56 inches	IGNITION	Storage battery
WHEELS	Wood	STARTING SYSTEM . .	Two unit
FRONT TIRES	36 x 4½ inches, cord	STARTER OPERATED .	Gear to fly wheel
REAR TIRES	36 x 4½ inches, cord	LIGHTING SYSTEM . .	Electric
SERVICE BRAKE . . .	External contracting on rear wheels	VOLTAGES	Six
		WIRING SYSTEM . . .	Single
		GASOLINE SYSTEM . .	Vacuum
EMERGENCY BRAKE .	Internal expanding on rear wheels	CLUTCH	Cone
		TRANSMISSION . . .	Selective sliding
CYLINDERS	Six	GEAR CHANGES . . .	Three forward, one reverse
ARRANGED	Vertically		
CAST	En bloc	DRIVE	Spiral bevel
HORSEPOWER	48.6	REAR AXLE	Full floating
(N. A. C. C. Rating)		STEERING GEAR . . .	Worm and sector

In addition to above specifications, price includes top, top
hood, windshield, speedometer, ammeter and demountable rims

COLE MOTOR
CAR COMPANY

INDIANAPOLIS
INDIANA

Price $1595
Three-Passenger Roadster . . 1595

COLE TOURING CAR—860-G

COLOR	Norland green	BORE AND STROKE .	3½ x 4½ inches
SEATING CAPACITY .	Seven persons	LUBRICATION	Force feed
POSITION OF DRIVER .	Left side	RADIATOR	Cellular
WHEELBASE	127 inches	COOLING	Water pump
GAUGE	56 inches	IGNITION	Storage battery
WHEELS	Wood	STARTING SYSTEM . .	Single unit
FRONT TIRES	35 x 4½ inches	STARTER OPERATED .	Gear to fly wheel
REAR TIRES	35 x 4½ inches, anti-skid	LIGHTING SYSTEM . .	Electric
		VOLTAGES	Six
SERVICE BRAKE . . .	Contracting on rear wheels	WIRING SYSTEM . . .	Single
		GASOLINE SYSTEM . .	Vacuum
EMERGENCY BRAKE .	Expanding on rear wheels	CLUTCH	Cone
		TRANSMISSION . . .	Selective sliding
CYLINDERS	Eight	GEAR CHANGES . . .	Three forward, one reverse
ARRANGED	V-type, 90 degrees		
CAST	En bloc	DRIVE	Spiral bevel
HORSEPOWER	39.2	REAR AXLE	Full floating
(N. A. C. C. Rating)		STEERING GEAR . . .	Worm and sector

In addition to above specifications, price includes top, top hood, windshield, speedometer, ammeter, voltmeter and demountable rims

**INTER-STATE
MOTOR
COMPANY**

Price $850
Roadster . . 850

M U N C I E
I N D I A N A

INTER-STATE TOURING CAR—T

COLOR	Blue
SEATING CAPACITY .	Five persons
POSITION OF DRIVER.	Left side
WHEELBASE	110 inches
GAUGE.	56 inches
WHEELS	Wood
FRONT TIRES	33 x 4 inches
REAR TIRES	33 x 4 inches, anti-skid
SERVICE BRAKE . . .	External on rear axle
EMERGENCY BRAKE .	Internal on rear axle
CYLINDERS	Four
ARRANGED	Vertically
CAST	En bloc
HORSEPOWER	19.6
(N. A. C. C. Rating)	
BORE AND STROKE .	3½ x 5 inches

LUBRICATION	Splash with cir-culating pump
RADIATOR	Cellular
COOLING	Thermo-syphon
IGNITION	Storage battery
STARTING SYSTEM . .	Two unit
STARTER OPERATED .	Gear to fly wheel
LIGHTING SYSTEM . .	Electric
VOLTAGES	Six
WIRING SYSTEM. . .	Single
GASOLINE SYSTEM . .	Gravity
CLUTCH	Cone
TRANSMISSION . . .	Selective sliding
GEAR CHANGES . . .	Three forward, one reverse
DRIVE	Plain bevel
REAR AXLE	Three-quarters floating
STEERING GEAR . .	Worm and gear

In addition to above specifications, price includes top, top hood,
windshield, speedometer, electrical indicator and demountable rims

**PIERCE-ARROW
MOTOR CAR
COMPANY**

**BUFFALO
NEW YORK**

Price	$4300
Two-Passenger Runabout . . .	4300
Three-Passenger Runabout . . .	4300
Two-Passenger Coupe	5000
Three-Passenger Coupe	5000
Four-Passenger Touring	4300
Brougham	5200
Landaulet	5200
Sedan	5200
Brougham-Landaulet	5200
Vestibule Brougham	5350
Vestibule Landaulet	5350
Vestibule Brougham-Landaulet .	5350

PIERCE-ARROW FIVE-PASSENGER TOURING CAR—38-C-4

COLOR	Optional	RADIATOR	Cellular
SEATING CAPACITY .	Five persons	COOLING	Water
POSITION OF DRIVER	Right side	IGNITION	High-tension magneto and storage battery
WHEELBASE	134 inches		
GAUGE	56 inches		
WHEELS	Wood	STARTING SYSTEM . .	Two unit
FRONT TIRES	36 x 4½ inches	STARTER OPERATED .	Gear to fly wheel
REAR TIRES	36 x 4½ inches	LIGHTING SYSTEM . .	Electric
SERVICE BRAKE . . .	Expanding on rear wheels	VOLTAGES	Six
		WIRING SYSTEM . . .	Single
EMERGENCY BRAKE .	Contracting on rear wheels	GASOLINE SYSTEM . .	Pressure
CYLINDERS	Six	CLUTCH	Cone
ARRANGED	Vertically under hood	TRANSMISSION . . .	Selective sliding
		GEAR CHANGES . . .	Four forward, one reverse
CAST	In pairs		
HORSEPOWER	38.4 (N. A. C. C. Rating)	DRIVE	Spiral bevel
BORE AND STROKE . .	4 x 5½ inches	REAR AXLE	Semi-floating
LUBRICATION	Force feed	STEERING GEAR . . .	Screw and nut

In addition to above specifications, price includes top, top hood, windshield, speedometer, autometer, clock and demountable rims

PIERCE-ARROW
MOTOR CAR
COMPANY

BUFFALO
NEW YORK

Price	$4300
Two-Passenger Runabout	4300
Four-Passenger Touring	4300
Two-Passenger Coupe	5000
Three-Passenger Coupe	5000
Five-Passenger Touring	4300
Brougham	5200
Landaulet	5200
Sedan	5200
Brougham-Landaulet	5200
Vestibule Brougham	5350
Vestibule Landaulet	5350
Vestibule Brougham-Landaulet	5350

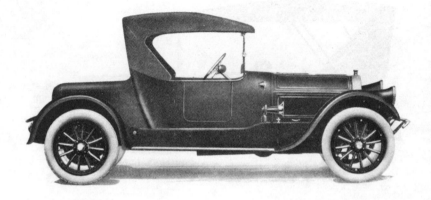

PIERCE-ARROW THREE-PASSENGER RUNABOUT—38-C-4

COLOR	Optional	RADIATOR	Cellular
SEATING CAPACITY	Four persons	COOLING	Water
POSITION OF DRIVER	Right side	IGNITION	High-tension magneto and storage battery
WHEELBASE	134 inches		
GAUGE	56 inches		
WHEELS	Wood	STARTING SYSTEM	Two unit
FRONT TIRES	36 x 4½ inches	STARTER OPERATED	Gear to fly wheel
REAR TIRES	36 x 4½ inches	LIGHTING SYSTEM	Electric
SERVICE BRAKE	Expanding on rear wheels	VOLTAGES	Six
		WIRING SYSTEM	Single
EMERGENCY BRAKE	Contracting on rear wheels	GASOLINE SYSTEM	Pressure
		CLUTCH	Cone
CYLINDERS	Six	TRANSMISSION	Selective sliding
ARRANGED	Vertically	GEAR CHANGES	Four forward, one reverse
CAST	In pairs		
HORSEPOWER	38.4 (N. A. C. C. Rating)	DRIVE	Spiral bevel
BORE AND STROKE	4 x 5½ inches	REAR AXLE	Semi-floating
LUBRICATION	Force feed	STEERING GEAR	Screw and nut

In addition to above specifications, price includes top, top hood,
windshield, speedometer, autometer, clock and demountable rims

PIERCE-ARROW MOTOR CAR COMPANY
BUFFALO NEW YORK

Price	$5000
Two-Passenger Runabout	4300
Three-Passenger Runabout	4300
Two-Passenger Coupe	5000
Four-Passenger Touring	4300
Five-Passenger Touring	4300
Brougham	5200
Brougham-Landaulet	5200
Vestibule Landaulet	5350
Vestibule Brougham	5350
Vestibule Brougham-Landaulet	5350
Landaulet	5200
Sedan	5200

PIERCE-ARROW THREE-PASSENGER COUPE—38-C-4

COLOR	Optional	RADIATOR	Cellular
SEATING CAPACITY	Four persons	COOLING	Water
POSITION OF DRIVER	Right side	IGNITION	High-tension magneto and storage battery
WHEELBASE	134 inches		
GAUGE	56 inches		
WHEELS	Wood	STARTING SYSTEM	Two unit
FRONT TIRES	36 x 4½ inches	STARTER OPERATED	Gear to fly wheel
REAR TIRES	36 x 4½ inches	LIGHTING SYSTEM	Electric
SERVICE BRAKE	Expanding on rear wheels	VOLTAGES	Six
		WIRING SYSTEM	Single
EMERGENCY BRAKE	Contracting on rear wheels	GASOLINE SYSTEM	Pressure
CYLINDERS	Six	CLUTCH	Cone
ARRANGED	Vertically	TRANSMISSION	Selective sliding
CAST	In pairs	GEAR CHANGES	Four forward, one reverse
HORSEPOWER	38.4 (N. A. C. C. Rating)	DRIVE	Spiral bevel
BORE AND STROKE	4 x 5½ inches	REAR AXLE	Semi-floating
LUBRICATION	Force feed	STEERING GEAR	Screw and nut

In addition to above specifications, price includes windshield, speedometer, autometer, clock and demountable rims

PIERCE-ARROW
MOTOR CAR
COMPANY

BUFFALO
NEW YORK

Price	$5200
Two-Passenger Runabout . . .	4300
Three-Passenger Runabout . .	4300
Two-Passenger Coupe	5000
Three-Passenger Coupe	5000
Four-Passenger Touring	4300
Five-Passenger Touring	4300
Brougham	5200
Landaulet	5200
Sedan	5200
Vestibule Brougham	5350
Vestibule Landaulet	5350
Vestibule Brougham-Landaulet .	5350

PIERCE-ARROW BROUGHAM—38-C-4

COLOR	Optional		RADIATOR	Cellular
SEATING CAPACITY .	Seven persons		COOLING	Water
POSITION OF DRIVER	Right side		IGNITION	High-tension magneto and storage battery
WHEELBASE	134 inches			
GAUGE	56 inches			
WHEELS	Wood		STARTING SYSTEM . .	Two unit
FRONT TIRES	36 x 4½ inches		STARTER OPERATED .	Gear to fly wheel
REAR TIRES	36 x 4½ inches		LIGHTING SYSTEM . .	Electric
SERVICE BRAKE . .	Expanding on rear wheels		VOLTAGES	Six
			WIRING SYSTEM . . .	Single
EMERGENCY BRAKE .	Contracting on rear wheels		GASOLINE SYSTEM . .	Pressure
CYLINDERS	Six		CLUTCH	Cone
ARRANGED	Vertically		TRANSMISSION . . .	Selective sliding
CAST	In pairs		GEAR CHANGES . . .	Four forward, one reverse
HORSEPOWER	38.4 (N. A. C. C. Rating)		DRIVE	Spiral bevel
BORE AND STROKE .	4 x 5½ inches		REAR AXLE	Semi-floating
LUBRICATION	Force feed		STEERING GEAR . . .	Screw and nut

In addition to above specifications, price includes windshield, speedometer, autometer, clock and demountable rims

**PIERCE-ARROW
MOTOR CAR
COMPANY**

**BUFFALO
NEW YORK**

Price	$5200
Two-Passenger Runabout	4300
Three-Passenger Runabout . . .	4300
Two-Passenger Coupe	5000
Three-Passenger Coupe	5000
Four-Passenger Touring	4300
Five-Passenger Touring	4300
Landaulet	5200
Sedan	5200
Brougham	5200
Vestibule Brougham	5350
Vestibule Landaulet	5350
Vestibule Brougham-Landaulet .	5350

PIERCE-ARROW BROUGHAM-LANDAULET—38-C-4

COLOR	Optional		LUBRICATION	Force feed
SEATING CAPACITY .	Seven persons		RADIATOR	Cellular
POSITION OF DRIVER	Right side		COOLING	Water
WHEELBASE	134 inches		IGNITION	High-tension magneto and storage battery
GAUGE	56 inches			
WHEELS	Wood		STARTING SYSTEM . .	Two unit
FRONT TIRES	36 x 4½ inches		STARTER OPERATED .	Gear to fly wheel
REAR TIRES	36 x 4½ inches		LIGHTING SYSTEM . .	Electric
SERVICE BRAKE . .	Expanding on rear wheels		VOLTAGES	Six
			WIRING SYSTEM . . .	Single
EMERGENCY BRAKE	Contracting on rear wheels		GASOLINE SYSTEM . .	Pressure
			CLUTCH	Cone
CYLINDERS	Six		TRANSMISSION . . .	Selective sliding
ARRANGED	Vertically		GEAR CHANGES . . .	Four forward, one reverse
CAST	In pairs			
HORSEPOWER	38.4		DRIVE	Spiral bevel
(N. A. C. C. Rating)			REAR AXLE	Semi-floating
BORE AND STROKE .	4 x 5½ inches		STEERING GEAR . . .	Screw and nut

In addition to above specifications, price includes windshield,
speedometer, autometer, clock and demountable rims

PIERCE-ARROW
MOTOR CAR
COMPANY

BUFFALO
NEW YORK

Price	$5000
Two-Passenger Runabout	4900
Three-Passenger Runabout	4900
Two-Passenger Coupe	5700
Three-Passenger Coupe	5700
Four-Passenger Touring	4900
Five-Passenger Touring	4900
Suburban	6000
Landau	6000
Brougham	5800
Suburban-Landau	6000
Vestibule Suburban	6200
Vestibule Landau	6200
Vestibule Brougham	5950
Vestibule Suburban-Landau	6200

PIERCE-ARROW SEVEN-PASSENGER TOURING CAR—48-B-4

COLOR	Optional
SEATING CAPACITY	Seven persons
POSITION OF DRIVER	Right side
WHEELBASE	142 inches
GAUGE	56 inches
WHEELS	Wood
FRONT TIRES	37 x 5 inches
REAR TIRES	37 x 5 inches
SERVICE BRAKE	Expanding on rear wheels
EMERGENCY BRAKE	Contracting on rear wheels
CYLINDERS	Six
ARRANGED	Vertically
CAST	In pairs
HORSEPOWER	48.6 (N. A. C. C. Rating)
BORE AND STROKE	$4\frac{1}{2}$ x $5\frac{1}{2}$ inches
LUBRICATION	Force feed

RADIATOR	Cellular
COOLING	Water
IGNITION	High-tension magneto and storage battery
STARTING SYSTEM	Two unit
STARTER OPERATED	Gear to fly wheel
LIGHTING SYSTEM	Electric
VOLTAGES	Six
WIRING SYSTEM	Single
GASOLINE SYSTEM	Pressure
CLUTCH	Cone
TRANSMISSION	Selective sliding
GEAR CHANGES	Four forward, one reverse
DRIVE	Spiral bevel
REAR AXLE	Semi-floating
STEERING GEAR	Screw and nut

In addition to above specifications, price includes top, top hood,
windshield, speedometer, autometer, clock and demountable rims

PIERCE-ARROW
MOTOR CAR
COMPANY

BUFFALO
NEW YORK

Price	$6000
Two-Passenger Runabout . . .	4900
Three-Passenger Runabout . . .	4900
Two-Passenger Coupe	5700
Three-Passenger Coupe.	5700
Four-Passenger Touring	4900
Five-Passenger Touring.	4900
Seven-Passenger Touring	5000
Landau	6000
Brougham	5800
Suburban	6000
Vestibule Suburban	6200
Vestibule Landau	6200
Vestibule Brougham	5950
Vestibule Suburban-Landau . .	6200

PIERCE-ARROW SUBURBAN LANDAU—48-B-4

COLOR	Optional		RADIATOR	Cellular
SEATING CAPACITY .	Seven persons		COOLING	Water
POSITION OF DRIVER	Right side		IGNITION	High-tension magneto and storage battery
WHEELBASE	142 inches			
GAUGE	56 inches			
WHEELS	Wood		STARTING SYSTEM . .	Two unit
FRONT TIRES	37 x 5 inches		STARTER OPERATED .	Gear to fly wheel
REAR TIRES	37 x 5 inches		LIGHTING SYSTEM . .	Electric
SERVICE BRAKE. . .	Expanding on rear wheels		VOLTAGES	Six
			WIRING SYSTEM. . .	Single
EMERGENCY BRAKE .	Contracting on rear wheels		GASOLINE SYSTEM. .	Pressure
CYLINDERS	Six		CLUTCH	Cone
ARRANGED	Vertically		TRANSMISSION . . .	Selective sliding
CAST	In pairs		GEAR CHANGES . . .	Four forward, one reverse
HORSEPOWER	48.6			
(N. A. C. C. Rating)			DRIVE	Spiral bevel
BORE AND STROKE. .	4½ x 5½ inches		REAR AXLE	Semi-floating
LUBRICATION	Force feed		STEERING GEAR. . .	Screw and nut

In addition to above specifications, price includes windshield, speedometer, autometer, clock and demountable rims

PIERCE-ARROW
MOTOR CAR
COMPANY

BUFFALO
NEW YORK

Price.	$6000
Two-Passenger Runabout . . .	4900
Three-Passenger Runabout . . .	4900
Two-Passenger Coupe	5700
Three-Passenger Coupe	5700
Four-Passenger Touring	4900
Five-Passenger Touring. . . .	4900
Seven-Passenger Touring	5000
Suburban Landau	6000
Landau	6000
Brougham	5800
Vestibule Suburban.	6200
Vestibule Landau	6200
Vestibule Brougham	5950
Vestibule Suburban-Landau . .	6200

PIERCE-ARROW SUBURBAN—48-B-4

COLOR	Optional		RADIATOR	Cellular
SEATING CAPACITY .	Seven persons		COOLING	Water
POSITION OF DRIVER	Right side		IGNITION	High-tension magneto and storage battery
WHEELBASE	142 inches			
GAUGE	56 inches		STARTING SYSTEM .	Two unit
WHEELS	Wood		STARTER OPERATED .	Gear to fly wheel
FRONT TIRES	37 x 5 inches		LIGHTING SYSTEM . .	Electric
REAR TIRES	37 x 5 inches		VOLTAGES	Six
SERVICE BRAKE . . .	Expanding on rear wheels		WIRING SYSTEM . .	Single
EMERGENCY BRAKE	Contracting on rear wheels		GASOLINE SYSTEM . .	Pressure
			CLUTCH	Cone
CYLINDERS	Six		TRANSMISSION . . .	Selective sliding
ARRANGED	Vertically		GEAR CHANGES . . .	Four forward, one reverse
CAST	In pairs			
HORSEPOWER	48.6 (N. A. C. C. Rating)		DRIVE	Spiral bevel
BORE AND STROKE .	4½ x 5½ inches		REAR AXLE	Semi-floating
LUBRICATION	Force feed		STEERING GEAR . . .	Screw and nut

In addition to above specifications, price includes windshield, speedometer, autometer, clock and demountable rims

PIERCE-ARROW
MOTOR CAR
COMPANY

BUFFALO
NEW YORK

Price	$6000
Two-Passenger Runabout . . .	4900
Three-Passenger Runabout . .	4900
Two-Passenger Coupe	5700
Three-Passenger Coupe	5700
Four-Passenger Touring	4900
Five-Passenger Touring	4900
Seven-Passenger Touring	5000
Suburban	6000
Brougham	5800
Suburban-Landau	6000
Vestibule Suburban	6200
Vestibule Landau	6200
Vestibule Brougham	5950
Vestibule Suburban-Landau . .	6200

PIERCE-ARROW LANDAU—48-B-4

COLOR	Optional		RADIATOR	Cellular
SEATING CAPACITY .	Seven persons		COOLING	Water
POSITION OF DRIVER	Right side		IGNITION	High-tension magneto and storage battery
WHEELBASE	142 inches			
GAUGE	56 inches			
WHEELS	Wood		STARTING SYSTEM . .	Two unit
FRONT TIRES	37 x 5 inches		STARTER OPERATED .	Gear to fly wheel
REAR TIRES	37 x 5 inches		LIGHTING SYSTEM . .	Electric
SERVICE BRAKE . . .	Expanding on rear wheels		VOLTAGES	Six
			WIRING SYSTEM . .	Single
EMERGENCY BRAKE .	Contracting on rear wheels		GASOLINE SYSTEM . .	Pressure
CYLINDERS	Six		CLUTCH	Cone
ARRANGED	Vertically		TRANSMISSION . . .	Selective sliding
CAST	In pairs		GEAR CHANGES . . .	Four forward, one reverse
HORSEPOWER	48.6 (N. A. C. C. Rating)		DRIVE	Spiral bevel
BORE AND STROKE .	4½ x 5½ inches		REAR AXLE	Semi-floating
LUBRICATION	Force feed		STEERING GEAR . . .	Screw and nut

In addition to above specifications, price includes windshield, speedometer, autometer, clock and demountable rims

PIERCE-ARROW
MOTOR CAR
COMPANY

B U F F A L O
N E W Y O R K

Price	**$7200**
Two-Passenger Runabout . . .	5900
Three-Passenger Runabout . . .	5900
Two-Passenger Coupe	6700
Three-Passenger Coupe	6700
Four-Passenger Touring	5900
Five-Passenger Touring	5900
Seven-Passenger Touring	6000
Suburban	7000
Landau	7000
Brougham	6800
Suburban-Landau	7000
Vestibule Landau	7200
Vestibule Brougham	6950
Vestibule Suburban-Landau . .	7200

PIERCE-ARROW VESTIBULE SUBURBAN—66-A-4

COLOR	Optional		LUBRICATION	Force feed
SEATING CAPACITY .	Seven persons		RADIATOR	Cellular
POSITION OF DRIVER	Right side		COOLING	Water
WHEELBASE	147½ inches		IGNITION	High-tension magneto and storage battery
GAUGE	57 inches			
WHEELS	Wood		STARTING SYSTEM .	Two unit
FRONT TIRES	37 x 5 inches		STARTER OPERATED .	Gear to fly wheel
REAR TIRES	38 x 5½ inches		LIGHTING SYSTEM . .	Electric
SERVICE BRAKE . . .	Expanding on rear wheels		VOLTAGES	Six
			WIRING SYSTEM . .	Single
EMERGENCY BRAKE .	Contracting on rear wheels		GASOLINE SYSTEM . .	Pressure
			CLUTCH	Cone
CYLINDERS	Six		TRANSMISSION . . .	Selective sliding
ARRANGED	Vertically		GEAR CHANGES . . .	Four forward, one reverse
CAST	In pairs			
HORSEPOWER	60		DRIVE	Spiral bevel
	(N. A. C. C. Rating)		REAR AXLE	Semi-floating
BORE AND STROKE .	5 x 7 inches		STEERING GEAR . . .	Screw and nut

In addition to above specifications, price includes windshield, speedometer, autometer, clock and demountable rims

**PIERCE-ARROW
MOTOR CAR
COMPANY**

**B U F F A L O
N E W   Y O R K**

Price	$6000
Two-Passenger Runabout	5900
Three-Passenger Runabout . .	5900
Two-Passenger Coupe	6700
Three-Passenger Coupe	6700
Four-Passenger Touring . . .	5900
Five-Passenger Touring	5900
Suburban	7000
Landau	7000
Brougham	6800
Suburban-Landau	7000
Vestibule Landau	7200
Vestibule Suburban	7200
Vestibule Brougham	6950
Vestibule Suburban-Landau . .	7200

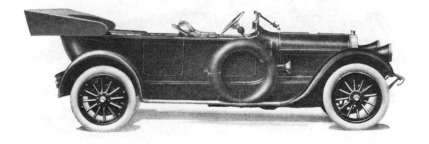

PIERCE-ARROW SEVEN-PASSENGER TOURING CAR—66-A-4

COLOR	Optional		RADIATOR	Cellular
SEATING CAPACITY .	Seven persons		COOLING	Water
POSITION OF DRIVER .	Right side		IGNITION	High tension magneto and storage battery
WHEELBASE	147½ inches			
GAUGE	57 inches			
WHEELS	Wood		STARTING SYSTEM . .	Two unit
FRONT TIRES	37 x 5 inches		STARTER OPERATED .	Gear to fly wheel
REAR TIRES	38 x 5½ inches		LIGHTING SYSTEM . .	Electric
SERVICE BRAKE . . .	Expanding on rear wheels		VOLTAGES	Six
			WIRING SYSTEM . . .	Single
EMERGENCY BRAKE .	Contracting on rear wheels		GASOLINE SYSTEM . .	Pressure
			CLUTCH	Cone
CYLINDERS	Six		TRANSMISSION . . .	Selective sliding
ARRANGED	Vertically		GEAR CHANGES . . .	Four forward, one reverse
CAST	In pairs			
HORSEPOWER	60 (N. A. C. C. Rating)		DRIVE	Spiral bevel
BORE AND STROKE . .	5 x 7 inches		REAR AXLE	Semi-floating
LUBRICATION	Force feed		STEERING GEAR . .	Screw and nut

In addition to above specifications, price includes top, top hood,
windshield, speedometer, autometer, clock and demountable rims

**S C R I P P S -
B O O T H
C O M P A N Y**

**D E T R O I T
M I C H I G A N**

SCRIPPS-BOOTH ROADSTER—D

COLOR	Biscuit, gray or royal blue	LUBRICATION	Force feed
SEATING CAPACITY .	Three persons	RADIATOR	Cellular
POSITION OF DRIVER	Left side	COOLING	Thermo-syphon
WHEELBASE	110 inches	IGNITION	Storage battery
GAUGE	56 inches	STARTING SYSTEM . .	Double unit
WHEELS	Wire	STARTER OPERATED .	Gear to fly wheel
FRONT TIRES	32 x 4 inches		
REAR TIRES	32 x 4 inches anti-skid	LIGHTING SYSTEM . .	Electric
SERVICE BRAKE . . .	Contracting on rear wheels	VOLTAGES	Six
		WIRING SYSTEM . . .	Single
EMERGENCY BRAKE .	Expanding on rear wheels	GASOLINE SYSTEM . .	Vacuum
CYLINDERS	Eight	CLUTCH	Dry multiple disc
ARRANGED	V type, 90 degrees	TRANSMISSION . . .	Selective sliding
CAST	En bloc with crank case	GEAR CHANGES . . .	Three forward
		DRIVE	Plain bevel
HORSEPOWER	22.05	REAR AXLE	Three-quarters floating
(N. A. C. C. Rating)			
BORE AND STROKE .	2⅝ x 3¾ inches	STEERING GEAR . . .	Worm and gear

In addition to above specifications, price includes top,
top hood, windshield, speedometer and demountable wheel

GREAT WESTERN
A U T O M O B I L E
C O M P A N Y

Price, $1185

PERU,   INDIANA

GREAT WESTERN 1916 TOURING CAR

COLOR	Black	LUBRICATION	Splash with circulating pump
SEATING CAPACITY .	Five persons		
POSITION OF DRIVER .	Left side	RADIATOR	Cellular
WHEELBASE	118 inches	COOLING	Water pump
GAUGE	56 inches	IGNITION	Storage battery
WHEELS	Wood	STARTING SYSTEM . .	Single unit
FRONT TIRES	32 x 3½ or 33 x 4 inches	STARTER OPERATED .	Chain to crank shaft
REAR TIRES	32 x 3½ or 33 x 4 inches	LIGHTING SYSTEM . .	Electric
		VOLTAGES	Six
SERVICE BRAKE . .	Contracting on rear wheels	WIRING SYSTEM . . .	Double
EMERGENCY BRAKE .	Expanding on rear wheels	GASOLINE SYSTEM . .	Vacuum
		CLUTCH	Multiple disc
CYLINDERS	Six	TRANSMISSION . . .	Selective sliding
ARRANGED	Vertically	GEAR CHANGES . . .	Three forward, one reverse
CAST	En bloc	DRIVE	Plain bevel
HORSEPOWER	21.6	REAR AXLE	Semi-floating
(N. A. C. C. Rating)		STEERING GEAR . . .	Worm and gear
BORE AND STROKE .	3 x 5 inches		

In addition to above specifications, price includes top, top
hood, windshield, speedometer, ammeter and demountable rim

VELIE MOTOR VEHICLE COMPANY
MOLINE ILLINOIS

Price $1065
With winter top 1240
Two-Passenger Roadster 1045
Four-Passenger Coupe . 1750

VELIE BILTWEL SIX—22

COLOR	Velie blue		RADIATOR	Cellular
SEATING CAPACITY .	Five persons		COOLING	Water pump
POSITION OF DRIVER	Left side		IGNITION	Storage battery
WHEELBASE	115 inches		STARTING SYSTEM . .	Two unit
GAUGE	56 inches		STARTER OPERATED .	Gear to fly wheel
WHEELS	Wood		LIGHTING SYSTEM . .	Electric
FRONT TIRES	32 x 4 inches		VOLTAGES	Six
REAR TIRES	32 x 4 inches, anti-skid		WIRING SYSTEM . . .	Single
SERVICE BRAKE . . .	Rear axle		GASOLINE SYSTEM . .	Vacuum
EMERGENCY BRAKE .	Rear axle		CLUTCH	Dry multiple disc
CYLINDERS	Six		TRANSMISSION . . .	Selective sliding
ARRANGED	Vertically		GEAR CHANGES . . .	Three forward, one reverse
CAST	En bloc		DRIVE	Spiral bevel
HORSEPOWER . . . . 25.35 (N. A. C. C. Rating)			REAR AXLE	Three-quarters floating
BORE AND STROKE . .	3¼ x 4½ inches		STEERING GEAR . . .	Worm and gear
LUBRICATION	Force feed and splash			

In addition to above specifications, price includes top, top
hood, windshield, speedometer, ammeter and demountable rims

**WESTCOTT
MOTOR CAR
COMPANY**

**RICHMOND
INDIANA**

Price $1595
Three-Passenger Cloverleaf
    Roadster 1595
Seven-Passenger Sedan . . 1945

WESTCOTT TOURING CAR—51

COLOR	Dark green or dark gray		BORE AND STROKE . .	3½ x 5¼ inches
SEATING CAPACITY .	Seven persons		LUBRICATION	Force feed and splash
POSITION OF DRIVER .	Left side		RADIATOR	Cellular
WHEELBASE	126 inches		COOLING	Water pump
GAUGE	56 inches		IGNITION	Storage battery
WHEELS	Wood		STARTING SYSTEM . .	Single unit
FRONT TIRES	35 x 4½ inches, anti-skid		STARTER OPERATED .	Gear to fly wheel
REAR TIRES	35 x 4½ inches, anti-skid		LIGHTING SYSTEM . .	Electric
			VOLTAGES	Six
SERVICE BRAKE . . .	Contracting on rear wheels		WIRING SYSTEM . . .	Single
EMERGENCY BRAKE .	Expanding on rear wheels		GASOLINE SYSTEM . .	Vacuum
			CLUTCH	Dry multiple disc
CYLINDERS	Six		TRANSMISSION . . .	Selective sliding
ARRANGED	Vertically		GEAR CHANGES . . .	Three forward, one reverse
CAST	En bloc		DRIVE	Spiral bevel
HORSEPOWER	29.4		REAR AXLE	Semi-floating
	(N. A. C. C. Rating)		STEERING GEAR . .	Worm and wheel

In addition to above specifications, price includes top, top hood, wind-shield, speedometer, ammeter, voltmeter, clock and demountable rims

WESTCOTT
MOTOR CAR
COMPANY

RICHMOND
INDIANA

Price	$1445
Three-Passenger Cloverleaf Roadster	1445
Three-Passenger Cloverleaf Cabriolet	1745

WESTCOTT TOURING CAR—42

COLOR	Dark green or dark gray		BORE AND STROKE . .	3½ x 5¼ inches
SEATING CAPACITY .	Five persons		LUBRICATION	Force feed and splash
POSITION OF DRIVER .	Left side		RADIATOR	Cellular
WHEELBASE	121 inches		COOLING	Water pump
GAUGE	56 inches		IGNITION.	Storage battery
WHEELS	Wood		STARTING SYSTEM . .	Single unit
FRONT TIRES	34 x 4 inches, anti-skid		STARTER OPERATED .	Gear to fly wheel
REAR TIRES	34 x 4 inches, anti-skid		LIGHTING SYSTEM . .	Electric
			VOLTAGES	Six
			WIRING SYSTEM . .	Single
SERVICE BRAKE. . .	Contracting on rear wheels		GASOLINE SYSTEM. .	Vacuum
EMERGENCY BRAKE .	Expanding on rear wheels		CLUTCH	Dry multiple disc
			TRANSMISSION . . .	Selective sliding
CYLINDERS	Six		GEAR CHANGES . . .	Three forward, one reverse
ARRANGED	Vertically			
CAST	En bloc		DRIVE	Spiral bevel
HORSEPOWER 29.4			REAR AXLE	Semi-floating
(N. A. C. C. Rating)			STEERING GEAR. . .	Worm and wheel

In addition to above specifications, price includes top, top hood, windshield, speedometer, ammeter, voltmeter, clock and demountable rims

CHEVROLET
MOTOR
COMPANY
OF MICHIGAN

FLINT
MICHIGAN

Price, $750

CHEVROLET ROYAL MAIL—TYPE H-2½

COLOR	Body and wheels, Chevrolet green; chassis and fenders, black	BORE AND STROKE .	3¹¹⁄₁₆ x 4 inches	
		LUBRICATION	Splash with circulating pump	
SEATING CAPACITY .	Two persons	RADIATOR	Cellular	
POSITION OF DRIVER.	Left side	COOLING	Thermo-syphon	
WHEELBASE	106 inches	IGNITION	Storage battery	
GAUGE.	56 inches	STARTING SYSTEM . .	Single unit	
WHEELS	Wood	STARTER OPERATED .	Gear to fly wheel	
FRONT TIRES	32 x 3½ inches	LIGHTING SYSTEM . .	Electric	
REAR TIRES	32 x 3½ inches, anti-skid	VOLTAGES	Six	
		WIRING SYSTEM. . .	Single; double on starting motor	
SERVICE BRAKE. . .	Rear wheel	GASOLINE SYSTEM. .	Pressure	
EMERGENCY BRAKE .	Internal expanding	CLUTCH	Cone	
		TRANSMISSION . . .	Selective sliding	
CYLINDERS	Four	GEAR CHANGES . . .	Three forward, one reverse	
ARRANGED	Vertically			
CAST	En bloc	DRIVE	Plain bevel	
HORSEPOWER	21.74	REAR AXLE	Semi-floating	
(N. A. C. C. Rating)		STEERING GEAR. . .	Worm and gear	

In addition to above specifications, price includes top, top
hood, windshield, speedometer, ammeter and demountable rims

CHEVROLET
MOTOR
COMPANY
OF MICHIGAN

FLINT
MICHIGAN

Price, $750

CHEVROLET BABY GRAND—TYPE H-4

COLOR	Body and wheels, Chevrolet green; chassis and fenders, black	BORE AND STROKE .	$3\frac{11}{16}$ x 4 inches
		LUBRICATION	Splash with circulating pump
SEATING CAPACITY .	Five persons	RADIATOR	Cellular
POSITION OF DRIVER	Left side	COOLING	Thermo-syphon
WHEELBASE	106 inches	IGNITION.	Storage battery
GAUGE.	56 inches	STARTING SYSTEM . .	Single unit
WHEELS	Wood	STARTER OPERATED .	Gear to fly wheel
FRONT TIRES	32 x 3½ inches	LIGHTING SYSTEM . .	Electric
REAR TIRES	32 x 3½ inches, anti-skid	VOLTAGES	Six
		WIRING SYSTEM. . .	Single; double on starting motor
SERVICE BRAKE. . .	Rear wheels	GASOLINE SYSTEM . .	Pressure
EMERGENCY BRAKE .	Internal expanding	CLUTCH	Cone
		TRANSMISSION . . .	Selective sliding
CYLINDERS	Four	GEAR CHANGES . . .	Three forward, one reverse
ARRANGED	Vertically		
CAST	En bloc	DRIVE	Plain bevel
HORSEPOWER	21.74	REAR AXLE	Semi-floating
(N. A. C. C. Rating)		STEERING GEAR. . .	Worm and gear

In addition to above specifications, price includes top, top
hood, windshield, speedometer, ammeter and demountable rims

CHEVROLET
M O T O R
C O M P A N Y
OF MICHIGAN

F L I N T
M I C H I G A N

Price $490
With Electric Lighting and
    Starting 550

CHEVROLET FOUR NINETY—TYPE 490

COLOR	Ebony black
SEATING CAPACITY .	Five persons
POSITION OF DRIVER	Left side
WHEELBASE	102 inches
GAUGE.	56 inches
WHEELS	Wood
FRONT TIRES	30 x 3 inches
REAR TIRES	30 x 3½ inches
SERVICE BRAKE. . .	Rear wheels
EMERGENCY BRAKE .	Internal expanding
CYLINDERS	Four
ARRANGED	Vertically
CAST	En bloc
HORSEPOWER. . . .	21.74 (N. A. C. C. Rating)
BORE AND STROKE .	3¹¹⁄₁₆ x 4 inches

LUBRICATION	Splash with circulating pump
RADIATOR	Cellular
COOLING	Thermo-syphon
IGNITION.	High-tension magneto
STARTING SYSTEM . .	Single unit
STARTER OPERATED .	Gear to fly wheel
LIGHTING SYSTEM . .	Gas
GASOLINE SYSTEM . .	Gravity
CLUTCH	Cone
TRANSMISSION . . .	Selective sliding
GEAR CHANGES . . .	Three forward, one reverse
DRIVE	Plain bevel
REAR AXLE	Three-quarters floating
STEERING GEAR. . .	Spur gears and sector

In addition to above specifications, price
includes top, top hood and windshield

**W. A. PATERSON
C O M P A N Y**

**F   L   I   N   T
M I C H I G A N**

Price $985
Seven-Passenger .   1060

PATERSON TOURING CAR—6-42

COLOR	Blue	LUBRICATION	Force feed and splash
SEATING CAPACITY .	Five persons	RADIATOR	Tubular
POSITION OF DRIVER	Left side	COOLING	Water pump
WHEELBASE	117 inches	IGNITION.	Delco distributor and storage battery
GAUGE	56 inches		
WHEELS	Wood		
FRONT TIRES	32 x 4 inches	STARTING SYSTEM . .	Two unit
REAR TIRES	32 x 4 inches, anti-skid	STARTER OPERATED .	Gear to fly wheel
		LIGHTING SYSTEM . .	Electric
SERVICE BRAKE. . .	Contracting on rear wheels	VOLTAGES	Six
		WIRING SYSTEM. . .	Single
EMERGENCY BRAKE .	Expanding on rear wheels	GASOLINE SYSTEM. .	Vacuum
		CLUTCH	Cone
CYLINDERS	Six	TRANSMISSION . . .	Selective sliding
ARRANGED	Vertically	GEAR CHANGES . . .	Three forward
CAST	En bloc	DRIVE	Plain bevel
HORSEPOWER	25.35	REAR AXLE	Three-quarters floating
(N. A. C. C. Rating)			
BORE AND STROKE . .	3¼ x 4½ inches	STEERING GEAR . . .	Worm and nut

In addition to above specifications, price includes top, top
hood, windshield, speedometer, ammeter and demountable rims

**C A D I L L A C
M O T O R   C A R
C O M P A N Y**

**D E T R O I T
M I C H I G A N**

Price, $2080

CADILLAC ROADSTER—TYPE 53

COLOR	Royal green	LUBRICATION	Force feed
SEATING CAPACITY .	Two persons	RADIATOR	Tubular
POSITION OF DRIVER	Left side	COOLING	Water pump
WHEELBASE	122 inches	IGNITION	Generator and storage battery
GAUGE	56 or 61 inches		
WHEELS	Wood	STARTING SYSTEM . .	Single unit
FRONT TIRES	36 x 4½ inches	STARTER OPERATED .	Gear to fly wheel
REAR TIRES	36 x 4½ inches, anti-skid	LIGHTING SYSTEM . .	Electric
		VOLTAGES	Six
SERVICE BRAKE . . .	Contracting on rear wheels	WIRING SYSTEM . . .	Single
		GASOLINE SYSTEM . .	Pressure
EMERGENCY BRAKE .	Expanding on rear wheels	CLUTCH	Dry multiple disc
CYLINDERS	Eight	TRANSMISSION . . .	Selective sliding
ARRANGED	V type, 90 degrees	GEAR CHANGES . . .	Three forward and reverse
CAST	In fours	DRIVE	Spiral bevel
HORSEPOWER	31.25 (N. A. C. C. Rating)	REAR AXLE	Full floating
BORE AND STROKE .	3⅛ x 5⅛ inches	STEERING GEAR . . .	Worm and sector

In addition to above specifications, price includes top, top hood,
windshield, speedometer, ammeter, clock and demountable rims

C A D I L L A C
M O T O R   C A R
C O M P A N Y

D E T R O I T
M I C H I G A N

Price . . $2400
Coupe .   2800

CADILLAC VICTORIA—TYPE 53

COLOR	Calumet green and black
SEATING CAPACITY .	Three persons
POSITION OF DRIVER	Left side
WHEELBASE	122 inches
GAUGE	56 or 61 inches
WHEELS	Wood
FRONT TIRES	36 x 4½ inches
REAR TIRES	36 x 4½ inches, anti-skid
SERVICE BRAKE . . .	Contracting on rear wheels
EMERGENCY BRAKE .	Expanding on rear wheels
CYLINDERS	Eight
ARRANGED	V type, 90 degrees
CAST	In fours
HORSEPOWER	31.25 (N. A. C. C. Rating)

BORE AND STROKE .	3⅛ x 5⅛ inches
LUBRICATION	Force feed circulating
RADIATOR	Tubular
COOLING	Water pump
IGNITION	Generator and storage battery
STARTING SYSTEM . .	Single unit
STARTER OPERATED .	Gear to fly wheel
LIGHTING SYSTEM . .	Electric
VOLTAGES	Six
WIRING SYSTEM . . .	Single
GASOLINE SYSTEM . .	Pressure
CLUTCH	Dry multiple disc
TRANSMISSION . . .	Selective sliding
GEAR CHANGES . . .	Three forward, one reverse
DRIVE	Spiral bevel
REAR AXLE	Full floating
STEERING GEAR . . .	Worm and sector

In addition to above specifications, price includes top hood,
windshield, speedometer, ammeter, clock and demountable rims

CADILLAC
MOTOR CAR
COMPANY

DETROIT
MICHIGAN

Price $2080
Five-Passenger Salon . . 2080

CADILLAC SEVEN-PASSENGER CAR—TYPE 53

COLOR	Royal green	RADIATOR	Tubular
SEATING CAPACITY .	Seven persons	COOLING	Water pump
POSITION OF DRIVER	Left side	IGNITION	Generator and storage battery
WHEELBASE	122 inches		
GAUGE	56 or 61 inches	STARTING SYSTEM . .	Single unit
WHEELS	Wood	STARTER OPERATED .	Gear to fly wheel
FRONT TIRES	36 x 4½ inches	LIGHTING SYSTEM . .	Electric
REAR TIRES	36 x 4½ inches, anti-skid	VOLTAGES	Six
		WIRING SYSTEM . . .	Single
SERVICE BRAKE . . .	Contracting on rear wheels	GASOLINE SYSTEM . .	Pressure
EMERGENCY BRAKE .	Expanding on rear wheels	CLUTCH	Dry multiple disc
CYLINDERS	Eight	TRANSMISSION . . .	Selective sliding
ARRANGED	V-type, 90 degrees	GEAR CHANGES . . .	Three forward and reverse
CAST	In fours		
HORSEPOWER	31.25	DRIVE	Spiral bevel
(N. A. C. C. Rating)		REAR AXLE	Full floating
BORE AND STROKE .	3⅛ x 5⅛ inches	STEERING GEAR . . .	Worm and sector
LUBRICATION	Force feed		

In addition to above specifications, price includes top, top hood
windshield, speedometer, ammeter, clock and demountable rims

CADILLAC
MOTOR CAR
COMPANY

DETROIT
MICHIGAN

Price, $2950

CADILLAC BROUGHAM—TYPE 53

COLOR	Calumet green and black	LUBRICATION	Force feed circulating
SEATING CAPACITY	Five persons	RADIATOR	Tubular
POSITION OF DRIVER	Left side	COOLING	Water pump
WHEELBASE	122 inches	IGNITION	Generator and storage battery
GAUGE	56 or 61 inches		
WHEELS	Wood	STARTING SYSTEM	Single unit
FRONT TIRES	36 x 4½ inches	STARTER OPERATED	Gear to fly wheel
REAR TIRES	36 x 4½ inches, anti-skid	LIGHTING SYSTEM	Electric
		VOLTAGES	Six
SERVICE BRAKE	Contracting on rear wheels	WIRING SYSTEM	Single
		GASOLINE SYSTEM	Pressure
EMERGENCY BRAKE	Expanding on rear wheels	CLUTCH	Dry multiple disc
CYLINDERS	Eight	TRANSMISSION	Selective sliding
ARRANGED	V type, 90 degrees	GEAR CHANGES	Three forward, one reverse
CAST	In fours		
HORSEPOWER	31.25	DRIVE	Spiral bevel
(N. A. C. C. Rating)		REAR AXLE	Full floating
BORE AND STROKE	3⅛ x 5⅛ inches	STEERING GEAR	Worm and sector

In addition to above specifications, price includes windshield, speedometer, ammeter, clock and demountable rims

CADILLAC
MOTOR CAR
COMPANY

DETROIT
MICHIGAN

Price . . $3450
Berlin . 3600

CADILLAC LIMOUSINE—TYPE 53

COLOR	Calumet green and black		BORE AND STROKE .	3⅛ x 5⅛ inches
SEATING CAPACITY .	Seven persons		LUBRICATION	Force feed
POSITION OF DRIVER	Left side		RADIATOR	Tubular
WHEELBASE	122 inches		COOLING	Water pump
GAUGE	56 or 61 inches		IGNITION	Generator and storage battery
WHEELS	Wood		STARTING SYSTEM . .	Single unit
FRONT TIRES	36 x 4½ inches		STARTER OPERATED .	Gear to fly wheel
REAR TIRES	36 x 4½ inches, anti-skid		LIGHTING SYSTEM . .	Electric
			VOLTAGES	Six
SERVICE BRAKE . . .	Contracting on rear wheels		WIRING SYSTEM . . .	Single
			GASOLINE SYSTEM . .	Pressure
EMERGENCY BRAKE .	Expanding on rear wheels		CLUTCH	Dry multiple disc
CYLINDERS	Eight		TRANSMISSION . . .	Selective sliding
ARRANGED	V type, 90 degrees		GEAR CHANGES . . .	Three forward and reverse
CAST	In fours		DRIVE	Spiral bevel
HORSEPOWER	31.25		REAR AXLE	Full floating
(N. A. C. C. Rating)			STEERING GEAR . . .	Worm and sector

In addition to above specifications, price includes windshield, speedometer, ammeter, clock and demountable rims

ALLEN   MOTOR
C O M P A N Y

FOSTORIA, OHIO

Price . . . $795
Roadster . 795

ALLEN TOURING CAR—37

COLOR	Body, olive green; running gear, black		BORE AND STROKE . .	3¾ x 5 inches
			LUBRICATION	Splash with circulating pump
SEATING CAPACITY .	Five persons		RADIATOR	Tubular
POSITION OF DRIVER	Left side		COOLING	Water
WHEELBASE	112 inches		IGNITION	Storage battery
GAUGE	56 inches		STARTING SYSTEM . .	Two unit
WHEELS	Wood		STARTER OPERATED .	Gear to fly wheel
FRONT TIRES	32 x 3½ inches		LIGHTING SYSTEM . .	Electric
REAR TIRES	32 x 3½ inches, anti-skid		VOLTAGES	Six
			WIRING SYSTEM . .	Single
SERVICE BRAKE . . .	Contracting on rear wheels		GASOLINE SYSTEM . .	Vacuum
EMERGENCY BRAKE .	Expanding on rear wheels		CLUTCH	Cone
			TRANSMISSION . . .	Selective sliding
CYLINDERS	Four		GEAR CHANGES . . .	Three
ARRANGED	Vertically		DRIVE	Plain bevel
CAST	En bloc		REAR AXLE	Full floating
HORSEPOWER	22.5 (N. A. C. C. Rating)		STEERING GEAR . .	Worm and gear

In addition to above specifications, price includes top, top hood, windshield, speedometer, ammeter and demountable rims

MAXWELL
MOTOR COM-
PANY, Inc.

DETROIT
MICHIGAN

Price	$655
Roadster . .	635
Cabriolet . .	865
Sedan . . .	935
Town Car . .	915

MAXWELL TOURING CAR

COLOR	Black	LUBRICATION	Splash with circulating pump
SEATING CAPACITY .	Five persons		
POSITION OF DRIVER	Left side	RADIATOR	Tubular
WHEELBASE	103 inches	COOLING	Thermo-syphon
GAUGE	56 or 60 inches	IGNITION	High-tension magneto
WHEELS	Wood		
FRONT TIRES	30 x 3½ inches	STARTING SYSTEM . .	Single unit
REAR TIRES	30 x 3½ inches, anti-skid	STARTER OPERATED .	Gear to fly wheel
		LIGHTING SYSTEM . .	Electric
SERVICE BRAKE . . .	Contracting on rear wheels	VOLTAGES	Lighting, six; starting, twelve
EMERGENCY BRAKE .	Expanding on rear wheels	WIRING SYSTEM . . .	Single
		GASOLINE SYSTEM . .	Gravity
CYLINDERS	Four	CLUTCH	Cone in oil
ARRANGED	Vertically	TRANSMISSION . . .	Selective sliding
CAST	En bloc	GEAR CHANGES . . .	Three forward
HORSEPOWER	21.03	DRIVE	Plain bevel
(N. A. C. C. Rating)		REAR AXLE.	Three-quarters floating
BORE AND STROKE .	3⅝ x 4½ inches	STEERING GEAR . . .	Worm and sector

In addition to above specifications, price includes top, top
hood, windshield, speedometer, ammeter and demountable rims

**M O L I N E
AUTOMOBILE
C O M P A N Y**

**E A S T M O L I N E
I L L I N O I S**

Price $2500
Roadster 2500
Limousine . . . 3800
Sedan 3250

MOLINE-KNIGHT TOURING CAR—50

COLOR	Blue-black with gray striping
SEATING CAPACITY .	Seven persons
POSITION OF DRIVER	Left side
WHEELBASE	128 inches
GAUGE	56 inches
WHEELS	Wood
FRONT TIRES	36 x 4½ inches
REAR TIRES	36 x 4½ inches, anti-skid
SERVICE BRAKE . . .	Contracting on rear wheels
EMERGENCY BRAKE .	Expanding on rear wheels
CYLINDERS	Four
ARRANGED	Vertically
CAST	En bloc
HORSEPOWER	25.6 (N. A. C. C. Rating)
BORE AND STROKE .	4 x 6 inches

LUBRICATION	Force feed
RADIATOR	Tubular
COOLING	Thermo-syphon
IGNITION	High-tension magneto and dry batteries
STARTING SYSTEM . .	Two unit
STARTER OPERATED .	Gear to fly wheel
LIGHTING SYSTEM .	Electric
VOLTAGES	Starting, twelve; lighting, six
WIRING SYSTEM . . .	Double
GASOLINE SYSTEM . .	Pressure
CLUTCH	Cone
TRANSMISSION . . .	Selective sliding
GEAR CHANGES . . .	Four
DRIVE	Spiral bevel
REAR AXLE	Full floating
STEERING GEAR . . .	Screw and nut

In addition to above specifications, price includes top, top hood, windshield, speedometer, ammeter, voltmeter, clock and demountable rims

MOLINE AUTOMOBILE COMPANY

EAST MOLINE ILLINOIS

Price . . . $1450
Roadster . 1450

MOLINE-KNIGHT TOURING CAR—40

COLOR	Auto green and black with gold striping
SEATING CAPACITY .	Seven persons
POSITION OF DRIVER	Left side
Wheel base	118 inches
GAUGE	56 inches
WHEELS	Wood
FRONT TIRES	34 x 4 inches
REAR TIRES	34 x 4 inches, anti-skid
SERVICE BRAKE . . .	Contracting on rear wheels
EMERGENCY BRAKE .	Expanding on rear wheels
CYLINDERS	Four
ARRANGED	Vertically
CAST	En bloc
HORSEPOWER	22.5 (N. A. C. C. Rating)

BORE AND STROKE .	3¾ x 5 inches
LUBRICATION	Force feed
RADIATOR	Tubular
COOLING	Thermo-syphon
IGNITION	High tension battery
STARTING SYSTEM . .	Two unit
STARTER OPERATED .	Gear to fly wheel
LIGHTING SYSTEM . .	Electric
VOLTAGES	Six
WIRING SYSTEM . . .	Single
GASOLINE SYSTEM . .	Vacuum
CLUTCH	Cone
TRANSMISSION . . .	Selective sliding
GEAR CHANGES . . .	Three
DRIVE	Spiral bevel
REAR AXLE	Three-quarters floating
STEERING GEAR . . .	Worm and sector

In addition to above specifications, price includes top, top hood, windshield, speedometer, ammeter, voltmeter, clock and demountable rims

**MITCHELL-
LEWIS MOTOR
COMPANY**

**R A C I N E
W I S C O N S I N**

Price $1250
Three-Passenger . . 1250
Seven-Passenger . . 1285

MITCHELL—THE SIX OF '16

COLOR	Body, dark Mitchell blue; running gear, black	BORE AND STROKE . .	3½ x 5 inches
		LUBRICATION	Pump over and splash
SEATING CAPACITY .	Five persons	RADIATOR	Cellular
POSITION OF DRIVER	Left side	COOLING	Water pump
WHEELBASE	125 inches	IGNITION	Storage battery
GAUGE	56 or 60 inches	STARTING SYSTEM . .	Single unit
WHEELS	Wood	STARTER OPERATED .	Chain to crank shaft
FRONT TIRES	34 x 4 inches		
REAR TIRES	34 x 4 inches, anti-skid	LIGHTING SYSTEM . .	Electric
		VOLTAGES	Lighting, six; starting, twelve
SERVICE BRAKE . . .	Contracting on rear wheels	WIRING SYSTEM . . .	Double
		GASOLINE SYSTEM . .	Vacuum
EMERGENCY BRAKE .	Expanding on rear wheels	CLUTCH	Cone
		TRANSMISSION . . .	Selective sliding
CYLINDERS	Six	GEAR CHANGES . . .	Three forward, one reverse
ARRANGED	Vertically		
CAST	En bloc	DRIVE	Plain bevel
HORSEPOWER	29.4	REAR AXLE	Full floating
(N. A. C. C. Rating)		STEERING GEAR . .	Worm and gear

In addition to above specifications, price includes top, top hood,
windshield, speedometer, ammeter, voltmeter and demountable rims

NATIONAL
MOTOR
VEHICLE
COMPANY

INDIANAPOLIS
INDIANA

Price	$1990
Four-Passenger Touring	1990
Six-Passenger Touring	2020
Three-Passenger Roadster . . .	1990
Four Passenger Coupe	2650
Five-Passenger Sedan	3200

NATIONAL HIGHWAY TWELVE

COLOR	National dark blue	LUBRICATION	Full force feed
SEATING CAPACITY .	Three persons	RADIATOR	Cellular
POSITION OF DRIVER.	Left side	COOLING	Water pump
WHEELBASE	128 inches	IGNITION	High-tension magneto
GAUGE	56 inches	STARTING SYSTEM . .	Single unit
WHEELS	Wood	STARTER OPERATED .	Gear to fly wheel
FRONT TIRES	36 x 4½ inches	LIGHTING SYSTEM . .	Electric
REAR TIRES	36 x 4½ inches	VOLTAGES	Six
SERVICE BRAKE . . .	Contracting on rear wheels	WIRING SYSTEM . .	Single
EMERGENCY BRAKE .	Expanding on rear wheels	GASOLINE SYSTEM . .	Vacuum
CYLINDERS	Twelve	CLUTCH	Cone
ARRANGED	V-type, 60 degrees	TRANSMISSION . . .	Selective sliding
CAST	In sixes	GEAR CHANGES . . .	Three forward
HORSEPOWER	36.3	DRIVE	Spiral bevel
(N. A. C. C. Rating)		REAR AXLE	Full floating
BORE AND STROKE .	2¾ x 4¾ inches	STEERING GEAR . .	Worm and gear

In addition to above specifications, price includes top, top hood,
windshield, speedometer, ammeter and demountable rims

NATIONAL
MOTOR
VEHICLE
COMPANY

INDIANAPOLIS
INDIANA

| Price. . . . . $1690 |
| Six-Passenger Touring . . . 1720 |
| Three-Passenger Roadster . 1690 |
| Four-Passenger Coupe . . . 2350 |
| Five-Passenger Sedan. . . . 2900 |

NATIONAL HIGHWAY SIX

COLOR.	National dark blue		LUBRICATION	Splash with circulating pump
SEATING CAPACITY .	Four persons		RADIATOR	Cellular
POSITION OF DRIVER	Left side		COOLING.	Water pump
WHEELBASE	128 inches		IGNITION.	High-tension magneto
GAUGE	56 inches			
WHEELS	Wood		STARTING SYSTEM . .	Single unit
FRONT TIRES	34 x 4½ inches		STARTER OPERATED .	Gear to fly wheel
REAR TIRES	34 x 4½ inches		LIGHTING SYSTEM . .	Electric
SERVICE BRAKE . .	Contracting on rear wheels		VOLTAGES	Six
			WIRING SYSTEM . .	Single
EMERGENCY BRAKE .	Expanding on rear wheels		GASOLINE SYSTEM. .	Vacuum
			CLUTCH	Cone
CYLINDERS.	Six		TRANSMISSION . . .	Selective sliding
ARRANGED	Vertically		GEAR CHANGES . . .	Three forward
CAST	En bloc		DRIVE	Spiral bevel
HORSEPOWER. . . .	29.4		REAR AXLE	Full floating
(N. A. C. C. Rating)			STEERING GEAR . .	Worm and gear
BORE AND STROKE .	3½ x 5¼ inches			

In addition to above specifications, price includes top, top hood,
windshield, speedometer, ammeter and demountable rims

**NATIONAL
MOTOR
VEHICLE
COMPANY**

**INDIANAPOLIS
INDIANA**

Price.	$2500
Four-Passenger Touring	2375
Five-Passenger Touring	2375
Seven-Passenger Touring	2400
Three-Passenger Roadster . . .	2375
Four-Passenger Coupe	2850
Five-Passenger Sedan.	3400

NATIONAL NEWPORT SIX

COLOR	Optional	LUBRICATION	Splash with circulating pump
SEATING CAPACITY .	Six persons		
POSITION OF DRIVER	Left side	RADIATOR	Cellular
WHEELBASE	134 inches	COOLING	Water pump
GAUGE	56 inches	IGNITION	High-tension magneto
WHEELS	Wood		
FRONT TIRES	37 x 5 inches	STARTING SYSTEM . .	Single unit
REAR TIRES	37 x 5 inches	STARTER OPERATED .	Gear to fly wheel
SERVICE BRAKE . .	Contracting on rear wheels	LIGHTING SYSTEM . .	Electric
		VOLTAGES	Six
EMERGENCY BRAKE .	Expanding on rear wheels	WIRING SYSTEM . .	Single
		GASOLINE SYSTEM . .	Pressure
CYLINDERS	Six	CLUTCH	Cone
ARRANGED	Vertically	TRANSMISSION . . .	Selective sliding
CAST	En bloc	GEAR CHANGES . . .	Three forward
HORSEPOWER. . . . 33.75 (N. A. C. C. Rating)		DRIVE	Spiral bevel
		REAR AXLE	Full floating
BORE AND STROKE .	3¾ x 5½ inches	STEERING GEAR . .	Worm and gear

In addition to above specifications, price includes top, top hood,
windshield, speedometer, ammeter and demountable rims

MOON MOTOR
CAR COMPANY

S T .   L O U I S
M I S S O U R I

Price . . . $1195
Roadster . 1195

MOON TOURING CAR—6-30

COLOR	Black or Brewster green		BORE AND STROKE .	3¼ x 4½ inches
SEATING CAPACITY .	Five persons		LUBRICATION	Pump over and splash
POSITION OF DRIVER	Left side		RADIATOR	Cellular
WHEELBASE	118 inches		COOLING	Water pump
GAUGE	56 inches		IGNITION	Storage battery
WHEELS	Wood		STARTING SYSTEM . .	Single unit
FRONT TIRES	33 x 4 inches		STARTER OPERATED .	Gear to fly wheel
REAR TIRES	33 x 4 inches, anti-skid		LIGHTING SYSTEM . .	Electric
SERVICE BRAKE . . .	Contracting on rear wheels		VOLTAGES	Six
			WIRING SYSTEM . . .	Single
EMERGENCY BRAKE .	Expanding on rear wheels		GASOLINE SYSTEM . .	Vacuum
			CLUTCH	Dry multiple disc
CYLINDERS	Six		TRANSMISSION . . .	Selective sliding
ARRANGED	Vertically		GEAR CHANGES . . .	Three and reverse
CAST	En bloc		DRIVE	Spiral bevel
HORSEPOWER	25.35 (N. A. C. C. Rating)		REAR AXLE	Full floating
			STEERING GEAR . . .	Worm and gear

In addition to above specifications, price includes top, top hood,
windshield, speedometer, ammeter and demountable rims

F. I. A. T.

POUGHKEEPSIE
NEW   YORK

Price	$4850
Limousine . .	5850
Landaulet . .	5950
Runabout . .	4850

F. I. A. T. RIVIERA—55

COLOR	F. I. A. T. blue, green, maroon or gray		BORE AND STROKE .	5⅛ x 6¾ inches
			LUBRICATION	Full-force feed
			RADIATOR	Honeycomb
SEATING CAPACITY .	Seven persons		COOLING	Water pump
POSITION OF DRIVER .	Right side		IGNITION	High-tension magneto
WHEELBASE	128 inches			
GAUGE	56 inches		STARTING SYSTEM . .	Two unit
WHEELS	Wood		STARTER OPERATED .	Gear to fly wheel
FRONT TIRES	36 x 4½ inches		LIGHTING SYSTEM . .	Electric
REAR TIRES	37 x 5 inches		VOLTAGES	Six
SERVICE BRAKE . . .	Contracting on rear wheels		WIRING SYSTEM . . .	Single
			GASOLINE SYSTEM . .	Pressure
EMERGENCY BRAKE .	Expanding on rear wheels		CLUTCH	Multiple disc
			TRANSMISSION . . .	Selective sliding
CYLINDERS	Four		GEAR CHANGES . . .	Four forward one reverse
ARRANGED	Vertically			
CAST	En bloc		DRIVE	Plain bevel
HORSEPOWER	42.03		REAR AXLE.	Semi-floating
(N. A. C. C. Rating)			STEERING GEAR. . .	Worm and wheel

In addition to above specifications, price includes top, top hood,
windshield, speedometer, ammeter, clock and demountable rims

PULLMAN
MOTOR CAR
COMPANY

YORK, PA

Price	$740
Two-Passenger Roadster . .	740
Three-Passenger Roadster . .	740
Coupe	990

PULLMAN 1916 FOUR

COLOR	Optional		RADIATOR	Cellular
SEATING CAPACITY .	Five persons		COOLING	Thermo-syphon
POSITION OF DRIVER	Left side		IGNITION	High-tension
WHEELBASE	114 inches			magneto
GAUGE	56 inches		STARTING SYSTEM . .	Single unit
WHEELS	Wood		STARTER OPERATED .	Chain to crank
FRONT TIRES	31 x 4 inches,			shaft
	anti-skid		LIGHTING SYSTEM . .	Electric
REAR TIRES	31 x 4 inches,		VOLTAGES	Starting, twelve;
	anti-skid			lighting, six
SERVICE BRAKE . . .	Contracting on		WIRING SYSTEM . . .	Single
	rear wheels		GASOLINE SYSTEM . .	Gravity
EMERGENCY BRAKE .	Expanding on		CLUTCH	Multiple disc
	rear wheels			in oil
CYLINDERS	Four		TRANSMISSION . . .	Selective sliding
ARRANGED	Vertically		GEAR CHANGES . . .	Three forward,
CAST	En bloc			one reverse
HORSEPOWER	22.5		DRIVE	Plain bevel
(N. A. C. C. Rating)			REAR AXLE	Full floating
BORE AND STROKE .	3¾ x 4¼ inches		STEERING GEAR . . .	Worm and wheel
LUBRICATION	Splash with cir-			
	culating pump			

In addition to above specifications, price includes top, top hood, windshield, speedometer, ammeter, voltmeter, clock and demountable rims

H A Y N E S
A U T O M O B I L E
C O M P A N Y

K O K O M O
I N D I A N A

Price, $1485

HAYNES ROADSTER—34

COLOR	Body, Brewster green; chassis, hood and fenders, black	LUBRICATION	Splash with circulating pump
SEATING CAPACITY .	Three persons	RADIATOR	Cellular
POSITION OF DRIVER .	Left side	COOLING	Water pump
WHEELBASE	121 inches	IGNITION	Generator and storage battery
GAUGE	56 inches	STARTING SYSTEM . .	Two unit
WHEELS	Wood	STARTER OPERATED .	Chain to crank shaft
FRONT TIRES	34 x 4 inches		
REAR TIRES	34 x 4 inches, anti-skid	LIGHTING SYSTEM . .	Electric
		VOLTAGES	Six
SERVICE BRAKE . . .	Expanding on rear wheels	WIRING SYSTEM . . .	Double
		GASOLINE SYSTEM . .	Vacuum
EMERGENCY BRAKE .	Expanding on rear wheels	CLUTCH	Dry multiple disc
		TRANSMISSION . . .	Selective sliding
CYLINDERS	Six	GEAR CHANGES . . .	Three forward, one reverse
ARRANGED	Vertically		
CAST	En bloc	DRIVE	Spiral bevel
HORSEPOWER	29.4	REAR AXLE	Full floating
(N. A. C. C. Rating)		STEERING GEAR . . .	Full worm
BORE AND STROKE . .	3½ x 5 inches		

In addition to above specifications, price includes top, top
hood, windshield, speedometer, clock and demountable rims

**H A Y N E S
AUTOMOBILE
C O M P A N Y**

**K O K O M O
I N D I A N A**

Price, $1385

HAYNES LIGHT SIX—34

COLOR	Body, Brewster green; chassis, hood and fenders, black.	BORE AND STROKE . .	3½ x 5 inches
		LUBRICATION	Splash with circulating pump
SEATING CAPACITY .	Five persons	RADIATOR	Cellular
POSITION OF DRIVER .	Left side	COOLING	Water pump
WHEELBASE	121 inches	IGNITION	Generator and storage battery
GAUGE	56 inches	STARTING SYSTEM . .	Two unit
WHEELS	Wood	STARTER OPERATED .	Chain to crank shaft
FRONT TIRES	34 x 4 inches		
REAR TIRES	34 x 4 inches, anti-skid	LIGHTING SYSTEM . .	Electric
		VOLTAGES	Six
SERVICE BRAKE . . .	Expanding on rear wheels	WIRING SYSTEM . . .	Double
		GASOLINE SYSTEM . .	Vacuum
EMERGENCY BRAKE .	Expanding on rear wheels	CLUTCH	Dry multiple disc
		TRANSMISSION . . .	Selective sliding
CYLINDERS	Six	GEAR CHANGES . . .	Three forward, one reverse
ARRANGED	Vertically		
CAST	En bloc	DRIVE	Spiral bevel
HORSEPOWER	29.4	REAR AXLE	Full floating
(N. A. C. C. Rating)		STEERING GEAR . . .	Full worm

In addition to above specifications, price includes top, top
hood, windshield, speedometer, clock and demountable rims

H A Y N E S
AUTOMOBILE
C O M P A N Y

K O K O M O
I N D I A N A

Price, $1495

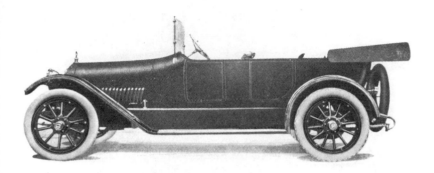

HAYNES KOKOMO SIX—35

COLOR	Body, Brewster green; chassis, hood and tenders, black
SEATING CAPACITY . .	Seven persons
POSITION OF DRIVER .	Left side
WHEELBASE	127 inches
GAUGE	56 inches
WHEELS	Wood
FRONT TIRES	35 x 4½ inches
REAR TIRES	35 x 4½ inches, anti-skid
SERVICE BRAKE . . .	Expanding on rear wheels
EMERGENCY BRAKE .	Expanding on rear wheels
CYLINDERS	Six
ARRANGED	Vertically
CAST	En bloc
HORSEPOWER	29.4 (N. A. C. C. Rating)
BORE AND STROKE . .	3½ x 5 inches

LUBRICATION	Splash with circulating pump
RADIATOR	Cellular
COOLING	Water pump
IGNITION	Generator and storage battery
STARTING SYSTEM . .	Two unit
STARTER OPERATED .	Chain to crankshaft
LIGHTING SYSTEM . .	Electric
VOLTAGES	Six
WIRING SYSTEM . . .	Double
GASOLINE SYSTEM . .	Vacuum
CLUTCH	Dry multiple disc
TRANSMISSION . . .	Selective sliding
GEAR CHANGES . . .	Three forward, one reverse
DRIVE	Spiral bevel
REAR AXLE	Full floating
STEERING GEAR . . .	Full worm

In addition to above specifications, price includes top, top
hood, windshield, speedometer, clock and demountable rims

**THE
LEXINGTON-
HOWARD CO.**

CONNERSVILLE
I N D I A N A

Price $1875
Clubster . . 1875

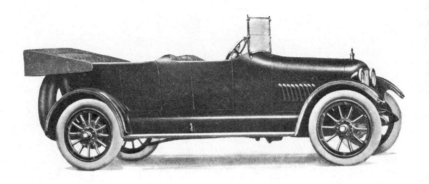

LEXINGTON TOURING CAR—6-N

COLOR	Optional
SEATING CAPACITY .	Six persons
POSITION OF DRIVER	Left side
WHEELBASE	132 inches
GAUGE	56 inches
WHEELS	Wood
FRONT TIRES	35 x 4½ inches
REAR TIRES	35 x 4½ inches, anti-skid
SERVICE BRAKE. . .	Internal expanding
EMERGENCY BRAKE .	Internal expanding
CYLINDERS	Six
ARRANGED	Vertically
CAST	En bloc
HORSEPOWER	29.4
(N. A. C. C. Rating)	
BORE AND STROKE .	3½ x 5¼ inches

LUBRICATION	Force feed and splash
RADIATOR	Cellular
COOLING	Water pump
IGNITION.	High-tension magneto
STARTING SYSTEM . .	Single unit
STARTER OPERATED .	Gear to fly wheel
LIGHTING SYSTEM . .	Electric
VOLTAGES	Six
WIRING SYSTEM. . .	Single
GASOLINE SYSTEM. .	Vacuum
CLUTCH	Dry multiple disc
TRANSMISSION . . .	Selective sliding
GEAR CHANGES . . .	Three forward, one reverse
DRIVE	Spiral bevel
REAR AXLE	Full floating
STEERING GEAR. . .	Worm and gear

In addition to above specifications, price includes top, top hood,
windshield, speedometer, ammeter, voltmeter and demountable rims

THE   THOMAS
B. JEFFERY
C O M P A N Y
K E N O S H A
W I S C O N S I N

Price $1035
Five-Passenger Touring . . . 1000
Seven-Passenger Sedan . . . 1200
Five-Passenger Sedan 1165
Three-Passenger Roadster . . 1000

JEFFERY TOURING CAR—462

COLOR	Brewster green and black		LUBRICATION	Force feed and splash
SEATING CAPACITY .	Seven persons		RADIATOR	Cellular
POSITION OF DRIVER	Left side		COOLING	Water pump
WHEELBASE	116 inches		IGNITION	High-tension magneto
GAUGE	56 inches			
WHEELS	Wood		STARTING SYSTEM . .	Two unit
FRONT TIRES	34 x 4 inches		STARTER OPERATED .	Gear to fly wheel
REAR TIRES	34 x 4 inches		LIGHTING SYSTEM . .	Electric
SERVICE BRAKE . . .	Contracting on rear wheels		VOLTAGES	Six
			WIRING SYSTEM . . .	Single
EMERGENCY BRAKE .	Contracting on drive shaft		GASOLINE SYSTEM . .	Vacuum
			CLUTCH	Plate
CYLINDERS	Four		TRANSMISSION . . .	Selective sliding
ARRANGED	Vertically		GEAR CHANGES . . .	Three forward
CAST	En bloc		DRIVE	Spiral bevel
HORSEPOWER	22.5		REAR AXLE	Semi-floating
(N. A. C. C. Rating)			STEERING GEAR . . .	Worm and wheel
BORE AND STROKE .	3¾ x 5¼ inches			

In addition to above specifications, price includes top, top hood, windshield, speedometer, ammeter, voltmeter, clock and demountable rims

J. I. CASE T. M.
COMPANY, Inc.

Price . . . $1090

R A C I N E
W I S C O N S I N

CASE TOURING CAR

COLOR	Body, Brewster green; chassis, black
SEATING CAPACITY .	Seven persons
POSITION OF DRIVER	Left side
WHEELBASE	120 inches
GAUGE	56 inches
WHEELS	Wood
FRONT TIRES	34 x 4 inches
REAR TIRES	34 x 4 inches, anti-skid
SERVICE BRAKE . . .	External on rear wheels
EMERGENCY BRAKE .	Internal on rear wheels
CYLINDERS	Four
ARRANGED	Vertically
CAST	En bloc
HORSEPOWER	21.03 (N. A. C. C. Rating)

BORE AND STROKE .	3⅝ x 6 inches
LUBRICATION	Force feed and splash
RADIATOR	Cellular
COOLING	Thermo-syphon
IGNITION	Storage battery
STARTING SYSTEM . .	Two unit
STARTER OPERATED .	Gear to fly wheel
LIGHTING SYSTEM . .	Electric
VOLTAGES	Six.
WIRING SYSTEM . . .	Single
GASOLINE SYSTEM . .	Gravity
CLUTCH	Cone
TRANSMISSION . . .	Selective sliding
GEAR CHANGES . . .	Three forward, one reverse
DRIVE	Spiral bevel
REAR AXLE	Three-quarters floating
STEERING GEAR . . .	Screw and nut

In addition to above specifications, price includes top, top hood,
windshield, speedometer, ammeter, voltmeter and demountable rims

CHANDLER
MOTOR CAR
COMPANY

CLEVELAND, OHIO

Price	$1295
Roadster	1295
Limousine	2450
Sedan	2250
Convertible Sedan	1795
Coupe	1950
Cabriolet	1650

CHANDLER TOURING CAR

COLOR	Dark blue and black	LUBRICATION	Splash with circulating pump
SEATING CAPACITY	Seven persons	RADIATOR	Cellular
POSITION OF DRIVER	Left side	COOLING	Water pump
WHEELBASE	123 inches	IGNITION	High tension magneto
GAUGE	56 inches		
WHEELS	Wood	STARTING SYSTEM	Two unit
FRONT TIRES	34 x 4 inches	STARTER OPERATED	Gear to fly wheel
REAR TIRES	34 x 4 inches	LIGHTING SYSTEM	Electric
SERVICE BRAKE	Contracting on rear wheels	VOLTAGES	Six
		WIRING SYSTEM	Single
EMERGENCY BRAKE	Expanding on rear wheels	GASOLINE SYSTEM	Vacuum
		CLUTCH	Dry multiple disc
CYLINDERS	Six	TRANSMISSION	Selective sliding
ARRANGED	Vertically	GEAR CHANGES	Three and reverse
CAST	In threes	DRIVE	Spiral bevel
HORSEPOWER	27.34 (N. A. C. C. Rating)	REAR AXLE	Three-quarters floating
BORE AND STROKE	3⅜ x 5 inches	STEERING GEAR	Worm and sector

In addition to above specifications, price includes top, top
hood, windshield, speedometer and demountable rims

**THE
PATHFINDER
COMPANY**

**INDIANAPOLIS
INDIANA**

Price $2475
Clover Leaf Roadster . 2750

PATHFINDER LA SALLE—1-B

COLOR	Body, blue ; running gear, black	BORE AND STROKE .	2⅞ x 5 inches
		LUBRICATION	Full force feed
SEATING CAPACITY .	Seven persons	RADIATOR	Cellular
POSITION OF DRIVER	Left side	COOLING	Water pump
WHEELBASE	130 inches	IGNITION	Storage battery
GAUGE	56 inches	STARTING SYSTEM . .	Single unit
WHEELS	Wire	STARTER OPERATED .	Gear to fly wheel
FRONT TIRES	35 x 5 inches	LIGHTING SYSTEM . .	Electric
REAR TIRES	35 x 5 inches, anti-skid	VOLTAGES	Six
		WIRING SYSTEM . . .	Single
SERVICE BRAKE . . .	Expanding on rear axle	GASOLINE SYSTEM . .	Vacuum
		CLUTCH	Dry multiple disc
EMERGENCY BRAKE .	Expanding on rear wheels	TRANSMISSION . . .	Selective sliding
CYLINDERS	Twelve	GEAR CHANGES . . .	Three forward, one reverse
ARRANGED	V-type, 60 degrees		
CAST	In threes	DRIVE	Spiral bevel
HORSEPOWER	30.68	REAR AXLE	Full floating
(N. A. C. C. Rating)		STEERING GEAR . . .	Worm

In addition to above specifications, price includes top, top hood,
windshield, speedometer, ammeter, clock and demountable rims

**JAS. CUNNINGHAM
SON & COMPANY**

R O C H E S T E R
N E W   Y O R K

Price	$3750
Runabout	3500
Four Passenger	3750
Limousine	5000
Landaulet	5000

CUNNINGHAM TOURING CAR—S

COLOR	Optional	RADIATOR	Cellular
SEATING CAPACITY .	Seven persons	COOLING	Water pump
POSITION OF DRIVER	Left side	IGNITION	High-tension magneto
WHEELBASE	129 inches		
GAUGE	56 inches	STARTING SYSTEM . .	Electric
WHEELS	Wood	STARTER OPERATED .	Gear in trans- mission
FRONT TIRES	37 x 5 inches		
REAR TIRES	37 x 5 inches, anti-skid	LIGHTING SYSTEM .	Electric
		VOLTAGES	Six
SERVICE BRAKE . . .	Contracting on rear wheels	WIRING SYSTEM . . .	Single
		GASOLINE SYSTEM . .	Pressure
EMERGENCY BRAKE .	Internal expand- ing on rear wheels	CLUTCH	Dry multiple disc
CYLINDERS	Four	TRANSMISSION . . .	Selective sliding
ARRANGED	Vertically	GEAR CHANGES . . .	Three forward, one reverse
CAST	In pairs		
HORSEPOWER	36.1 (N. A. C. C. Rating)	DRIVE	Spiral bevel
BORE AND STROKE .	4¾ x 5¾ inches	REAR AXLE	Full floating
LUBRICATION	Full force feed	STEERING GEAR . . .	Worm and sector

In addition to above specifications, price includes top, top hood, windshield, speedometer, ammeter, voltmeter and demountable rims

**LOCOMOBILE
COMPANY
OF AMERICA**

**BRIDGEPORT
CONNECTICUT**

Price.	$4400
Six-Passenger Touring . . .	4400
Seven-Passenger Limousine .	5400
Seven-Passenger Landaulet .	5500
Seven-Passenger Berline . .	5700

LOCOMOBILE " 38 " TOURING CAR—R-6

COLOR	Optional	LUBRICATION	Pressure and internal circulating system
SEATING CAPACITY .	Seven persons		
POSITION OF DRIVER	Left side	RADIATOR	Cellular
WHEELBASE	140 inches	COOLING	Water pump
GAUGE	56 inches	IGNITION	High-tension magneto and storage battery
WHEELS	Wood		
FRONT TIRES	36 x 4½ inches		
REAR TIRES	37 x 5 inches	STARTING SYSTEM . .	Two unit
SERVICE BRAKE . . .	Contracting on rear wheels	STARTER OPERATED .	Gear to fly wheel
		LIGHTING SYSTEM . .	Electric
EMERGENCY BRAKE .	Expanding on rear wheels	VOLTAGES	Six
		WIRING SYSTEM . . .	Single
CYLINDERS	Six	GASOLINE SYSTEM . .	Pressure
ARRANGED	Vertically	CLUTCH	Dry multiple disc
CAST	In pairs	TRANSMISSION . . .	Selective sliding
HORSEPOWER	43.35	GEAR CHANGES . . .	Four forward
(N. A. C. C. Rating)		DRIVE	Spiral bevel
BORE AND STROKE .	4¼ x 5 inches	REAR AXLE	Full floating
		STEERING GEAR . . .	Worm and gear

In addition to above specifications, price includes top, top hood, windshield, speedometer, ammeter, voltmeter, clock and demountable rims

LOCOMOBILE
COMPANY
OF AMERICA

BRIDGEPORT
CONNECTICUT

Price. $6200
Six-Passenger Touring 5100
Seven-Passenger Touring 5100
Seven-Passenger Landaulet . . . 6300
Seven-Passenger Berline 6500

LOCOMOBILE " 48 " LIMOUSINE—M-6

COLOR.	Optional		LUBRICATION	Pressure and internal circulating system
SEATING CAPACITY .	Seven persons			
POSITION OF DRIVER	Left side		RADIATOR	Cellular
WHEELBASE	143 inches		COOLING.	Water pump
GAUGE	56 inches		IGNITION.	High-tension magneto and storage battery
WHEELS	Wood			
FRONT TIRES	37 x 5 inches			
REAR TIRES	37 x 5 inches		STARTING SYSTEM . .	Two unit
SERVICE BRAKE. . .	Contracting on rear wheels		STARTER OPERATED .	Gear to fly wheel
			LIGHTING SYSTEM . .	Electric
EMERGENCY BRAKE .	Expanding on rear wheels		VOLTAGES	Six
			WIRING SYSTEM. . .	Double
CYLINDERS	Six		GASOLINE SYSTEM. .	Pressure
ARRANGED	Vertically		CLUTCH	Dry multiple disc
CAST	In pairs		TRANSMISSION . . .	Selective sliding
HORSEPOWER. . . . 48.6 (N. A. C. C. Rating)			GEAR CHANGES . . .	Four forward
			DRIVE.	Spiral bevel
			REAR AXLE	Full floating
BORE AND STROKE .	4½ x 5½ inches		STEERING GEAR. . .	Worm and gear

In addition to above specifications, price includes windshield,
speedometer, ammeter, voltmeter, clock and demountable rims

THE WILLYS-
OVERLAND
COMPANY

Price . . . $615
Roadster . 595

TOLEDO, OHIO

OVERLAND TOURING CAR—75

COLOR	Black	BORE AND STROKE .	3⅛ x 5 inches
SEATING CAPACITY .	Five persons	LUBRICATION	Splash with circulating pump
POSITION OF DRIVER	Left side	RADIATOR	Cellular
WHEELBASE	104 inches	COOLING	Thermo-syphon
GAUGE	56 or 60 inches	IGNITION	High-tension magneto
WHEELS	Wood	STARTING SYSTEM . .	Two unit
FRONT TIRES	31 x 4 inches	STARTER OPERATED .	Gear to fly wheel
REAR TIRES	31 x 4 inches, anti-skid	LIGHTING SYSTEM . .	Electric
		VOLTAGES	Six
SERVICE BRAKE . . .	Contracting on rear wheels	WIRING SYSTEM . . .	Single
		GASOLINE SYSTEM . .	Gravity
EMERGENCY BRAKE .	Expanding on rear wheels	CLUTCH	Cone
		TRANSMISSION . . .	Selective sliding
CYLINDERS	Four	GEAR CHANGES . . .	Three forward, one reverse
ARRANGED	Vertically		
CAST	En bloc	DRIVE	Plain bevel
HORSEPOWER 15.63		REAR AXLE	Full floating
(N. A. C. C. Rating)		STEERING GEAR . .	Worm and gear

In addition to above specifications, price includes top, top
hood, windshield, speedometer, ammeter and demountable rims

THE WILLYS-OVERLAND COMPANY

TOLEDO, OHIO

Price	$750
Roadster	725
Panel Delivery .	750
Open Delivery .	725
Limousine . . .	950
Coupe	875

OVERLAND TOURING CAR—83

COLOR	Body, Brewster green; fenders and radiator, black	BORE AND STROKE .	4⅛ x 4½ inches
		LUBRICATION	Splash with circulating pump
SEATING CAPACITY .	Five persons	RADIATOR	Cellular
POSITION OF DRIVER	Left side	COOLING	Thermo-syphon
WHEELBASE	106 inches	IGNITION	High-tension magneto
GAUGE	56 or 60 inches		
WHEELS	Wood	STARTING SYSTEM . .	Two unit
FRONT TIRES	33 x 4 inches	STARTER OPERATED .	Gear to fly wheel
REAR TIRES	33 x 4 inches, anti-skid	LIGHTING SYSTEM . .	Electric
		VOLTAGES	Six
SERVICE BRAKE . . .	Contracting on rear wheels	WIRING SYSTEM . .	Single
		GASOLINE SYSTEM . .	Gravity
EMERGENCY BRAKE .	Expanding on rear wheels	CLUTCH	Cone
		TRANSMISSION . . .	Selective sliding
CYLINDERS	Four	GEAR CHANGES . . .	Three forward, one reverse
ARRANGED	Vertically		
CAST	Separately	DRIVE	Plain bevel
HORSEPOWER	27.23	REAR AXLE	Three-quarters floating
(N. A. C. C. Rating)		STEERING GEAR . .	Worm and gear

In addition to above specifications, price includes top, top hood, windshield, speedometer, ammeter and demountable rims

THE WILLYS-OVERLAND COMPANY

Price, $1145

TOLEDO, OHIO

OVERLAND TOURING CAR—86

COLOR	Body, Brewster green; fenders and radiator, black	BORE AND STROKE	3½ x 5¼ inches
		LUBRICATION	Force feed and splash
SEATING CAPACITY	Seven persons	RADIATOR	Cellular
POSITION OF DRIVER	Left side	COOLING	Water pump
WHEELBASE	125 inches	IGNITION	High tension magneto
GAUGE	56 inches	STARTING SYSTEM	Two unit
WHEELS	Wood	STARTER OPERATED	Gear to fly wheel
FRONT TIRES	35 x 4½ inches	LIGHTING SYSTEM	Electric
REAR TIRES	35 x 4½ inches, anti-skid	VOLTAGES	Six
		WIRING SYSTEM	Single
SERVICE BRAKE	Contracting on rear wheels	GASOLINE SYSTEM	Vacuum
		CLUTCH	Cone
EMERGENCY BRAKE	Expanding on rear wheels	TRANSMISSION	Selective sliding
		GEAR CHANGES	Three forward, one reverse
CYLINDERS	Six		
ARRANGED	Vertically	DRIVE	Plain bevel
CAST	En bloc	REAR AXLE	Full floating
HORSEPOWER	29.4	STEERING GEAR	Worm and gear
(N. A. C. C. Rating)			

In addition to above specifications, price includes top, top
hood, windshield, speedometer, ammeter and demountable rims

THE WILLYS-
OVERLAND
COMPANY

TOLEDO, OHIO

Price $1125
Roadster . . 1095
Coupe . . . 1500
Limousine . 1750

WILLYS-KNIGHT TOURING CAR—84 B

COLOR	Body, royal blue; wheels, gray; fenders, black		BORE AND STROKE .	$4\frac{1}{8}$ x $4\frac{1}{2}$ inches
SEATING CAPACITY .	Five persons		LUBRICATION	Force feed and splash
POSITION OF DRIVER	Left side		RADIATOR	Cellular
WHEELBASE	114 inches		COOLING	Thermo-syphon
GAUGE	56 inches		IGNITION	High-tension magneto
WHEELS	Wood		STARTING SYSTEM . .	Two unit
FRONT TIRES	34 x 4 inches		STARTER OPERATED .	Gear to fly wheel
REAR TIRES	34 x 4 inches, anti-skid		LIGHTING SYSTEM . .	Electric
SERVICE BRAKE . . .	Contracting on rear wheels		VOLTAGES	Six
			WIRING SYSTEM . . .	Single
EMERGENCY BRAKE .	Expanding on rear wheels		GASOLINE SYSTEM . .	Vacuum
CYLINDERS	Four		CLUTCH	Cone
ARRANGED	Vertically		TRANSMISSION . . .	Selective sliding
CAST	En bloc		GEAR CHANGES . . .	Three forward, one reverse
HORSEPOWER	27.23 (N. A. C. C. Rating)		DRIVE	Spiral bevel
			REAR AXLE	Full floating
			STEERING GEAR . .	Worm and gear

In addition to above specifications, price includes top, top
hood, windshield, speedometer, ammeter and demountable rims

**OLDS MOTOR
W O R K S**

L A N S I N G
M I C H I G A N

Price $1095
Roadster . . 1095

OLDSMOBILE TOURING CAR—43

COLOR	Orriford lake or Brewster green with natural wood wheels
SEATING CAPACITY .	Five persons
POSITION OF DRIVER.	Left side
WHEELBASE	120 inches
GAUGE	56 inches
WHEELS	Wood
FRONT TIRES	33 x 4 inches
REAR TIRES	33 x 4 inches, anti-skid
SERVICE BRAKE. . .	Contracting on rear wheels
EMERGENCY BRAKE .	Expanding on rear wheels
CYLINDERS	Four
ARRANGED	Vertically
CAST	En bloc
HORSEPOWER 19.6	
(N. A. C. C. Rating)	

BORE AND STROKE .	3½ x 5 inches
LUBRICATION	Full splash
RADIATOR	Cellular
COOLING	Water pump
IGNITION	Delco system
STARTING SYSTEM . .	Single unit
STARTER OPERATED .	Gear to fly wheel
LIGHTING SYSTEM . .	Electric
VOLTAGES	Six
WIRING SYSTEM . . .	Single
GASOLINE SYSTEM . .	Vacuum
CLUTCH	Cone
TRANSMISSION . . .	Selective sliding
GEAR CHANGES . . .	Three forward
DRIVE	Spiral bevel
REAR AXLE	Three-quarters floating
STEERING GEAR . . .	Screw and nut

In addition to above specifications, price includes top, top hood, windshield, speedometer, ammeter, clock and demountable rims

**OLDS MOTOR
W O R K S**

L A N S I N G
M I C H I G A N

Price $1195
Roadster . . 1195

OLDSMOBILE TOURING CAR—44

COLOR	Royal green with natural wood wheels
SEATING CAPACITY .	Five persons
POSITION OF DRIVER .	Left side
WHEELBASE	120 inches
GAUGE	56 inches
WHEELS	Wood
FRONT TIRES	33 x 4 inches
REAR TIRES	33 x 4 inches anti-skid
SERVICE BRAKE . . .	Contracting on rear wheels
EMERGENCY BRAKE .	Expanding on rear wheels
CYLINDERS	Eight
ARRANGED	V type, 90 degrees
CAST	En bloc with half of crank case
HORSEPOWER	26.45
(N. A. C. C. Rating)	
BORE AND STROKE .	2⅞ x 4¾ inches
LUBRICATION	Full force feed
RADIATOR	Cellular
COOLING	Water pump
IGNITION	Delco system
STARTING SYSTEM . .	Three unit
STARTER OPERATED .	Gear to fly wheel
LIGHTING SYSTEM . .	Electric
VOLTAGES	Six
WIRING SYSTEM . . .	Single
GASOLINE SYSTEM . .	Vacuum
CLUTCH	Cone
TRANSMISSION . . .	Selective sliding
GEAR CHANGES . . .	Three forward
DRIVE	Spiral bevel
REAR AXLE	Full floating
STEERING GEAR . . .	Screw and nut

In addition to above specifications, price includes top, top hood, windshield, speedometer, ammeter, clock and demountable rims

PAIGE-DETROIT MOTOR CAR COMPANY

DETROIT MICHIGAN

Price, $1050

PAIGE FLEETWOOD SIX—38

COLOR	Body, Richelieu blue with straw colored wheels	LUBRICATION	Force feed and splash
SEATING CAPACITY .	Five persons	RADIATOR	Cellular
POSITION OF DRIVER	Left side	COOLING	Water pump
WHEELBASE	117 inches	IGNITION	High tension magneto and storage battery
GAUGE	56 or 60 inches		
WHEELS	Wood	STARTING SYSTEM . .	Two unit
FRONT TIRES	32 x 4 inches	STARTER OPERATED .	Gear to fly wheel
REAR TIRES	32 x 4 inches, anti-skid	LIGHTING SYSTEM . .	Electric
SERVICE BRAKE . . .	Contracting on rear wheels	VOLTAGES	Six
		WIRING SYSTEM . .	Single
EMERGENCY BRAKE .	Expanding on rear wheels	GASOLINE SYSTEM . .	Gravity
		CLUTCH	Multiple disc in oil
CYLINDERS	Six	TRANSMISSION . . .	Selective sliding
ARRANGED	Vertically	GEAR CHANGES . . .	Three forward
CAST	En bloc	DRIVE	Spiral bevel
HORSEPOWER	23.44 (N. A. C. C. Rating)	REAR AXLE	Three-quarters floating
BORE AND STROKE .	3⅛ x 5 inches	STEERING GEAR . . .	Screw and split sleeve

In addition to above specifications, price includes top, top hood. windshield, speedometer, ammeter and demountable rims

**PAIGE-DETROIT
MOTOR CAR
COMPANY**

**DETROIT
MICHIGAN**

Price	$1295
Seven-Passenger Sedan . . .	1900
Three-Passenger Cabriolet. .	1600
Three-Passenger Coupe . . .	1700
Seven-Passenger Town Car .	2250
Three-Passenger Roadster .	1295

PAIGE FAIRFIELD SIX—46

COLOR	Body, Richelieu blue; running gear, red	BORE AND STROKE .	$3\frac{1}{2}$ x $5\frac{1}{4}$ inches
		LUBRICATION	Force feed and splash
SEATING CAPACITY .	Seven persons	RADIATOR	Cellular
POSITION OF DRIVER	Left side	COOLING	Water pump
WHEELBASE	124 inches	IGNITION	Storage battery
GAUGE	56 inches	STARTING SYSTEM . .	Two unit
WHEELS	Wood	STARTER OPERATED .	Gear to fly wheel
FRONT TIRES	34 x 4 inches	LIGHTING SYSTEM . .	Electric
REAR TIRES	34 x 4 inches, anti-skid	VOLTAGES	Six
		WIRING SYSTEM. . .	Single
SERVICE BRAKE . . .	Contracting on rear wheels	GASOLINE SYSTEM . .	Gravity
		CLUTCH	Multiple disc in oil
EMERGENCY BRAKE .	Expanding on rear wheels	TRANSMISSION . . .	Selective sliding
		GEAR CHANGES . . .	Three
CYLINDERS	Six	DRIVE	Spiral bevel
ARRANGED	Vertically	REAR AXLE.	Three-quarters floating
CAST	En bloc		
HORSEPOWER	29.4 (N. A. C. C. Rating)	STEERING GEAR . . .	Screw and split sleeve

In addition to above specifications, price includes top, top hood, windshield, speedometer, ammeter and demountable rims

THE F. B.
STEARNS
COMPANY

CLEVELAND, OHIO

Price, $1395

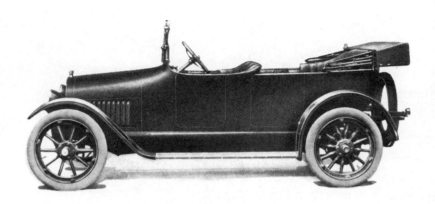

STEARNS-KNIGHT TOURING CAR—L-4

COLOR	Body, Stearns Royal green; running gear, black	BORE AND STROKE . .	3¾ x 5⅝ inches
SEATING CAPACITY .	Five persons	LUBRICATION	Full force feed
POSITION OF DRIVER .	Left side	RADIATOR	Cellular
WHEELBASE	119 inches	COOLING	Water pump
GAUGE	56 inches	IGNITION	Storage battery
WHEELS	Wood	STARTING SYSTEM . .	Two unit
FRONT TIRES	34 x 4 inches,	STARTER OPERATED .	Gear to fly wheel
REAR TIRES	34 x 4 inches,	LIGHTING SYSTEM . .	Electric
SERVICE BRAKE . . .	Contracting on transmission shaft	VOLTAGES	Twelve
EMERGENCY BRAKE .	Expanding on rear wheels	WIRING SYSTEM . . .	Single
CYLINDERS	Four	GASOLINE SYSTEM . .	Gravity
ARRANGED	Vertically	CLUTCH	Cone
CAST	En bloc	TRANSMISSION . . .	Selective sliding
HORSEPOWER	22.5 (N. A. C. C. Rating)	GEAR CHANGES . . .	Three
		DRIVE	Spiral bevel
		REAR AXLE	Semi-floating
		STEERING GEAR . .	Worm and gear

In addition to above specifications, price includes top, top
hood, windshield, speedometer, ammeter and demountable rims

THE F. B.
STEARNS
COMPANY
CLEVELAND, OHIO

Price, $2050

STEARNS-KNIGHT EIGHT

COLOR	Body, Stearns Brewster green; running gear, black	BORE AND STROKE . .	3¼ x 5 inches
SEATING CAPACITY .	Seven persons	LUBRICATION	Full force feed
POSITION OF DRIVER .	Left side	RADIATOR	Cellular
WHEELBASE	123 inches	COOLING	Thermo-syphon
GAUGE	56 inches	IGNITION	Storage battery
WHEELS	Wood	STARTING SYSTEM . .	Two unit
FRONT TIRES	35 x 4½ inches	STARTER OPERATED .	Gear to fly wheel
REAR TIRES	35 x 4½ inches	LIGHTING SYSTEM . .	Electric
SERVICE BRAKE . . .	Contracting on transmission shaft	VOLTAGES	Twelve
		WIRING SYSTEM . . .	Single
EMERGENCY BRAKE .	Expanding on rear wheels	GASOLINE SYSTEM . .	Vacuum
CYLINDERS	Eight	CLUTCH	Dry multiple disc
ARRANGED	V-type, 90 degrees	TRANSMISSION . . .	Selective sliding
CAST	In fours	GEAR CHANGES . . .	Three
HORSEPOWER	33.8	DRIVE	Spiral bevel
	(N. A. C. C. Rating)	REAR AXLE	Semi-floating
		STEERING GEAR . .	Worm and gear

In addition to above specifications, price includes top, top hood,
windshield, speedometer, ammeter, clock and demountable rims

APPERSON
BROTHERS
AUTOMOBILE
COMPANY

KOKOMO
INDIANA

Price $1850
Four-Passenger Roadster . 1850

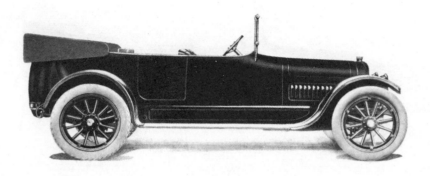

APPERSON LIGHT EIGHT TOURING CAR—8-16

COLOR	Blue or green	BORE AND STROKE .	3⅛ x 5 inches
SEATING CAPACITY .	Seven persons	LUBRICATION	Full force feed
POSITION OF DRIVER	Left side	RADIATOR . . . , .	Cellular
Wheel base	128 inches	COOLING	Thermo-syphon
GAUGE	56 inches	IGNITION	Storage battery
WHEELS	Wood	STARTING SYSTEM . .	Two unit
FRONT TIRES	35 x 4½ inches	STARTER OPERATED .	Gear to fly wheel
REAR TIRES	35 x 4½ inches, anti-skid	LIGHTING SYSTEM . .	Electric
		VOLTAGES	Six
SERVICE BRAKE . . .	Contracting on rear wheels	WIRING SYSTEM . . .	Double
		GASOLINE SYSTEM . .	Vacuum
EMERGENCY BRAKE .	Expanding on rear wheels	CLUTCH	Plate
		TRANSMISSION . . .	Selective sliding
CYLINDERS	Eight	GEAR CHANGES . . .	Three forward, one reverse
ARRANGED	V type, 90 degrees	DRIVE	Spiral bevel
CAST -.	En bloc	REAR AXLE	Semi-floating
HORSEPOWER	31.25 (N. A. C. C. Rating)	STEERING GEAR . . .	Worm and wheel

In addition to above specifications, price includes top, top hood,
windshield, speedometer, ammeter, clock and demountable rims

A P P E R S O N
B R O T H E R S
A U T O M O B I L E
C O M P A N Y
K O K O M O
I N D I A N A

Price $1550
Four-Passenger Roadster . . . 1550
Five-Passenger Touring Car . . 1485

APPERSON LIGHT SIX TOURING CAR—6-16

COLOR	Blue or green	BORE AND STROKE .	3½ x 5 inches
SEATING CAPACITY .	Seven persons	LUBRICATION	Full force feed
POSITION OF DRIVER	Left side	RADIATOR	Cellular
Wheel base	128 inches	COOLING	Water pump
GAUGE	56 inches	IGNITION	Storage battery
WHEELS	Wood	STARTING SYSTEM . .	Two unit
FRONT TIRES	34 x 4 inches	STARTER OPERATED .	Gear to fly wheel
REAR TIRES	34 x 4 inches, anti-skid	LIGHTING SYSTEM . .	Electric
		VOLTAGES	Six
SERVICE BRAKE . . .	Contracting on rear wheels	WIRING SYSTEM . . .	Double
		GASOLINE SYSTEM . .	Vacuum
EMERGENCY BRAKE .	Expanding on rear wheels	CLUTCH	Plate
		TRANSMISSION . . .	Selective sliding
CYLINDERS	Six	GEAR CHANGES . . .	Three forward, one reverse
ARRANGED	Vertically		
CAST	En bloc	DRIVE	Spiral bevel
HORSEPOWER	29.4 (N. A. C. C. Rating)	REAR AXLE	Semi-floating
		STEERING GEAR . . .	Worm and wheel

In addition to above specifications, price includes top, top hood,
windshield, speedometer, ammeter, clock and demountable rims

**PACKARD
MOTOR CAR
COMPANY**

**DETROIT
MICHIGAN**

Price.	$3150
Seven-Passenger Salon Touring .	3150
Six-Passenger Salon Touring . .	3150
Five-Passenger Phaeton	3150
Five-Passenger Salon Phaeton .	3150

PACKARD STANDARD TOURING CAR—1-35

COLOR.	Body and door panels, Packard blue, striped with cream yellow; wheels, cream yellow, striped with black; chassis, black	HORSEPOWER	43.2	
			(N. A. C. C. Rating)	
		BORE AND STROKE. .	3 x 5 inches	
		LUBRICATION	Full force feed	
		RADIATOR	Vertical tube	
		COOLING	Water pump	
		IGNITION	Generator with storage battery	
SEATING CAPACITY .	Seven persons			
POSITION OF DRIVER .	Left side	STARTING SYSTEM . .	Two unit	
WHEELBASE	135 inches	STARTER OPERATED .	Gear to fly wheel	
GAUGE	56 inches	LIGHTING SYSTEM . .	Electric	
WHEELS	Wood	VOLTAGES	Seven	
FRONT TIRES	36 x 4½ inches, cord	WIRING SYSTEM. . .	Double	
		GASOLINE SYSTEM .	Pressure	
REAR TIRES	37 x 5 inches, cord	CLUTCH	Dry multiple disc	
SERVICE BRAKE. . .	Contracting on rear wheels	TRANSMISSION . . .	Selective sliding	
EMERGENCY BRAKE .	Expanding on rear wheels	GEAR CHANGES . . .	Three forward, one reverse	
CYLINDERS	Twelve	DRIVE	Spiral bevel	
ARRANGED	V-type, 60 degrees	REAR AXLE	Non-floating	
CAST	In sixes	STEERING GEAR. . .	Worm and nut	

In addition to above specifications, price includes top, top hood,
windshield, speedometer, ammeter, clock and demountable rims

P A C K A R D
M O T O R   C A R
C O M P A N Y

D E T R O I T
M I C H I G A N

Price.	$4650
Seven-Passenger Imperial Limousine	4800
Seven-Passenger Salon Limousine	4750
Seven-Passenger Limousine with Cab Sides	4650
Seven-Passenger Limousine without Cab Sides	4600
Six-Passenger Limousine without Cab Sides	4550
Six-Passenger Landaulet without Cab Sides	4550
Four-Passenger Brougham . . .	4600

PACKARD LANDAULET WITH CAB SIDES—1-35

COLOR	Body and door panels, Packard blue, striped with black; wheels, Packard blue, striped with black; chassis, black	HORSEPOWER	43.2 (N. A. C. C. Rating)	
		BORE AND STROKE .	3 x 5 inches	
		LUBRICATION	Force feed	
		RADIATOR	Vertical tube	
		COOLING	Water pump	
		IGNITION	Generator with storage battery	
SEATING CAPACITY .	Seven persons			
POSITION OF DRIVER	Left side	STARTING SYSTEM . .	Two unit	
WHEELBASE	135 inches	STARTER OPERATED .	Gear to fly wheel	
GAUGE.	56 inches	LIGHTING SYSTEM . . .	Electric	
WHEELS	Wood	VOLTAGES	Seven	
FRONT TIRES	36 x 4½ inches, cord	WIRING SYSTEM. . .	Double	
REAR TIRES	37 x 5 inches, cord	GASOLINE SYSTEM. .	Pressure	
SERVICE BRAKE. . .	Contracting on rear wheels	CLUTCH	Dry multiple disc	
		TRANSMISSION . . .	Selective sliding	
EMERGENCY BRAKE .	Expanding on rear wheels	GEAR CHANGES . . .	Three forward, one reverse	
CYLINDERS	Twelve	DRIVE	Spiral bevel	
ARRANGED.	V-type, 60 degrees	REAR AXLE	Non-floating	
CAST	In sixes	STEERING GEAR . . .	Worm and nut	

In addition to above specifications, price includes
speedometer, ammeter, clock and demountable rims

PACKARD
MOTOR CAR
COMPANY

DETROIT
MICHIGAN

Price	$2750
Seven-Passenger Touring	2750
Seven Passenger Salon Touring	2750
Five-Passenger Salon Phaeton	2750
Two-Passenger Runabout	2750
Six-Passenger Limousine	4150
Six-Passenger Landaulet.	4150
Four-Passenger Brougham . . .	4200
Three-Passenger Coupe	3700

PACKARD PHAETON—1-25

COLOR	Body and door panels, Packard blue, striped with cream yellow; wheels, cream yellow, striped with black; chassis, black	CAST	In sixes
		HORSEPOWER	43.2 (N. A. C. C. Rating)
		BORE AND STROKE. .	3 x 5 inches
		LUBRICATION	Force feed
		RADIATOR	Vertical tube
		COOLING	Water pump
SEATING CAPACITY .	Five persons	IGNITION	Generator with storage battery
POSITION OF DRIVER .	Left side	STARTING SYSTEM . .	Two unit
WHEELBASE	125 inches	STARTER OPERATED .	Gear to fly wheel
GAUGE	56 inches	LIGHTING SYSTEM . .	Electric
WHEELS	Wood	VOLTAGES	Seven
FRONT TIRES	36 x 4½ inches, cord	WIRING SYSTEM . . .	Double
		GASOLINE SYSTEM .	Pressure
REAR TIRES	37 x 5 inches, cord	CLUTCH	Dry multiple disc
SERVICE BRAKE . . .	Contracting on rear wheels	TRANSMISSION . . .	Selective sliding
		GEAR CHANGES . . .	Three forward, one reverse
EMERGENCY BRAKE .	Expanding on rear wheels	DRIVE	Spiral bevel
CYLINDERS	Twelve	REAR AXLE	Non-floating
ARRANGED	V-type, 60 degrees	STEERING GEAR . . .	Worm and nut

In addition to above specifications, price includes top, top hood,
windshield, speedometer, ammeter, clock and demountable rims

STUTZ MOTOR
CAR COMPANY

INDIANAPOLIS
INDIANA

Price . . . $2100
Bearcat . 2000
Bulldog . 2250

STUTZ ROADSTER—C

COLOR	Yellow, mercedes red, vermillion, or monitor gray
SEATING CAPACITY .	Two persons
POSITION OF DRIVER	Right side
WHEELBASE	120 inches
GAUGE	56½ inches
WHEELS	Wood
FRONT TIRES	34 x 4½ inches
REAR TIRES	34 x 4½ inches,
SERVICE BRAKE . . .	Expanding on rear wheels
EMERGENCY BRAKE .	Expanding on rear wheels
CYLINDERS	Four
ARRANGED	Vertically
CAST	In pairs
HORSEPOWER	36.1
(N. A. C. C. Rating)	
BORE AND STROKE .	4¾ x 5½ inches

LUBRICATION	Force feed and splash
RADIATOR	Cellular
COOLING	Water pump
IGNITION	High-tension magneto and storage battery
STARTING SYSTEM . .	Two unit
STARTER OPERATED .	Gear to fly wheel
LIGHTING SYSTEM . .	Electric
VOLTAGES	Six
WIRING SYSTEM . . .	Single
GASOLINE SYSTEM . .	Gravity
CLUTCH	Cone
TRANSMISSION . . .	Selective sliding
GEAR CHANGES . . .	Three forward, one reverse
DRIVE	Plain bevel
REAR AXLE	Three-quarters floating
STEERING GEAR . . .	Worm and gear

In addition to above specifications, price includes
ammeter, voltmeter and demountable rims

STUTZ MOTOR
CAR COMPANY

INDIANAPOLIS
I N D I A N A

Price $2550
Touring . . 2300

STUTZ BULLDOG SPECIAL—C

COLOR	Battleship gray, azure blue or mercedes red		LUBRICATION	Force feed and splash
SEATING CAPACITY .	Four persons		RADIATOR	Cellular
POSITION OF DRIVER	Right side		COOLING	Water pump
WHEELBASE	130 inches		IGNITION	High-tension magneto and storage battery
GAUGE	56½ inches			
WHEELS	Wire		STARTING SYSTEM . .	Two unit
FRONT TIRES	33 x 5 inches, cord		STARTER OPERATED .	Gear to fly wheel
REAR TIRES	33 x 5 inches, cord		LIGHTING SYSTEM . .	Electric
SERVICE BRAKE . .	Contracting on rear wheels		VOLTAGES	Six
			WIRING SYSTEM . . .	Single
EMERGENCY BRAKE .	Expanding on rear wheels		GASOLINE SYSTEM . .	Pressure
			CLUTCH	Cone
CYLINDERS	Four		TRANSMISSION . . .	Selective sliding
ARRANGED	Vertically		GEAR CHANGES . . .	Three forward, one reverse
CAST	In pairs		DRIVE	Plain bevel
HORSEPOWER	36.1 (N. A. C. C. Rating)		REAR AXLE	Three-quarters floating
BORE AND STROKE .	4¾ x 5½ inches		STEERING GEAR . . .	Worm and gear

In addition to above specifications, price includes top, top hood, wind-shield, speedometer, ammeter, voltmeter and demountable rims

**SAXON MOTOR
COMPANY**

**DETROIT
MICHIGAN**

Price $395
With winter top .   455

SAXON ROADSTER—14

COLOR	Body, green or blue; running gear, black	BORE AND STROKE. .	2¾ x 4 inches
SEATING CAPACITY .	Two persons	LUBRICATION	Splash with circulating pump
POSITION OF DRIVER	Left side	RADIATOR	Cellular
WHEELBASE	96 inches	COOLING	Thermo-syphon
GAUGE	54 inches	IGNITION	Dry cells
WHEELS	Wood	LIGHTING SYSTEM . .	Gas
FRONT TIRES	28 x 3 inches	GASOLINE SYSTEM . .	Gravity
REAR TIRES	28 x 3 inches,	CLUTCH	Dry multiple disc
SERVICE BRAKE. . .	Contracting on rear wheels	TRANSMISSION . . .	Selective sliding
EMERGENCY BRAKE .	Expanding on rear wheels	GEAR CHANGES . . .	Three forward, one reverse
CYLINDERS	Four	DRIVE	Plain bevel
ARRANGED	Vertically	REAR AXLE	Semi-floating
CAST	En bloc	STEERING GEAR. . .	Gear and sector
HORSEPOWER. . . .	12.10 (N. A. C. C. Rating)		

In addition to above specifications, price
includes top, top hood and windshield

SAXON MOTOR
COMPANY

D E T R O I T
M I C H I G A N

Price $785
With winter top . . 935

SAXON TOURING CAR—S-2

COLOR	Body, green; running gear, black	LUBRICATION	Splash with circulating pump
SEATING CAPACITY .	Five persons	RADIATOR	Cellular
POSITION OF DRIVER	Left side	COOLING	Thermo-syphon
WHEELBASE	112 inches	IGNITION	Storage battery
GAUGE	54 inches	STARTING SYSTEM . .	Two unit
WHEELS	Wood	STARTER OPERATED .	Gear to fly wheel
FRONT TIRES	32 x 3½ inches	LIGHTING SYSTEM . .	Electric
REAR TIRES	32 x 3½ inches, anti-skid	VOLTAGES	Six
		WIRING SYSTEM . . .	Single
SERVICE BRAKE . . .	Contracting on rear wheels	GASOLINE SYSTEM . .	Gravity
EMERGENCY BRAKE .	Expanding on rear wheels	CLUTCH	Dry multiple disc
CYLINDERS	Six	TRANSMISSION . . .	Selective sliding
ARRANGED	Vertically	GEAR CHANGES . . .	Three forward, one reverse
CAST	En bloc	DRIVE	Spiral bevel
HORSEPOWER	19.84 (N. A. C. C. Rating)	REAR AXLE	Semi-floating
BORE AND STROKE . .	2⅞ x 4½ inches	STEERING GEAR . . .	Worm and nut

In addition to above specifications, price includes top, top hood, windshield, speedometer, ammeter, voltmeter and demountable rim

REO MOTOR
CAR COMPANY

Price $875
Three-Passenger Runabout. . 875

LANSING
MICHIGAN

REO THE FIFTH TOURING CAR—R

COLOR	Body, golden olive; running gear, black	BORE AND STROKE . .	4⅛ x 4½ inches
		LUBRICATION	Splash with circulating pump
SEATING CAPACITY .	Five persons	RADIATOR	Tubular
POSITION OF DRIVER	Left side	COOLING	Water pump
WHEEL BASE	115 inches	IGNITION	Storage battery
GAUGE	56 inches	STARTING SYSTEM . .	Two unit
WHEELS	Wood	STARTER OPERATED .	Chain to transmission shaft
FRONT TIRES	34 x 4 inches		
REAR TIRES	34 x 4 inches, anti-skid	LIGHTING SYSTEM . .	Electric
		VOLTAGES	Six
SERVICE BRAKE . . .	Contracting on rear wheels	WIRING SYSTEM. . .	Double
		GASOLINE SYSTEM. .	Gravity
EMERGENCY BRAKE .	Expanding on rear wheels	CLUTCH	Dry multiple disc
		TRANSMISSION . . .	Selective sliding
CYLINDERS	Four	GEAR CHANGES . . .	Three forward, one reverse
ARRANGED	Vertically		
CAST	In pairs	DRIVE	Plain bevel
HORSEPOWER	27.23	REAR AXLE	Semi-floating
	(N. A. C. C. Rating)	STEERING GEAR . . .	Pinion and sector

In addition to above specifications, price includes top, top
hood, windshield, speedometer, ammeter and demountable rims

**REO MOTOR
CAR COMPANY**

Price, $1250

**L A N S I N G
M I C H I G A N**

REO TOURING CAR—M

COLOR	Body, golden olive; running gear, black		BORE AND STROKE .	$3\frac{9}{16}$ x $5\frac{1}{8}$ inches
			LUBRICATION	Splash with circulating pump
SEATING CAPACITY .	Seven persons		RADIATOR	Tubular
POSITION OF DRIVER .	Left side		COOLING	Water pump
WHEELBASE	126 inches		IGNITION	Storage battery
GAUGE	56 inches		STARTING SYSTEM . .	Two unit
WHEELS	Wood		STARTER OPERATED .	Chain to transmission shaft
FRONT TIRES	34 x 4½ inches			
REAR TIRES	34 x 4½ inches, anti-skid		LIGHTING SYSTEM . .	Electric
			VOLTAGES	Six
SERVICE BRAKE . .	Contracting on rear wheels		WIRING SYSTEM . . .	Double
			GASOLINE SYSTEM . .	Vacuum
EMERGENCY BRAKE .	Expanding on rear wheels		CLUTCH	Dry multiple disc
			TRANSMISSION . . .	Selective sliding
CYLINDERS	Six		GEAR CHANGES . . .	Three forward, one reverse
ARRANGED	Vertically			
CAST	In threes		DRIVE	Spiral bevel
HORSEPOWER	30.4 (N. A. C. C. Rating)		REAR AXLE	Full floating
			STEERING GEAR . . .	Pinion and sector

In addition to above specifications, price includes top, top
hood, windshield, speedometer, ammeter and demountable rims

**STUDEBAKER
CORPORATION
OF AMERICA**

D E T R O I T
M I C H I G A N

Price. $845
Three-Passenger Roadster . . . 825
Three-Passenger Landau Road-
    ster 1145

STUDEBAKER FOUR TOURING CAR—SF

COLOR	Body, blue; chassis, black
SEATING CAPACITY .	Seven persons
POSITION OF DRIVER	Left side
WHEELBASE	112 inches
GAUGE	56 inches
WHEELS	Wood
FRONT TIRES	34 x 4 inches
REAR TIRES	34 x 4 inches, anti-skid
SERVICE BRAKE . . .	Contracting on rear wheels
EMERGENCY BRAKE .	Expanding on rear wheels
CYLINDERS	Four
ARRANGED	Vertically
CAST	En bloc
HORSEPOWER	24.03 (N. A. C. C. Rating)

BORE AND STROKE .	3⅞ x 5 inches
LUBRICATION	Splash with circulating pump
RADIATOR	Tubular
COOLING	Water pump
IGNITION	Storage battery
STARTING SYSTEM . .	Two unit
STARTER OPERATED .	Chain to crank shaft
LIGHTING SYSTEM . .	Electric
VOLTAGES	Six
WIRING SYSTEM . . .	Single
GASOLINE SYSTEM . .	Vacuum
CLUTCH	Cone
TRANSMISSION . . .	Selective sliding
GEAR CHANGES . . .	Three forward, one reverse
DRIVE	Plain bevel
REAR AXLE	Full floating
STEERING GEAR . . .	Worm and gear

In addition to above specifications, price includes top, top hood,
windshield, speedometer, battery indicator and demountable rims

**STUDEBAKER
CORPORATION
OF AMERICA**

**D E T R O I T
M I C H I G A N**

Price											$1050
Three-Passenger Roadster								. . .			1025
Three-Passenger Landau Roadster											1350
Four-Passenger Coupe						. . . . .					1600
Seven-Passenger Sedan						. . . .					1675
Seven-Passenger Limousine						. . .					2500

STUDEBAKER SIX TOURING CAR—ED

COLOR	Body, blue; chassis, black	LUBRICATION	Splash with circulating pump
SEATING CAPACITY .	Seven persons	RADIATOR	Cellular
POSITION OF DRIVER	Left side	COOLING	Water pump
WHEELBASE	122 inches	IGNITION	Storage battery
GAUGE	56 inches	STARTING SYSTEM . .	Two unit
WHEELS	Wood	STARTER OPERATED .	Chain to crank shaft
FRONT TIRES	34 x 4 inches		
REAR TIRES	34 x 4 inches, anti-skid	LIGHTING SYSTEM . .	Electric
		VOLTAGES	Six
SERVICE BRAKE . . .	Contracting on rear wheels	WIRING SYSTEM . . .	Single
EMERGENCY BRAKE .	Expanding on rear wheels	GASOLINE SYSTEM . .	Vacuum
		CLUTCH	Cone
CYLINDERS	Six	TRANSMISSION . . .	Selective sliding
ARRANGED	Vertically	GEAR CHANGES . . .	Three forward, one reverse
CAST	En bloc		
HORSEPOWER	36.04 (N. A. C. C. Rating)	DRIVE	Plain bevel
		REAR AXLE	Full floating
BORE AND STROKE .	3⅞ x 5 inches	STEERING GEAR . . .	Worm and gear

In addition to above specifications, price includes top, top hood, windshield, speedometer, battery indicator and demountable rims

OAKLAND
MOTOR CAR
COMPANY

PONTIAC
MICHIGAN

Price . . . $795
Roadster .   795

OAKLAND TOURING CAR—32

COLOR	Blue or black	LUBRICATION	Splash with circulating pump
SEATING CAPACITY	Five persons	RADIATOR	Tubular
POSITION OF DRIVER	Left side	COOLING	Water pump
WHEELBASE	110 inches	IGNITION	Storage battery
GAUGE	56 or 60 inches	STARTING SYSTEM	Two unit
WHEELS	Wood	STARTER OPERATED	Gear to fly wheel
FRONT TIRES	32 x 3½ inches	LIGHTING SYSTEM	Electric
REAR TIRES	32 x 3½ inches, anti-skid	VOLTAGES	Six
SERVICE BRAKE	Contracting on rear wheels	WIRING SYSTEM	Single
		GASOLINE SYSTEM	Vacuum
EMERGENCY BRAKE	Expanding on rear wheels	CLUTCH	Cone
		TRANSMISSION	Selective sliding
CYLINDERS	Six	GEAR CHANGES	Three forward, one reverse
ARRANGED	Vertically		
CAST	En bloc	DRIVE	Plain bevel
HORSEPOWER	18.88	REAR AXLE	Full floating
(N. A. C. C. Rating)		STEERING GEAR	Worm and split nut
BORE AND STROKE	2¹³⁄₁₆ x 4¾ inches		

In addition to above specifications, price includes top,
top hood, windshield, speedometer and demountable rims

OAKLAND
MOTOR CAR
COMPANY

PONTIAC
MICHIGAN

Price $1050
Roadster . .   1050
Speedster . . 1050

OAKLAND TOURING CAR—38

COLOR	Blue or gray; chassis, black	LUBRICATION	Splash with circulating pump
SEATING CAPACITY .	Five persons	RADIATOR	Tubular
POSITION OF DRIVER	Left side	COOLING	Water pump
WHEELBASE	112 inches	IGNITION	Storage battery
WHEELS	Wood	STARTING SYSTEM . .	Single unit
FRONT TIRES	33 x 4 inches	STARTER OPERATED .	Gears to fly wheel
REAR TIRES	33 x 4 inches, anti-skid	LIGHTING SYSTEM . .	Electric
		VOLTAGES	Six
SERVICE BRAKE . . .	Contracting on rear wheels	WIRING SYSTEM . .	Single
EMERGENCY BRAKE .	Expanding on rear wheels	GASOLINE SYSTEM . .	Vacuum
		CLUTCH	Cone
CYLINDERS	Four	TRANSMISSION . . .	Selective sliding gear
ARRANGED	Vertically	GEAR CHANGES . . .	Three forward, one reverse
CAST	En bloc		
HORSEPOWER . . . . 19.6 (N. A. C. C. Rating)		DRIVE	Plain bevel
		REAR AXLE	Full floating
BORE AND STROKE .	3½ x 5 inches	STEERING GEAR . . .	Worm and split nut

In addition to above specifications, price includes top, top
hood, windshield, speedometer, ammeter and demountable rims

**O A K L A N D
M O T O R   C A R
C O M P A N Y**

**P O N T I A C
M I C H I G A N**

OAKLAND TOURING CAR—50

COLOR	Body, green; chassis, black	BORE AND STROKE .	3½ x 4½ inches
SEATING CAPACITY .	Seven persons	LUBRICATION	Force feed and splash
POSITION OF DRIVER	Left side	RADIATOR	Cellular
WHEELBASE	127 inches	COOLING	Water pump
GAUGE	56 inches	IGNITION	Storage battery
WHEELS	Wood	STARTING SYSTEM . .	Two unit
FRONT TIRES	34 x 4½ inches	STARTER OPERATED .	Gear to fly wheel
REAR TIRES	34 x 4½ inches, anti-skid	LIGHTING SYSTEM . .	Electric
		VOLTAGES	Six
SERVICE BRAKE. . .	Contracting on rear wheels	WIRING SYSTEM. . .	Single
		GASOLINE SYSTEM. .	Vacuum
EMERGENCY BRAKE .	Expanding on rear wheels	CLUTCH	Cone
		TRANSMISSION . . .	Selective sliding
CYLINDERS	Eight	GEAR CHANGES . . .	Three forward, one reverse
ARRANGED	V type, 90 degrees	DRIVE	Spiral bevel
CAST	In fours	REAR AXLE	Full floating
HORSEPOWER	39.2 (N. A. C. C. Rating)	STEERING GEAR. . .	Worm and split nut

In addition to above specifications, price includes top, top
hood, windshield, speedometer, ammeter and demountable rims

JACKSON
AUTOMOBILE
COMPANY

JACKSON
MICHIGAN

Price $985
With Detachable Sedan Top . 1195
Three-Passenger Roadster . . 985

JACKSON TOURING CAR—34

COLOR	Brewster green		LUBRICATION	Force feed and splash
SEATING CAPACITY .	Five persons		RADIATOR	Tubular
POSITION OF DRIVER	Left side		COOLING	Water pump
WHEELBASE	112 inches		IGNITION	Storage battery and dry cells
GAUGE	56 inches			
WHEELS	Wood		STARTING SYSTEM . .	Two unit
FRONT TIRES	32 x 4 inches		STARTER OPERATED .	Gear to fly wheel
REAR TIRES	32 x 4 inches, anti-skid		LIGHTING SYSTEM . .	Electric
SERVICE BRAKE . . .	Contracting on rear wheels		VOLTAGES	Six
			WIRING SYSTEM . . .	Double
EMERGENCY BRAKE .	Expanding on rear wheels		GASOLINE SYSTEM . .	Vacuum
			CLUTCH	Cone
CYLINDERS	Four		TRANSMISSION . . .	Selective sliding
ARRANGED	Vertically		GEAR CHANGES . . .	Three
CAST	En bloc		DRIVE	Plain bevel
HORSEPOWER	19.6 (N. A. C. C. Rating)		REAR AXLE	Three-quarters floating
BORE AND STROKE . .	3½ x 5 inches		STEERING GEAR . . .	Worm and sector

In addition to above specifications, price includes top, top
hood, windshield, speedometer, ammeter and demountable rims

**JACKSON
AUTOMOBILE
COMPANY**

**JACKSON
MICHIGAN**

Price $1195
With Detachable Sedan Top . 1405
Three-Passenger Roadster . . 1195

JACKSON TOURING CAR—348

COLOR	Dark green with natural wood wheels	LUBRICATION	Full force feed
SEATING CAPACITY .	Five persons	RADIATOR	Tubular
POSITION OF DRIVER	Left side	COOLING	Water pump
WHEELBASE	112 inches	IGNITION	Storage battery and dry cells
GAUGE	56 inches		
WHEELS	Wood	STARTING SYSTEM . .	Two unit
FRONT TIRES	32 x 4 inches	STARTER OPERATED .	Gear to fly wheel
REAR TIRES	32 x 4 inches, anti-skid	LIGHTING SYSTEM . .	Electric
		VOLTAGES	Six
SERVICE BRAKE . . .	Contracting on rear wheels	WIRING SYSTEM . . .	Double
		GASOLINE SYSTEM . .	Vacuum
EMERGENCY BRAKE .	Expanding on rear wheels	CLUTCH	Cone
CYLINDERS	Eight	TRANSMISSION . . .	Selective sliding
ARRANGED	V type, 90 degrees	GEAR CHANGES . . .	Three
CAST	In fours	DRIVE	Plain bevel
HORSEPOWER	26.45	REAR AXLE	Three-quarters floating
	(N. A. C. C. Rating)		
BORE AND STROKE .	2⅞ x 4¾ inches	STEERING GEAR . .	Worm and sector

In addition to above specifications, price includes top, top hood,
windshield, speedometer, ammeter and demountable rims

**J A C K S O N
A U T O M O B I L E
C O M P A N Y**

**J A C K S O N
M I C H I G A N**

Price $1685
With Detachable Sedan Top . 1925

JACKSON TOURING CAR—68

COLOR	Dark blue		BORE AND STROKE . .	3½ x 4½ inches
SEATING CAPACITY .	Seven persons		LUBRICATION	Full force feed
POSITION OF DRIVER	Left side		RADIATOR	Cellular
WHEELBASE	124 inches		COOLING	Water pump
GAUGE	56 inches		IGNITION	Storage battery and dry cells
WHEELS	Wood		STARTING SYSTEM . .	Two unit
FRONT TIRES	34 x 4½ inches		STARTER OPERATED .	Gear to fly wheel
REAR TIRES	34 x 4½ inches, anti-skid		LIGHTING SYSTEM . .	Electric
SERVICE BRAKE . . .	Contracting on rear wheels		VOLTAGES	Six
			WIRING SYSTEM . .	Double
EMERGENCY BRAKE .	Expanding on rear wheels		GASOLINE SYSTEM . .	Vacuum
			CLUTCH	Cone
CYLINDERS	Eight		TRANSMISSION . . .	Selective sliding
ARRANGED	V type, 90 degrees		GEAR CHANGES . . .	Three
CAST	In fours		DRIVE	Spiral bevel
HORESPOWER	39.2		REAR AXLE	Full floating
(N. A. C. C. Rating)			STEERING GEAR . . .	Worm and gear

In addition to above specifications, price includes top, top hood,
windshield, speedometer, ammeter and demountable rims

**NORDYKE &
MARMON
COMPANY, INC.**

INDIANAPOLIS
INDIANA

Price.	$2750
Four-Passenger Club Roadster .	2700
Three-Passenger Club Roadster .	2700
Five-Passenger Touring Car . .	2700

MARMON 34 TOURING CAR

COLOR.	Body, dark blue; running gear, black; wheels, cream		BORE AND STROKE .	3¾ x 5⅛ inches
			LUBRICATION	Full force feed
			RADIATOR	Cellular
SEATING CAPACITY .	Seven persons		COOLING	Water pump
POSITION OF DRIVER	Left side		IGNITION.	High-tension magneto
WHEELBASE	136 inches			
GAUGE	56 inches		STARTING SYSTEM . .	Two unit
WHEELS	Wire		STARTER OPERATED .	Gear to fly wheel
FRONT TIRES	34 x 4½ inches, cord		LIGHTING SYSTEM . .	Electric
REAR TIRES	34 x 4½ inches, cord		VOLTAGES	Twelve
			WIRING SYSTEM. . .	Single
SERVICE BRAKE. . .	Contracting on rear wheels		GASOLINE SYSTEM. .	Gravity
			CLUTCH	Cone
EMERGENCY BRAKE .	Expanding on rear wheels		TRANSMISSION . . .	Selective sliding
			GEAR CHANGES . . .	Three
CYLINDERS	Six		DRIVE.	Spiral bevel
ARRANGED	Vertically		REAR AXLE	Three-quarters floating
CAST	En bloc			
HORSEPOWER	33.75		STEERING GEAR . .	Worm and worm wheel
(N. A. C. C. Rating)				

In addition to above specifications, price includes top, top hood,
windshield, speedometer, ammeter, clock and extra wheel

BUICK MOTOR
C O M P A N Y

▬▬▬▬▬▬▬▬▬▬

F L I N T
M I C H I G A N

Price $985
Roadster . . 950
Coupe . . . 1350
Sedan . . . 1875

BUICK—D-6-45

COLOR	Blue-black		LUBRICATION	Splash with circulating pump
SEATING CAPACITY .	Five persons		RADIATOR	Cellular
POSITION OF DRIVER	Left side		COOLING	Water pump
WHEELBASE	115 inches		IGNITION	Storage battery
GAUGE	56 inches		STARTING SYSTEM . .	Single unit
WHEELS	Wood		STARTER OPERATED . .	Gear to fly wheel
FRONT TIRES	32 x 4 inches		LIGHTING SYSTEM . .	Electric
REAR TIRES	32 x 4 inches, anti-skid		VOLTAGES	Six
SERVICE BRAKE . .	Contracting on rear wheels		WIRING SYSTEM . . .	Single
			GASOLINE SYSTEM .	Vacuum
EMERGENCY BRAKE .	Expanding on rear wheels		CLUTCH	Cone
			TRANSMISSION . . .	Selective sliding
CYLINDERS	Six		GEAR CHANGES . . .	Three forward, one reverse
ARRANGED	Vertically			
CAST	En bloc		DRIVE	Spiral bevel
HORSEPOWER	25.35		REAR AXLE	Full floating
(N. A. C. C. Rating)			STEERING GEAR . . .	Split nut and worm
BORE AND STROKE .	3¼ x 4½ inches			

In addition to above specifications, price includes top, top
hood, windshield, speedometer, ammeter and demountable rims

BUICK MOTOR COMPANY

FLINT MICHIGAN

Price . . . $1485
Roadster . 1450

BUICK—D-6-55

COLOR	Royal green with black stripe	LUBRICATION	Splash with circulating pump
SEATING CAPACITY. .	Seven persons	RADIATOR	Cellular
POSITION OF DRIVER	Left side	COOLING	Water pump
WHEELBASE	130 inches	IGNITION	Storage battery
GAUGE	56 inches	STARTING SYSTEM . .	Single unit
WHEELS	Wood	STARTER OPERATED .	Gear to fly wheel
FRONT TIRES	36 x 4½ inches	LIGHTING SYSTEM . .	Electric
REAR TIRES	36 x 4½ inches, anti-skid	VOLTAGES	Six
SERVICE BRAKE . . .	Contracting on rear wheels	WIRING SYSTEM. . .	Single
		GASOLINE SYSTEM . .	Vacuum
EMERGENCY BRAKE .	Expanding on rear wheels	CLUTCH	Cone
		TRANSMISSION . . .	Selective sliding
CYLINDERS	Six	GEAR CHANGES . . .	Three forward, one reverse
ARRANGED	Vertically		
CAST	In pairs	DRIVE	Spiral bevel
HORSEPOWER . . . . 33.75 (N. A. C. C. Rating)		REAR AXLE	Full floating
		STEERING GEAR. . .	Split nut and worm
BORE AND STROKE .	3¾ x 5 inches		

In addition to above specifications, price includes top, top hood, windshield, speedometer, ammeter and demountable rims

ELKHART
CARRIAGE AND
MOTOR CAR
COMPANY

ELKHART
INDIANA

Price $795
Runabout . . $795

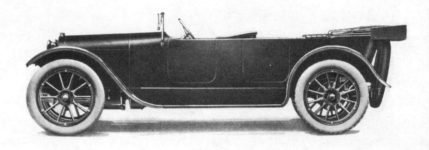

ELCAR TOURING CAR—A

COLOR	Body, black; running gear, gray	BORE AND STROKE .	3½ x 5 inches
		LUBRICATION	Splash with circulating pump
SEATING CAPACITY .	Five persons	RADIATOR	Tubular
POSITION OF DRIVER	Left side	COOLING	Thermo-syphon
WHEELBASE	114 inches	IGNITION	Storage battery
GAUGE	56 inches	STARTING SYSTEM . .	Single unit
WHEELS	Wood	STARTER OPERATED .	Chain to crank-shaft
FRONT TIRES	32 x 3½ inches		
REAR TIRES	32 x 3½ inches, anti-skid	LIGHTING SYSTEM . .	Electric
		VOLTAGES	Starting, twelve; lighting, six
SERVICE BRAKE . . .	Expanding on rear wheels	WIRING SYSTEM . .	Single
		GASOLINE SYSTEM . .	Vacuum
EMERGENCY BRAKE .	Expanding on rear wheels	CLUTCH	Cone
		TRANSMISSION . . .	Selective sliding
CYLINDERS	Four	GEAR CHANGES . . .	Three
ARRANGED	Vertically	DRIVE	Plain bevel
CAST	En bloc	REAR AXLE	Full floating
HORSEPOWER	19.6	STEERING GEAR . . .	Worm and sector
(N. A. C. C. Rating)			

In addition to above specifications, price includes top, top
hood, windshield, speedometer, ammeter and demountable rims

**CHALMERS
MOTOR
COMPANY**

Price, $1350

**DETROIT
MICHIGAN**

CHALMERS TOURING CAR SIX—40

COLOR	Body, Chalmers meteor blue and coupe green; running gear, black	BORE AND STROKE . .	3⅛ x 5 inches
		LUBRICATION	Force feed and splash
		RADIATOR	Cellular
SEATING CAPACITY .	Seven persons	COOLING	Thermo-syphon
POSITION OF DRIVER.	Left side	IGNITION	Storage battery
WHEELBASE	124 inches	STARTING SYSTEM . .	Two unit
GAUGE	56 inches	STARTER OPERATED .	Gear to fly wheel
WHEELS	Wood	LIGHTING SYSTEM . .	Electric
FRONT TIRES	34 x 4 inches	VOLTAGES	Six
REAR TIRES	34 x 4 inches, anti-skid	WIRING SYSTEM . . .	Single
		GASOLINE SYSTEM . .	Gravity
SERVICE BRAKE . . .	Contracting on rear wheels	CLUTCH	Dry multiple disc
EMERGENCY BRAKE .	Expanding on rear wheels	TRANSMISSION . . .	Selective sliding
		GEAR CHANGES . . .	Three and reverse
CYLINDERS	Six		
ARRANGED	Vertically	DRIVE	Spiral bevel
CAST	En bloc	REAR AXLE	Three-quarters floating
HORSEPOWER. . . .	23.44		
(N. A. C. C. Rating)		STEERING GEAR. . .	Worm and gear

In addition to above specifications, price includes top, top hood,
windshield, speedometer, ammeter and demountable rims

CHALMERS
MOTOR
COMPANY

DETROIT
MICHIGAN

Price $1700
Three-Passenger Roadster . . . 1350
Victoria-Cabriolet 1450

CHALMERS PALANQUIN SIX—40

COLOR	Body, Chalmers meteor blue and coupe green; demountable top, black; running gear, black
SEATING CAPACITY .	Seven persons
POSITION OF DRIVER.	Left side
WHEELBASE	124 inches
GAUGE	56 inches
WHEELS	Wood
FRONT TIRES	34 x 4 inches
REAR TIRES	34 x 4½ inches, anti-skid
SERVICE BRAKE . . .	Contracting on rear wheels
EMERGENCY BRAKE .	Expanding on rear wheels
CYLINDERS	Six
ARRANGED	Vertically
CAST	En bloc

HORSEPOWER	23.44 (N. A. C. C. Rating)
BORE AND STROKE . .	3⅛ x 5 inches
LUBRICATION	Force feed and splash
RADIATOR	Cellular
COOLING	Thermo-syphon
IGNITION	Storage battery
STARTING SYSTEM . .	Two unit
STARTER OPERATED .	Gear to fly wheel
LIGHTING SYSTEM . .	Electric
VOLTAGES	Six
WIRING SYSTEM . . .	Single
GASOLINE SYSTEM . .	Gravity
CLUTCH	Dry multiple disc
TRANSMISSION . . .	Selective sliding
GEAR CHANGES . . .	Three and reverse
DRIVE	Spiral bevel
REAR AXLE	Three-quarters floating
STEERING GEAR . . .	Worm and gear

In addition to above specifications, price includes top, top hood, windshield, speedometer, ammeter and demountable rims

KING MOTOR CAR COMPANY

DETROIT MICHIGAN

Price, $1350

KING CORSAIR—E

COLOR	Deep blue
SEATING CAPACITY .	Five persons
POSITION OF DRIVER	Left side
WHEELBASE	120 inches
GAUGE	56 inches
WHEELS	Wood
FRONT TIRES	34 x 4 inches
REAR TIRES	34 x 4 inches, anti-skid
SERVICE BRAKE . .	Rear wheels
EMERGENCY BRAKE .	Contracting on propeller shaft
CYLINDERS	Eight
ARRANGED	V-type, 90 degrees
CAST	In fours
HORSEPOWER	28.8 (N. A. C. C. Rating)

BORE AND STROKE .	3 x 5 inches
LUBRICATION	Force feed
RADIATOR	Cellular
COOLING	Thermo-syphon
IGNITION	Storage battery
STARTING SYSTEM . .	Two unit
STARTER OPERATED .	Gear to fly wheel
LIGHTING SYSTEM . .	Electric
VOLTAGES	Six
WIRING SYSTEM. . .	Single
GASOLINE SYSTEM. .	Vacuum
CLUTCH	Dry plate
TRANSMISSION . . .	Selective sliding
GEAR CHANGES . . .	Three forward, one reverse
DRIVE	Spiral bevel
REAR AXLE	Full floating
STEERING GEAR . .	Worm and gear

In addition to above specifications, price includes top, top
hood, windshield, speedometer, ammeter and demountable rims

KING MOTOR
CAR COMPANY

Price, $1150

DETROIT
MICHIGAN

KING RELIANCE—D

COLOR	Body, salon green; chassis, black	BORE AND STROKE	2⅞ x 5 inches
		LUBRICATION	Force feed
SEATING CAPACITY	Five persons	RADIATOR	Cellular
POSITION OF DRIVER	Left side	COOLING	Thermo-syphon
WHEELBASE	113 inches	IGNITION	Storage battery
GAUGE	56 inches	STARTING SYSTEM	Two unit
WHEELS	Wood	STARTER OPERATED	Gear to fly wheel
FRONT TIRES	33 x 4 inches	LIGHTING SYSTEM	Electric
REAR TIRES	33 x 4 inches anti-skid	VOLTAGES	Six
		WIRING SYSTEM	Double
SERVICE BRAKE	Contracting on rear wheels	GASOLINE SYSTEM	Vacuum
		CLUTCH	Multiple disc in oil
EMERGENCY BRAKE	Expanding on rear wheels	TRANSMISSION	Selective sliding
CYLINDERS	Eight	GEAR CHANGES	Three forward, one reverse
ARRANGED	V-type, 90 degrees		
CAST	In fours	DRIVE	Spiral bevel
HORSEPOWER	26.45	REAR AXLE	Full floating
	(N. A. C. C. Rating)	STEERING GEAR	Worm and gear

In addition to above specifications, price includes top, top hood, windshield, speedometer, ammeter and demountable rims

KING MOTOR
CAR COMPANY

D E T R O I T
M I C H I G A N

Price $1350
Roadster . . 1350
Sedan . . . 1900

KING CHALLENGER—E

COLOR	Deep blue		BORE AND STROKE .	3 x 5 inches
SEATING CAPACITY .	Seven persons		LUBRICATION	Force feed
POSITION OF DRIVER	Left side		RADIATOR	Cellular
WHEELBASE	120 inches		COOLING	Thermo-syphon
GAUGE	56 inches		IGNITION	Storage battery
WHEELS	Wood		STARTING SYSTEM . .	Two unit
FRONT TIRES	34 x 4 inches		STARTER OPERATED .	Gear to fly wheel
REAR TIRES	34 x 4 inches, anti-skid		LIGHTING SYSTEM . .	Electric
SERVICE BRAKE . .	Rear wheels		VOLTAGES	Six
EMERGENCY BRAKE .	Contracting on propeller shaft		WIRING SYSTEM . . .	Single
			GASOLINE SYSTEM . .	Vacuum
CYLINDERS	Eight		CLUTCH	Dry plate
ARRANGED	V-type, 90 degrees		TRANSMISSION . . .	Selective sliding
CAST	In fours		GEAR CHANGES . . .	Three forward, one reverse
HORSEPOWER . . . . 28.8 (N. A. C. C. Rating)			DRIVE	Spiral bevel
			REAR AXLE	Full floating
			STEERING GEAR . .	Worm and gear

In addition to above specifications, price includes top, top
hood, windshield, speedometer, ammeter and demountable rims

E M P I R E
AUTOMOBILE
C O M P A N Y

INDIANAPOLIS
I N D I A N A

Price, $1095

EMPIRE TOURING CAR—60

COLOR	Body, green or gray; running gear, black; wheels, red or green
SEATING CAPACITY .	Five persons
POSITION OF DRIVER	Left side
WHEELBASE	120 inches
GAUGE	56 inches
WHEELS	Wood
FRONT TIRES	34 x 4 inches
REAR TIRES	34 x 4 inches, anti-skid
SERVICE BRAKE . . .	Contracting on rear wheels
EMERGENCY BRAKE .	Expanding on rear wheels
CYLINDERS	Six
ARRANGED	Vertically
CAST	En bloc
HORSEPOWER	25.35
(N. A. C. C. Rating)	

BORE AND STROKE .	3¼ x 4½ inches
LUBRICATION	Force feed and splash
RADIATOR	Cellular
COOLING	Water pump
IGNITION	Storage battery
STARTING SYSTEM . .	Two unit
STARTER OPERATED .	Gear to fly wheel
LIGHTING SYSTEM . .	Electric
VOLTAGES	Six
WIRING SYSTEM . .	Single
GASOLINE SYSTEM . .	Vacuum
CLUTCH	Cone
TRANSMISSION . . .	Selective sliding
GEAR CHANGES . . .	Three forward, one reverse
DRIVE	Plain bevel
REAR AXLE	Three-quarters floating
STEERING GEAR . . .	Worm and gear

In addition to above specifications, price includes top, top
hood, windshield, speedometer, ammeter and demountable rims

REGAL MOTOR CAR COMPANY

D E T R O I T
M I C H I G A N

Price . . . **$650**
Roadster .   650

REGAL TOURING CAR—E

COLOR	Body and wheels, blue; fenders and hood, black	BORE AND STROKE .	3½ x 4 inches.
		LUBRICATION	Splash with circulating pump
SEATING CAPACITY .	Five persons	RADIATOR	Cellular
POSITION OF DRIVER	Left side	COOLING	Thermo-syphon
WHEELBASE	106 inches	IGNITION	Storage battery
GAUGE	56 inches	STARTING SYSTEM . .	Single unit
WHEELS	Wood	STARTER OPERATED .	Chain to crank shaft
FRONT TIRES	30 x 3½ inches		
REAR TIRES	30 x 3½ inches anti-skid	LIGHTING SYSTEM . .	Electric
		VOLTAGES	Twelve
SERVICE BRAKE . . .	Contracting on rear wheels	WIRING SYSTEM . . .	Double
		GASOLINE SYSTEM . .	Gravity
EMERGENCY BRAKE .	Expanding on rear wheels	CLUTCH	Cone
		TRANSMISSION . . .	Selective sliding
CYLINDERS	Four	GEAR CHANGES . . .	Three forward, one reverse
ARRANGED	Vertically		
CAST	En bloc	DRIVE	Plain bevel
HORSEPOWER	19.6	REAR AXLE	Full floating
(N. A. C. C. Rating)		STEERING GEAR . . .	Worm and gear

In addition to above specifications, price includes top, top
hood, windshield, speedometer and demountable rims

**A U B U R N
AUTOMOBILE
C O M P A N Y**

A U B U R N
I N D I A N A

Price $1050
Three-Passenger Roadster . 1050

AUBURN TOURING CAR—6-38

COLOR	Body, royal blue; hood, fenders and flashings, black.	BORE AND STROKE .	3 x 5 inches	
		LUBRICATION	Force feed and splash	
SEATING CAPACITY .	Five persons	RADIATOR	Cellular	
POSITION OF DRIVER	Left side	COOLING	Water pump	
WHEELBASE	120 inches	IGNITION	Storage battery	
GAUGE	56 inches	STARTING SYSTEM . .	Two unit	
WHEELS	Wood	STARTER OPERATED .	Gear to fly wheel	
FRONT TIRES	34 x 4 inches	LIGHTING SYSTEM . .	Electric	
REAR TIRES	34 x 4 inches	VOLTAGES	Six	
SERVICE BRAKE . . .	Contracting on rear wheels	WIRING SYSTEM . . .	Single	
EMERGENCY BRAKE .	Expanding on rear wheels	GASOLINE SYSTEM . .	Vacuum	
		CLUTCH	Cone	
CYLINDERS	Six	TRANSMISSION . . .	Selective sliding	
ARRANGED	Vertically	GEAR CHANGES . . .	Three forward, one reverse	
CAST	En bloc	DRIVE	Spiral bevel	
HORSEPOWER	21.6 (N. A. C. C. Rating)	REAR AXLE	Floating	
		STEERING GEAR . . .	Worm	

In addition to above specifications, price includes top, top hood,
windshield, speedometer, indicator and demountable rims

AUBURN
AUTOMOBILE
COMPANY

AUBURN
INDIANA

AUBURN TOURING CAR—6-40A

COLOR	Body, royal blue; fenders, hood and flashings, black.	LUBRICATION	Force feed and splash
SEATING CAPACITY .	Seven persons	RADIATOR	Cellular
POSITION OF DRIVER	Left side	COOLING	Water pump
WHEELBASE	126 inches	IGNITION	Storage battery
GAUGE	56 inches	STARTING SYSTEM . .	Single unit
WHEELS	Wood	STARTER OPERATED .	Gear to fly wheel
FRONT TIRES	35 x 4½ inches	LIGHTING SYSTEM . .	Electric
REAR TIRES	35 x 4½ inches	VOLTAGES	Six
SERVICE BRAKE . . .	Contracting on rear wheels	WIRING SYSTEM . . .	Single
EMERGENCY BRAKE .	Expanding on rear wheels	GASOLINE SYSTEM . .	Vacuum
		CLUTCH	Cone
CYLINDERS	Six	TRANSMISSION . . .	Selective sliding
ARRANGED	Vertically	GEAR CHANGES . . .	Three forward, one reverse
CAST	En bloc	DRIVE	Spiral bevel
HORSEPOWER	29.4 (N. A. C. C. Rating)	REAR AXLE	Foating
BORE AND STROKE .	3½ x 5 inches	STEERING GEAR . . .	Worm

In addition to above specifications, price includes top, top
hood, windshield, speedometer, indicator and demountable rims

**PREMIER
MOTOR MFG.
COMPANY**

**INDIANAPOLIS
INDIANA**

Price, $2300

PREMIER TOURING CAR—6-56

COLOR	Dark gun metal gray		LUBRICATION	Splash with circulating pump
SEATING CAPACITY .	Seven persons		RADIATOR	Cellular
POSITION OF DRIVER	Left side		COOLING	Water pump
WHEELBASE	134 inches		IGNITION	Storage battery
GAUGE	56 inches		STARTING SYSTEM . .	Two unit
WHEELS	Wood		STARTER OPERATED .	Gear to fly wheel
FRONT TIRES	36 x 4½ inches		LIGHTING SYSTEM . .	Electric
REAR TIRES	36 x 4½ inches, anti-skid		VOLTAGES	Six
SERVICE BRAKE. . .	Contracting on rear wheels		WIRING SYSTEM. . .	Single
			GASOLINE SYSTEM . .	Vacuum
EMERGENCY BRAKE .	Expanding on rear wheels		CLUTCH	Dry multiple disc
CYLINDERS	Six		TRANSMISSION . . .	Selective sliding
ARRANGED	Vertically		GEAR CHANGES. . .	Three forward, one reverse
CAST	In threes		DRIVE	Spiral bevel
HORSEPOWER	38.4 (N. A. C. C. Rating)		REAR AXLE	Full floating
BORE AND STROKE .	4 x 5½ inches		STEERING GEAR . . .	Worm and wheel

In addition to above specifications, price includes top, top hood,
windshield, speedometer, ammeter and demountable rims

P R E M I E R
M O T O R   M F G.
C O M P A N Y

Price, $2300

I N D I A N A P O L I S
I N D I A N A

PREMIER ROADSTER—6-56

COLOR	Dark gun metal gray	LUBRICATION	Splash with cir-culating pump
SEATING CAPACITY .	Three persons	RADIATOR	Cellular
POSITION OF DRIVER	Left side	COOLING	Water pump
WHEELBASE	134 inches	IGNITION	Storage battery
GAUGE	56 inches	STARTING SYSTEM . .	Two unit
WHEELS	Wire	STARTER OPERATED .	Gear to fly wheel
FRONT TIRES	34 x 4½ inches	LIGHTING SYSTEM . .	Electric
REAR TIRES	34 x 4½ inches, anti-skid	VOLTAGES	Six
SERVICE BRAKE. . .	Contracting on rear wheels	WIRING SYSTEM. . .	Single
		GASOLINE SYSTEM . .	Vacuum
EMERGENCY BRAKE .	Expanding on rear wheels	CLUTCH	Dry multiple disc
CYLINDERS	Six	TRANSMISSION . . .	Selective sliding
ARRANGED	Vertically	GEAR CHANGES . . .	Three forward, one reverse
CAST	In threes	DRIVE	Spiral bevel
HORSEPOWER	38.4 (N. A. C. C. Rating)	REAR AXLE	Full floating
BORE AND STROKE .	4 x 5½ inches	STEERING GEAR. . .	Worm and wheel

In addition to above specifications, price includes top, top
hood, windshield, speedometer, ammeter and demountable rims

**P R E M I E R
MOTOR   MFG.
C O M P A N Y**

INDIANAPOLIS
I N D I A N A

Price. $2300
Four-Passenger Yacht .   2300

PREMIER CLOVERLEAF ROADSTER—6-56

COLOR	Dark gun metal gray
SEATING CAPACITY .	Three persons
POSITION OF DRIVER	Left side
WHEELBASE	134 inches
GAUGE	56 inches
WHEELS	Wire
FRONT TIRES	34 x 4½ inches
REAR TIRES	34 x 4½ inches, anti-skid
SERVICE BRAKE . . .	Contracting on rear wheels
EMERGENCY BRAKE .	Expanding on rear wheels
CYLINDERS	Six
ARRANGED	Vertically
CAST	In threes
HORSEPOWER	38.4 (N. A. C. C. Rating)
BORE AND STROKE .	4 x 5½ inches

LUBRICATION	Splash with circulating pump
RADIATOR	Cellular
COOLING	Water pump
IGNITION	Storage battery
STARTING SYSTEM . .	Two unit
STARTER OPERATED .	Gear to fly wheel
LIGHTING SYSTEM . .	Electric
VOLTAGES	Six
WIRING SYSTEM . . .	Single
GASOLINE SYSTEM . .	Vacuum
CLUTCH	Dry multiple disc
TRANSMISSION . . .	Selective sliding
GEAR CHANGES . . .	Three forward, one reverse
DRIVE	Spiral bevel
REAR AXLE	Full floating
STEERING GEAR . . .	Worm and wheel

In addition to above specifications, price includes top, top
hood, windshield, speedometer, ammeter and demountable rims

**PREMIER
MOTOR   MFG.
COMPANY**

INDIANAPOLIS
INDIANA

Price. $2300
Two-Passenger Coupelet . . 2500

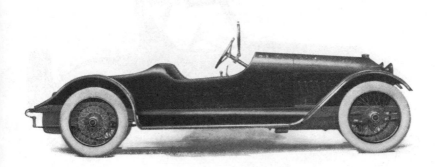

PREMIER SPEEDSTER—6-56

COLOR	Dark gun metal gray	LUBRICATION	Splash with circulating pump
SEATING CAPACITY .	Two persons	RADIATOR	Cellular
POSITION OF DRIVER	Left side	COOLING	Water pump
WHEELBASE	134 inches	IGNITION	Storage battery
GAUGE	56 inches	STARTING SYSTEM . .	Two unit
WHEELS	Wire	STARTER OPERATED .	Gear to fly wheel
FRONT TIRES	34 x 4½ inches	LIGHTING SYSTEM . .	Electric
REAR TIRES	34 x 4½ inches, anti-skid	VOLTAGES	Six
SERVICE BRAKE . . .	Contracting on rear wheels	WIRING SYSTEM . . .	Single
		GASOLINE SYSTEM . .	Vacuum
EMERGENCY BRAKE .	Expanding on rear wheels	CLUTCH	Dry multiple disc
CYLINDERS	Six	TRANSMISSION . . .	Selective sliding
ARRANGED	Vertically	GEAR CHANGES . . .	Three forward, one reverse
CAST	In threes	DRIVE	Spiral bevel
HOREPOWER . . . . 38.4 (N. A. C. C. Rating)		REAR AXLE	Full floating
BORE AND STROKE . 4 x 5½ inches		STEERING GEAR . . .	Worm and wheel

In addition to above specifications, price includes top, top
hood, windshield, speedometer, ammeter and demountable rims

**M E R C E R
AUTOMOBILE
C O M P A N Y**

**T R E N T O N
N E W   J E R S E Y**

Price, $2900

MERCER RUNABOUT—22-72

COLOR	Blue, green, gray or maroon		LUBRICATION	Force feed
SEATING CAPACITY .	Two persons		RADIATOR	Cellular
POSITION OF DRIVER	Left side		COOLING	Water pump
WHEELBASE	115 inches		IGNITION	High-tension magneto
GAUGE	56 inches			
WHEELS	Wood		STARTING SYSTEM . .	Single unit
FRONT TIRES	32 x 4 inches		STARTER OPERATED .	Fly-wheel generator and motor
REAR TIRES	32 x 4 inches			
SERVICE BRAKE . . .	Expanding on drive shaft		LIGHTING SYSTEM . .	Electric
			VOLTAGES	Twelve
EMERGENCY BRAKE .	Expanding on rear wheels		WIRING SYSTEM . . .	Single
			GASOLINE SYSTEM . .	Vacuum
CYLINDERS	Four		CLUTCH	Dry multiple disc
ARRANGED	Vertically		TRANSMISSION . . .	Selective sliding
CAST	En bloc		GEAR CHANGES . . .	Four forward, one reverse
HORSEPOWER	22.5			
(N. A. C. C. Rating)			DRIVE	Spiral bevel
			REAR AXLE	Full floating
BORE AND STROKE . .	3¾ x 6¾ inches		STEERING GEAR . . .	Worm and gear

In addition to above specifications, price includes top, top hood, windshield, speedometer, ammeter, voltmeter, clock and demountable rims

M E R C E R
A U T O M O B I L E
C O M P A N Y

T R E N T O N
N E W   J E R S E Y

Price $2750

MERCER RACEABOUT—22-72

COLOR	Yellow, gray or blue	BORE AND STROKE .	3¾ x 6¾ inches
SEATING CAPACITY .	Two persons	LUBRICATION	Force feed
POSITION OF DRIVER	Left side	RADIATOR	Cellular
WHEELBASE	115 inches	COOLING	Water pump
GAUGE	56 inches	IGNITION	High-tension magneto
WHEELS	Wire	LIGHTING SYSTEM . .	Electric
FRONT TIRES	32 x 4 inches	VOLTAGES	Twelve
REAR TIRES	32 x 4 inches	GASOLINE SYSTEM . .	Vacuum
SERVICE BRAKE . . .	Expanding on drive shaft	CLUTCH	Dry multiple disc
EMERGENCY BRAKE .	Expanding on rear wheels	TRANSMISSION . . .	Selective sliding
CYLINDERS	Four	GEAR CHANGES . . .	Four forward, one reverse
ARRANGED	Vertically	DRIVE	Spiral bevel
CAST	En bloc	REAR AXLE	Full floating
HORSEPOWER	22.5 (N. A. C. C. Rating)	STEERING GEAR. . .	Worm and gear

In addition to above specifications, price
includes speedometer, clock and wire wheels

M E R C E R
A U T O M O B I L E
C O M P A N Y

T R E N T O N
N E W   J E R S E Y

Price $3000
Four-Passenger Sporting . 3000

MERCER TOURING CAR—22-72

COLOR	Brown, blue, green, gray or red
SEATING CAPACITY .	Six persons
POSITION OF DRIVER	Left side
WHEELBASE	132 inches
GAUGE	56 inches
WHEELS	Wood
FRONT TIRES	34 x 4½ inches
REAR TIRES	34 x 4½ inches
SERVICE BRAKE. . .	Expanding on drive shaft
EMERGENCY BRAKE .	Expanding on rear wheels
CYLINDERS	Four
ARRANGED	Vertically
CAST	En bloc
HORSEPOWER	22.5 (N. A. C. C. Rating)
BORE AND STROKE .	3¾ x 6¾ inches

LUBRICATION	Force feed
RADIATOR	Cellular
COOLING	Water pump
IGNITION	High-tension magneto
STARTING SYSTEM . .	Single unit
STARTER OPERATED .	Fly wheel generator and motor
LIGHTING SYSTEM . .	Electric
VOLTAGES	Twelve
WIRING SYSTEM. . .	Single
GASOLINE SYSTEM. .	Vacuum
CLUTCH	Dry multiple disc
TRANSMISSION . . .	Selective sliding
GEAR CHANGES . . .	Four forward, one reverse
DRIVE	Spiral bevel
REAR AXLE	Full floating
STEERING GEAR. . .	Worm and gear

In addition to above specifications, price includes top, top hood, windshield, speedometer, ammeter, voltmeter, clock and demountable rims

B R I S C O E
M O T O R
COMPANY, INC.

J A C K S O N
M I C H I G A N

Price. $750
Three-Passenger Cloverleaf Roadster   750

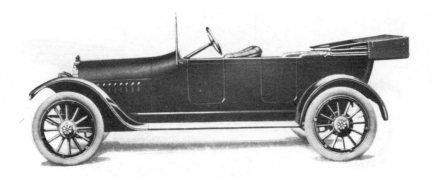

BRISCOE TOURING CAR—4-38

COLOR	Body, royal Briscoe green; running gear, black; wheels, cream
SEATING CAPACITY .	Five persons
POSITION OF DRIVER	Left side
WHEELBASE	114 inches
GAUGE	56 inches
WHEELS	Wood
FRONT TIRES	32 x 3½ inches
REAR TIRES	32 x 3½ inches
SERVICE BRAKE. . .	Contracting on rear wheels
EMERGENCY BRAKE .	Expanding on rear wheels
CYLINDERS	Four
ARRANGED	Vertically
CAST	En bloc
HORSEPOWER	18.9
(N. A. C. C. Rating)	

BORE AND STROKE .	$3\frac{7}{16}$ x 5⅛ inches
LUBRICATION	Splash with circulating pump
RADIATOR	Cellular
COOLING	Thermo-syphon
IGNITION	Storage battery
STARTING SYSTEM . .	Single unit
STARTER OPERATED .	Chain to transmission shaft
LIGHTING SYSTEM . .	Electric
VOLTAGES	Starting, twelve; lighting, six
WIRING SYSTEM. . .	Single
GASOLINE SYSTEM. .	Gravity
CLUTCH	Cone
TRANSMISSION . . .	Selective sliding
GEAR CHANGES . . .	Three forward, one reverse
DRIVE	Plain bevel
REAR AXLE	Full floating
STEERING GEAR. . .	Worm and sector

In addition to above specifications, price includes top,
top hood, windshield, speedometer and demountable rims

BRISCOE MOTOR COMPANY, INC.

JACKSON MICHIGAN

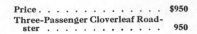

Price $950
Three-Passenger Cloverleaf Roadster 950

BRISCOE TOURING CAR—8-38

COLOR	Body, royal Briscoe green; running gear, black; wheels, cream	LUBRICATION	Full force feed
		RADIATOR	Cellular
		COOLING	Thermo-syphon
SEATING CAPACITY .	Five persons	IGNITION	Storage battery
POSITION OF DRIVER	Left side	STARTING SYSTEM . .	Single unit
WHEELBASE	114 inches	STARTER OPERATED .	Chain to transmission shaft
GAUGE	56 inches		
WHEELS	Wood	LIGHTING SYSTEM . .	Electric
FRONT TIRES	32 x 3½ inches	VOLTAGES	Starting, twelve; lighting, six
REAR TIRES	32 x 3½ inches		
SERVICE BRAKE . . .	Contracting on rear wheels	WIRING SYSTEM . . .	Single
		GASOLINE SYSTEM . .	Gravity
EMERGENCY BRAKE .	Expanding on rear wheels	CLUTCH	Cone
		TRANSMISSION . . .	Selective sliding
CYLINDERS	Eight	GEAR CHANGES . . .	Three forward, one reverse
ARRANGED	V-type, 90 degrees		
CAST	En bloc	DRIVE	Plain bevel
HORSEPOWER	28.8 (N. A. C. C. Rating)	REAR AXLE	Full floating
BORE AND STROKE .	3 x 3½ inches	STEERING GEAR . . .	Worm and sector

In addition to above specifications, price includes top, top
hood, windshield, speedometer and demountable rims

**CONSOLIDATED
CAR COMPANY**

**D E T R O I T
M I C H I G A N**

Price $1195
Two-Passenger Speedster . . . 1195
Four-Passenger Open-Type Road-
ster   250
Four-Passenger Motor Coach . . 1495
Five-Passenger Touring Sedan . 1795

ABBOTT-DETROIT TOURING CAR—6-44

COLOR	Black with cream wheels		LUBRICATION	Pump over and splash
SEATING CAPACITY .	Seven persons		RADIATOR	Tubular
POSITION OF DRIVER	Left side		COOLING	Water pump
WHEELBASE	122 inches		IGNITION	Storage battery
GAUGE	56 inches		STARTING SYSTEM . .	Two unit
WHEELS	Wood		STARTER OPERATED .	Gear to fly wheel
FRONT TIRES	32 x 4 inches		LIGHTING SYSTEM . .	Electric
REAR TIRES	32 x 4 inches		VOLTAGES	Six
SERVICE BRAKE . . .	Contracting on rear wheels		WIRING SYSTEM . . .	Single
EMERGENCY BRAKE .	Expanding on rear wheels		GASOLINE SYSTEM . .	Vacuum
CYLINDERS	Six		CLUTCH	Dry plate
ARRANGED	Vertically		TRANSMISSION . . .	Selective sliding
CAST	En bloc		GEAR CHANGES . . .	Three forward, and reverse
HORSEPOWER	25.35 (N. A. C. C. Rating)		DRIVE	Spiral bevel
BORE AND STROKE . .	3¼ x 4½ inches		REAR AXLE	Three-quarters floating
			STEERING GEAR . . .	Worm and wheel

In addition to above specifications, price includes top, top hood, windshield, speedometer, ammeter, voltmeter, clock and demountable rims

CONSOLIDATED CAR COMPANY

<hr>

DETROIT MICHIGAN

Price $1950
Racy Roadster . 1950

ABBOTT-DETROIT TOURING CAR—8-80

COLOR	Royal green		RADIATOR	Cellular
SEATING CAPACITY .	Seven persons		COOLING	Water pump
POSITION OF DRIVER	Left side		IGNITION	Storage battery and dry cells
WHEELBASE	121 inches			
GAUGE	56 inches		STARTING SYSTEM . .	Two unit
WHEELS	Wood		STARTER OPERATED .	Gear to fly wheel
FRONT TIRES	35 x 4½ inches		LIGHTING SYSTEM . .	Electric
REAR TIRES	35 x 4½ inches		VOLTAGES	Six .
SERVICE BRAKE . . .	Contracting on rear wheels		WIRING SYSTEM . . .	Double
EMERGENCY BRAKE .	Expanding on rear wheels		GASOLINE SYSTEM . .	Vacuum
CYLINDERS	Eight		CLUTCH	Dry multiple disc
ARRANGED	V-type, 90 degrees		TRANSMISSION . . .	Selective sliding
CAST	In fours		GEAR CHANGES . . .	Three forward, one reverse
HORSEPOWER	33.8			
(N. A. C. C. Rating)			DRIVE	Spiral bevel
BORE AND STROKE . .	3¼ x 5 inches		REAR AXLE	Three-quarters floating
LUBRICATION	Force feed and splash		STEERING GEAR . . .	Worm and wheel

In addition to above specifications, price includes top, top hood, windshield, speedometer, ammeter, voltmeter, clock and demountable rims

KISSEL MOTOR CAR COMPANY

HARTFORD WISCONSIN

Price	$1050
Four-Passenger Roadster	1150
Four-Passenger All-Year Road-ster	1450

KISSEL-KAR TOURING CAR—4-32

COLOR	Blue and black	BORE AND STROKE .	3⅞ x 5½ inches
SEATING CAPACITY .	Five persons	LUBRICATION	Splash with circulating pump
POSITION OF DRIVER	Left side		
WHEELBASE	115 inches	RADIATOR	Square tube
GAUGE	56 inches	COOLING	Water pump
WHEELS	Wood	IGNITION	Storage battery
FRONT TIRES	33 x 4 inches	STARTING SYSTEM . .	Single unit
REAR TIRES	33 x 4 inches, anti-skid	STARTER OPERATED .	Gear to fly wheel
		LIGHTING SYSTEM . .	Electric
SERVICE BRAKE . . .	Contracting on rear wheels	VOLTAGES	Six
		WIRING SYSTEM . . .	Single
EMERGENCY BRAKE .	Contracting on rear wheels	GASOLINE SYSTEM . .	Vacuum
		CLUTCH	Cone
CYLINDERS	Four	TRANSMISSION . . .	Selective sliding
ARRANGED	Vertically	GEAR CHANGES . . .	Three
CAST	En bloc	DRIVE	Spiral bevel
HORSEPOWER	24.03	REAR AXLE	Full floating
(N. A. C. C. Rating)		STEERING GEAR . . .	Split nut and worm

In addition to above specifications, price includes top, top hood, windshield, speedometer, ammeter, voltmeter and demountable rims

**KISSEL MOTOR
CAR COMPANY**

**H A R T F O R D
W I S C O N S I N**

Price	**$2000**
Four-Door Five-Passenger Touring .	1485
Four-Door Seven-Passenger Touring.	1585
Three-Door Five-Passenger Touring	1650
Three-Door Seven-Passenger Touring	1750
Roadster.	1650
Roadster Coupe	2000

KISSEL-KAR ALL-YEAR—6-42

COLOR	Blue and black
SEATING CAPACITY .	Five persons
POSITION OF DRIVER	Left side
WHEELBASE	126 inches
GAUGE	56 inches
WHEELS	Wood
FRONT TIRES	34 x 4 inches
REAR TIRES	34 x 4 inches, non-skid
SERVICE BRAKE . . .	Contracting on rear wheels
EMERGENCY BRAKE .	Contracting on rear wheels
CYLINDERS	Six
ARRANGED	Vertically
CAST	En bloc
HORSEPOWER . . . . 31.54 (N. A. C. C. Rating)	
BORE AND STROKE .	3⅝ x 5½ inches

LUBRICATION	Splash with circulating pump
RADIATOR	Square tube
COOLING	Water pump
IGNITION	High-tension magneto and storage battery
STARTING SYSTEM . .	Single unit
STARTER OPERATED .	Gear to fly wheel
LIGHTING SYSTEM . .	Electric
VOLTAGES	Six
WIRING SYSTEM . . .	Single
GASOLINE SYSTEM . .	Vacuum
CLUTCH	Cone
TRANSMISSION . . .	Selective sliding
GEAR CHANGES . . .	Three
DRIVE	Spiral bevel
REAR AXLE	Full floating
STEERING GEAR . .	Split nut worm

In addition to above specifications, price includes top, top hood, windshield, speedometer, ammeter, voltmeter, clock and demountable rims

**LEWIS SPRING
AND AXLE
COMPANY**

Price, $985

**J A C K S O N
AND CHELSEA
M I C H I G A N**

HOLLIER ROADSTER—158

COLOR	Optional		LUBRICATION	Force feed
SEATING CAPACITY .	Three persons		RADIATOR	Cellular
POSITION OF DRIVER	Left side		COOLING	Thermo-syphon
WHEELBASE	112 inches		IGNITION	Storage battery
GAUGE	56 inches		STARTING SYSTEM . .	Single unit
WHEELS	Wood		STARTER OPERATED .	Chain to crank shaft
FRONT TIRES	33 x 4 inches		LIGHTING SYSTEM . .	Electric
REAR TIRES	33 x 4 inches		VOLTAGES	Six and twelve
SERVICE BRAKE . . .	Contracting on rear wheels		WIRING SYSTEM . .	Single
EMERGENCY BRAKE .	Expanding on rear wheels		GASOLINE SYSTEM . .	Vacuum
CYLINDERS	Eight		CLUTCH	Cone
ARRANGED	V-type, 90 degrees		TRANSMISSION . . .	Selective sliding
CAST	En bloc		GEAR CHANGES . . .	Three forward, one reverse
HORSEPOWER	28.8 (N. A. C. C. Rating)		DRIVE	Plain bevel
BORE AND STROKE .	3 x 4¼ inches		REAR AXLE	Full floating
			STEERING GEAR . . .	Worm and worm gear

In addition to above specifications, price includes top, top hood, windshield, speedometer, ammeter, voltmeter, clock and demountable rims

LEWIS SPRING
AND AXLE
COMPANY

Price, $985

J A C K S O N
AND CHELSEA
M I C H I G A N

HOLLIER TOURING CAR—168

COLOR	Optional	LUBRICATION	Force feed
SEATING CAPACITY .	Five persons	RADIATOR	Cellular
POSITION OF DRIVER	Left side	COOLING	Thermo-syphon
WHEELBASE	112 inches	IGNITION	Storage battery
GAUGE	56 inches	STARTING SYSTEM . .	Single unit
WHEELS	Wood	STARTER OPERATED .	Chain to crank shaft
FRONT TIRES	33 x 4 inches	LIGHTING SYSTEM . .	Electric
REAR TIRES	33 x 4 inches	VOLTAGES	Six and twelve
SERVICE BRAKE . . .	Contracting on rear wheels	WIRING SYSTEM . . .	Double
EMERGENCY BRAKE .	Expanding on rear wheels	GASOLINE SYSTEM . .	Vacuum
		CLUTCH	Cone
CYLINDERS	Eight	TRANSMISSION . . .	Selective sliding
ARRANGED	V-type, 90 degrees	GEAR CHANGES . . .	Three forward, one reverse
CAST	En bloc	DRIVE	Plain bevel
HORSEPOWER	28.8	REAR AXLE	Full floating
(N. A. C. C. Rating)		STEERING GEAR . . .	Worm and worm gear
BORE AND STROKE .	3 x 4¼ inches		

In addition to above specifications, price includes top, top hood, windshield, speedometer, ammeter, voltmeter, clock and demountable rims

THE WINTON COMPANY

CLEVELAND, OHIO

Price.	$2285
Four-Passenger Touring	2285
Six-Passenger Touring	2435
Seven-Passenger Touring	2335
Runabout	2285
Three-Quarter Limousine . . .	3250
Full Four-Door Limousine . . .	3500
Sedan	3500
Limousine Landaulet.	3500
Coupe	3200

WINTON SIX-33 TOURING CAR

COLOR.	Optional		LUBRICATION	Force feed
SEATING CAPACITY .	Five persons		RADIATOR	Cellular
POSITION OF DRIVER	Left side		COOLING	Water pump
WHEELBASE	128 inches		IGNITION.	High-tension magneto and storage battery
GAUGE	56 inches			
WHEELS	Wood		STARTING SYSTEM . .	Two unit
FRONT TIRES. . . .	36 x 4½ inches		STARTER OPERATED .	Gear to fly wheel
REAR TIRES	36 x 4½ inches, anti-skid		LIGHTING SYSTEM . .	Electric
SERVICE BRAKE. . .	Contracting on rear wheels		VOLTAGES	Six
			WIRING SYSTEM. . .	Single
EMERGENCY BRAKE .	Expanding on rear wheels		GASOLINE SYSTEM. .	Vacuum
			CLUTCH	Dry multiple disc
CYLINDERS	Six		TRANSMISSION . . .	Selective sliding
ARRANGED	Vertically		GEAR CHANGES . . .	Four
CAST	In pairs		DRIVE.	Spiral bevel
HORSEPOWER. . . .	33.75 (N. A. C. C. Rating)		REAR AXLE	Full floating
BORE AND STROKE .	3¾ x 5¼ inches		STEERING GEAR. . .	Worm and gear

In addition to above specifications, price includes top, top hood, windshield, speedometer, ammeter, voltmeter, clock and demountable rims

THE WINTON COMPANY

CLEVELAND, OHIO

Price.	$3500
Four-Passenger Touring	3500
Five-Passenger Touring.	3500
Six-Passenger Touring	3500
Two-Passenger Roadster	3500
Runabout	3500
Three-Quarter Limousine . . .	4500
Full Four-Door Limousine . . .	4750
Sedan	4750
Limousine Landaulet.	4750
Coupe	4500

WINTON SIX-48 TOURING CAR

COLOR.	Optional	LUBRICATION	Force feed
SEATING CAPACITY .	Seven persons	RADIATOR	Cellular
POSITION OF DRIVER	Left side	COOLING	Water pump
WHEELBASE	138 inches	IGNITION	High-tension magneto and storage battery
GAUGE	56 inches		
WHEELS	Wood		
FRONT TIRES	37 x 5 inches	STARTING SYSTEM . .	Two unit
REAR TIRES	37 x 5 inches, anti-skid	STARTER OPERATED .	Gear to fly wheel
		LIGHTING SYSTEM . .	Electric
SERVICE BRAKE. . .	Contracting on rear wheels	VOLTAGES	Six
		WIRING SYSTEM . . .	Single
EMERGENCY BRAKE .	Expanding on rear wheels	GASOLINE SYSTEM . .	Vacuum
		CLUTCH	Dry multiple disc
CYLINDERS	Six	TRANSMISSION . . .	Selective sliding
ARRANGED	Vertically	GEAR CHANGES . . .	Four
CAST	In pairs	DRIVE.	Spiral bevel
HORSEPOWER . . . . (N. A. C. C. Rating)	48.6	REAR AXLE	Full floating
BORE AND STROKE .	4½ x 5½ inches	STEERING GEAR . . .	Worm and gear

In addition to above specifications, price includes top, top hood, windshield, speedometer, ammeter, voltmeter, clock and demountable rims

**A U S T I N
AUTOMOBILE
C O M P A N Y**

GRAND RAPIDS
M I C H I G A N

Price **$2800**
Four-Passenger Roadster . . **2800**
Sedan **3800**
Vestibule-Brougham **4000**

AUSTIN HIGHWAY KING—36-66

COLOR	Body, black; running gear, yellow		RADIATOR	Cellular
			COOLING	Water pump
SEATING CAPACITY .	Six persons		IGNITION	Storage battery
POSITION OF DRIVER	Left side		STARTING SYSTEM . .	Two unit
WHEELBASE	142 inches		STARTER OPERATED .	Gear to fly wheel
GAUGE	56 inches		LIGHTING SYSTEM . .	Electric
WHEELS	Wood or wire		VOLTAGES	Six
FRONT TIRES	34 x 4½ inches		WIRING SYSTEM . . .	Single
REAR TIRES	34 x 4½ inches		GASOLINE SYSTEM . .	Vacuum
SERVICE BRAKE . . .	Contracting on rear wheels		CLUTCH	Multiple disc in oil
EMERGENCY BRAKE .	Expanding on rear wheels		TRANSMISSION . . .	Selective sliding
CYLINDERS	Six		GEAR CHANGES . . .	Six forward, two reverse
ARRANGED	Vertically			
CAST	En bloc		DRIVE	Plain bevel
HORSEPOWER	36.04 (N. A. C. C. Rating)		REAR AXLE	Two-speed, full-floating
BORE AND STROKE .	3⅞ x 5¼ inches		STEERING GEAR . . .	Worm and sector
LUBRICATION	Force feed and splash			

In addition to above specifications, price includes top, top hood, windshield, speedometer, ammeter, clock and demountable rims

THE WHITE
COMPANY

CLEVELAND, OHIO

Price	$2700
Roadster	2650
Town Car	4000
Town Car Landaulet .	4000
Sedan	4000

WHITE TOURING CAR—30

COLOR	White special maroon, White special gray, Cleveland gray, Brewster green or cobalt blue
SEATING CAPACITY .	Five persons
POSITION OF DRIVER	Left side
WHEELBASE	115 inches
GAUGE	56 inches
WHEELS	Wood
FRONT TIRES	32 x 4 inches
REAR TIRES	32 x 4 inches
SERVICE BRAKE . . .	Contracting on rear wheels
EMERGENCY BRAKE .	Expanding on rear wheels
CYLINDERS	Four
ARRANGED	Vertically
CAST	En bloc
HORSEPOWER	22.5
(N. A. C. C. Rating)	

BORE AND STROKE .	$3\frac{3}{4}$ x $5\frac{1}{8}$ inches
LUBRICATION	Force feed and splash
RADIATOR	Honeycomb
COOLING	Water pump
IGNITION	High-tension magneto
STARTING SYSTEM . .	Single unit
STARTER OPERATED .	Chain to fly wheel sprocket
LIGHTING SYSTEM . .	Electric
VOLTAGES	Twenty-one
WIRING SYSTEM . .	Double
GASOLINE SYSTEM . .	Vacuum
CLUTCH	Single plate in oil
TRANSMISSION . . .	Selective sliding
GEAR CHANGES . . .	Four forward, one reverse
DRIVE	Plain bevel
REAR AXLE	Semi-floating
STEERING GEAR . .	Worm and sector

In addition to above specifications, price includes top,
top hood, windshield, speedometer and demountable rims

THE WHITE
COMPANY

CLEVELAND, OHIO

Price	$4000
Seven-Passenger Touring . .	2700
Three-Passenger Roadster .	2650
Sedan	4000
Town Car	4000

WHITE TOWN CAR LANDAULET—30

COLOR	White special maroon, White special gray, Cleveland gray, Brewster green or cobalt blue	BORE AND STROKE . .	$3\frac{3}{4}$ x $5\frac{1}{8}$ inches	
		LUBRICATION	Force feed and splash	
		RADIATOR	Honeycomb	
		COOLING	Water pump	
SEATING CAPACITY .	Six persons	IGNITION	High-tension magneto	
POSITION OF DRIVER	Left side			
WHEELBASE	115 inches	STARTING SYSTEM . .	Single unit	
GAUGE	56 inches	STARTER OPERATED .	Chain to fly wheel sprocket	
WHEELS	Wood	LIGHTING SYSTEM . .	Electric	
FRONT TIRES	32 x 4 inches	VOLTAGES	Twenty-one	
REAR TIRES	32 x 4 inches,	WIRING SYSTEM . . .	Double	
SERVICE BRAKE. . .	Contracting on rear wheels	GASOLINE SYSTEM. .	Vacuum	
		CLUTCH	Single plate in oil	
EMERGENCY BRAKE .	Expanding on rear wheels	TRANSMISSION . . .	Selective sliding	
CYLINDERS	Four	GEAR CHANGES . . .	Four forward, one reverse	
ARRANGED	Vertically			
CAST	En bloc	DRIVE	Plain bevel	
HORSEPOWER	22.5	REAR AXLE	Semi-floating	
(N. A. C. C. Rating)		STEERING GEAR. . .	Worm and sector	

In addition to above specifications, price includes
windshield, speedometer, clock and demountable rims

THE WHITE COMPANY

CLEVELAND, OHIO

Price	$3800
Limousine	5200
Laudaulet Limousine . .	5200
Semi-Touring	5300

WHITE TOURING CAR—45

COLOR	White special maroon, White special gray, Cleveland gray, Brewster green or cobalt blue	BORE AND STROKE .	4¼ x 6⅜ inches
		LUBRICATION	Force feed and splash
		RADIATOR	Honeycomb
		COOLING	Water pump
SEATING CAPACITY .	Seven persons	IGNITION	High-tension magneto
POSITION OF DRIVER	Left side		
WHEELBASE	133¾ inches	STARTING SYSTEM . .	Single unit
GAUGE	56 inches	STARTER OPERATED .	Chain to fly-wheel sprocket
WHEELS	Wood		
FRONT TIRES	36 x 4½ inches	LIGHTING SYSTEM . .	Electric
REAR TIRES	36 x 4½ inches	VOLTAGES	Twenty-one
SERVICE BRAKE . . .	Contracting on rear wheels	WIRING SYSTEM . .	Double
		GASOLINE SYSTEM . .	Vacuum
EMERGENCY BRAKE .	Expanding on rear wheels	CLUTCH	Single plate in oil
CYLINDERS	Four	TRANSMISSION . . .	Selective sliding
ARRANGED	Vertically	GEAR CHANGES . . .	Four forward, one reverse
CAST	En bloc	DRIVE	Plain bevel
HORSEPOWER	28.9 (N. A. C. C. Rating)	REAR AXLE	Semi-floating
		STEERING GEAR . .	Worm and sector

In addition to above specifications, price includes top, top hood, windshield, speedometer, clock and demountable rims

THE WHITE
COMPANY
▓▓▓▓▓▓▓▓▓▓▓▓▓▓▓▓▓▓▓
CLEVELAND, OHIO

Price $5200
Landaulet Limousine . 5200
Semi-touring 5300
Touring 3800

WHITE LIMOUSINE—45

COLOR	White special maroon, White special gray, Cleveland gray, Brewster green or cobalt blue
SEATING CAPACITY .	Seven persons
POSITION OF DRIVER	Left side
WHEELBASE	133¾ inches
GAUGE	56 inches
WHEELS	Wood
FRONT TIRES	36 x 4½ inches
REAR TIRES	36 x 4½ inches
SERVICE BRAKE . . .	Contracting on rear wheels
EMERGENCY BRAKE .	Expanding on rear wheels
CYLINDERS	Four
ARRANGED	Vertically
CAST	En bloc
HORSEPOWER	28.9
(N. A. C. C. Rating)	

BORE AND STROKE . .	4¼ x 6⅜ inches
LUBRICATION	Force feed and splash
RADIATOR	Honeycomb
COOLING	Water pump
IGNITION	High-tension magneto
STARTING SYSTEM . .	Single unit
STARTER OPERATED .	Chain to fly wheel sprocket
LIGHTING SYSTEM . .	Electric
VOLTAGES	Twenty-one
WIRING SYSTEM . . .	Double
GASOLINE SYSTEM . .	Vacuum
CLUTCH	Single plate in oil
TRANSMISSION . . .	Selective sliding
GEAR CHANGES . . .	Four forward, one reverse
DRIVE	Plain bevel
REAR AXLE	Semi-floating
STEERING GEAR . . .	Worm and sector

In addition to above specifications, price includes
windshield, speedometer, clock and demountable rims

A V E R Y
C O M P A N Y

P E O R I A
I L L I N O I S

Price $1095
Five-Passenger Touring . . 1095
Sedan 1295

GLIDE LIGHT SIX-40 TOURING CAR

COLOR	Body, Meteor blue; running-gear, black
SEATING CAPACITY .	Five persons
POSITION OF DRIVER	Left side
WHEELBASE	119 inches
GAUGE	56 inches
WHEELS	Wood
FRONT TIRES	34 x 4 inches
REAR TIRES	34 x 4 inches, anti-skid
SERVICE BRAKE. . .	Contracting on rear wheels
EMERGENCY BRAKE .	Expanding on rear wheels
CYLINDERS	Six
ARRANGED	Vertically
CAST	En bloc
HORSEPOWER	21.6 (N. A. C. C. Rating)
BORE AND STROKE .	3 x 5 inches
LUBRICATION	Splash with circulating pump
RADIATOR	Tubular
COOLING	Water pump
IGNITION	Storage battery
STARTING SYSTEM . .	Two unit
STARTER OPERATED .	Gear to fly wheel
LIGHTING SYSTEM . .	Electric
VOLTAGES	Six
WIRING SYSTEM. . .	Single
GASOLINE SYSTEM . .	Vacuum
CLUTCH	Dry multiple disc
TRANSMISSION . . .	Selective sliding
GEAR CHANGES . . .	Three forward, one reverse
DRIVE	Spiral bevel
REAR AXLE	Three-quarters floating
STEERING GEAR. . .	Screw and nut

In addition to above specifications, price includes top, top hood, windshield, speedometer, ammeter and demountable rims

M U T U A L
M O T O R S
C O M P A N Y

J A C K S O N
M I C H I G A N

Price, $1090

MARION TOURING CAR—K

COLOR	Wine with gold stripe, and black fenders	BORE AND STROKE . .	3 x 5 inches
		LUBRICATION	Force feed and splash
SEATING CAPACITY .	Five persons	RADIATOR	Cellular
POSITION OF DRIVER.	Left side	COOLING	Water pump
WHEELBASE	120 inches	IGNITION	Storage battery
GAUGE	56 inches	STARTING SYSTEM . .	Two unit
WHEELS	Wood	STARTER OPERATED .	Gear to fly wheel
FRONT TIRES	32 x 4 inches	LIGHTING SYSTEM . .	Electric
REAR TIRES	32 x 4 inches, anti-skid	VOLTAGES	Six
		WIRING SYSTEM . . .	Single
SERVICE BRAKE . . .	Contracting on rear wheels	GASOLINE SYSTEM . .	Vacuum
		CLUTCH	Dry multiple disc
EMERGENCY BRAKE .	Expanding on rear wheels	TRANSMISSION . . .	Selective sliding
		GEAR CHANGES . . .	Three forward and reverse
CYLINDERS	Six		
ARRANGED	Vertically	DRIVE	Spiral bevel
CAST	En bloc	REAR AXLE	Three-quarters floating
HORSEPOWER	21.6		
	(N. A. C. C. Rating)	STEERING GEAR . . .	Worm and sector

In addition to above specifications, price includes top, top
hood, windshield, speedometer, ammeter and demountable rims

**P E E R L E S S
M O T O R C A R
C O M P A N Y**

CLEVELAND, OHIO

Price $1890
Three-Passenger Roadster. . 1890
Seven-Passenger Limousine . 3060

PEERLESS TOURING—56

COLOR	Green	LUBRICATION	Full-force feed
SEATING CAPACITY .	Seven persons	RADIATOR	Tubular
POSITION OF DRIVER	Left side	COOLING	Water pump
WHEELBASE	125 inches	IGNITION	Storage battery and dry cells
GAUGE	56 inches		
WHEELS	Wood	STARTING SYSTEM . .	Two unit
FRONT TIRES	35 x 4½ inches	STARTER OPERATED .	Gear to fly wheel
REAR TIRES	35 x 4½ inches, anti-skid	LIGHTING SYSTEM . .	Electric
		VOLTAGES	Seven
SERVICE BRAKE . . .	Contracting on rear wheels	WIRING SYSTEM. . .	Single
		GASOLINE SYSTEM . .	Vacuum
EMERGENCY BRAKE .	Expanding on rear wheels	CLUTCH	Dry multiple disc
		TRANSMISSION . . .	Selective sliding
CYLINDERS	Eight	GEAR CHANGES . . .	Three forward, one reverse
ARRANGED	V-type, 90 degrees		
CAST	In fours	DRIVE	Spiral bevel
HORSEPOWER	33.8 (N. A. C. C. Rating)	REAR AXLE	Three-quarters floating
BORE AND STROKE .	3¼ x 5 inches	STEERING GEAR . . .	Worm and sector

In addition to above specifications, price includes top, top hood,
windshield, speedometer, ammeter, voltmeter and demountable rims

H U D S O N
M O T O R C A R
C O M P A N Y

D E T R O I T
M I C H I G A N

Price. $1375

HUDSON SUPER-SIX PHAETON

COLOR	Blue	RADIATOR	Cellular
SEATING CAPACITY .	Seven persons	COOLING	Water pump
POSITION OF DRIVER	Left side	IGNITION	Storage battery and generator
WHEELBASE	125½ inches		
GAUGE	56 inches	STARTING SYSTEM . .	Single unit
WHEELS	Wood	STARTER OPERATED .	Gear to fly wheel
FRONT TIRES	35 x 4½ inches		
REAR TIRES	35 x 4½ inches, anti-skid	LIGHTING SYSTEM . .	Electric
		VOLTAGES	Six
SERVICE BRAKE. . .	Contracting on rear wheels	WIRING SYSTEM . .	Single
		GASOLINE SYSTEM. .	Vacuum
EMERGENCY BRAKE .	Expanding on rear wheels	CLUTCH	Multiple disc in oil
CYLINDERS	Six		
ARRANGED	Vertically	TRANSMISSION . . .	Selective sliding
CAST	En bloc	GEAR CHANGES . . .	Three forward, one reverse
HORSEPOWER. . . .	29.4		
(N. A. C. C. Rating)		DRIVE	Spiral bevel
BORE AND STROKE .	3¼ x 5 inches	REAR AXLE	Live
LUBRICATION	Splash with circulating pump	STEERING GEAR . .	Worm and worm wheel

In addition to above specifications, price includes top, top
hood, windshield, speedometer, ammeter and demountable rims

H U D S O N
M O T O R   C A R
C O M P A N Y

D E T R O I T
M I C H I G A N

Price,   **$1900**

HUDSON SUPER-SIX TOURING SEDAN

COLOR	Blue	RADIATOR	Cellular
SEATING CAPACITY	Seven persons	COOLING	Water pump
POSITION OF DRIVER	Left side	IGNITION	Storage battery and generator
WHEELBASE	125½ inches		
GAUGE	56 inches	STARTING SYSTEM	Single unit
WHEELS	Wood	STARTER OPERATED	Gear to fly wheel
FRONT TIRES	35 x 4½ inches		
REAR TIRES	35 x 4½ inches, anti-skid	LIGHTING SYSTEM	Electric
		VOLTAGES	Six
SERVICE BRAKE	Contracting on rear wheels	WIRING SYSTEM	Single
		GASOLINE SYSTEM	Vacuum
EMERGENCY BRAKE	Expanding on rear wheels	CLUTCH	Multiple disc in oil
CYLINDERS	Six		
ARRANGED	Vertically	TRANSMISSION	Selective sliding
CAST	En bloc	GEAR CHANGES	Three forward, one reverse
HORSEPOWER	29.4		
(N. A. C. C. Rating)		DRIVE	Spiral bevel
BORE AND STROKE	3½ x 5 inches	REAR AXLE	Live
LUBRICATION	Splash with circulating pump	STEERING GEAR	Worm and worm wheel

In addition to above specifications, price includes
windshield, speedometer, ammeter and demountable rims

**H U D S O N
M O T O R C A R
C O M P A N Y**

**D E T R O I T
M I C H I G A N**

Price, . . . $1675
Roadster . 1375

HUDSON SUPER-SIX CABRIOLET

COLOR	Blue
SEATING CAPACITY .	Three persons
POSITION OF DRIVER	Left side
WHEELBASE	125½ inches
GAUGE	56 inches
WHEELS	Wood
FRONT TIRES	35 x 4½ inches
REAR TIRES	35 x 4½ inches, anti-skid
SERVICE BRAKE . . .	Contracting on rear wheels
EMERGENCY BRAKE .	Expanding on rear wheels
CYLINDERS	Six
ARRANGED	Vertically
CAST	En bloc
HORSEPOWER	29.4
(N. A. C. C. Rating)	
BORE AND STROKE .	3½ x 5 inches
LUBRICATION	Splash with circulating pump

RADIATOR	Cellular
COOLING	Water pump
IGNITION	Storage battery and generator
STARTING SYSTEM . .	Single unit
STARTER OPERATED .	Gear to fly wheel
LIGHTING SYSTEM . .	Electric
VOLTAGES	Six
WIRING SYSTEM . .	Single
GASOLINE SYSTEM . .	Vacuum
CLUTCH	Multiple disc in oil
TRANSMISSION . . .	Selective sliding
GEAR CHANGES . . .	Three forward, one reverse
DRIVE	Spiral bevel
REAR AXLE	Live
STEERING GEAR . .	Worm and worm wheel

In addition to above specifications, price includes top, top hood,
windshield, speedometer, ammeter and demountable rims

HUDSON
MOTOR CAR
COMPANY

DETROIT
MICHIGAN

Price $2500
Town Car . . 2500

HUDSON SUPER-SIX LIMOUSINE

COLOR	Blue
SEATING CAPACITY .	Seven persons
POSITION OF DRIVER	Left side
WHEELBASE	125½ inches
GAUGE	56 inches
WHEELS	Wood
FRONT TIRES	35 x 4½ inches
REAR TIRES	35 x 4½ inches, anti-skid
SERVICE BRAKE . . .	Contracting on rear wheels
EMERGENCY BRAKE .	Expanding on rear wheels
CYLINDERS	Six
ARRANGED	Vertically
CAST	En bloc
HORSEPOWER	29.4 (N. A. C. C. Rating)
BORE AND STROKE .	3½ x 5 inches
LUBRICATION	Splash with circulating pump
RADIATOR	Cellular
COOLING	Water pump
IGNITION	Storage battery and generator
STARTING SYSTEM . .	Single unit
STARTER OPERATED .	Gear to fly wheel
LIGHTING SYSTEM . .	Electric
VOLTAGES	Six
WIRING SYSTEM . .	Single
GASOLINE SYSTEM . .	Vacuum
CLUTCH	Multiple disc in oil
TRANSMISSION . . .	Selective sliding
GEAR CHANGES . . .	Three forward, one reverse
DRIVE	Spiral bevel
REAR AXLE	Live
STEERING GEAR . .	Worm and worm wheel

In addition to above specifications, price includes windshield, speedometer, ammeter and demountable rims

KLINE MOTOR CAR CORP.

RICHMOND VIRGINIA

Price, $1095

KLINE-KAR TOURING CAR—6-36

Color	Body, dark green; running gear, black; wheels, red or green	Bore and Stroke .	3¼ x 4½ inches
		Lubrication	Force feed and splash
Seating Capacity .	Five persons	Radiator	Cellular
Position of Driver	Left side	Cooling	Water pump
Wheelbase	120 inches	Ignition	Storage battery
Gauge	56 inches	Starting System .	Two unit
Wheels	Wood	Starter Operated .	Gear to fly wheel
Front Tires	34 x 4 inches	Lighting System . .	Electric
Rear Tires	34 x 4 inches, anti-skid	Voltages	Six
		Wiring System . .	Single
Service Brake . . .	Contracting on rear wheels	Gasoline System . .	Vacuum
		Clutch	Dry multiple disc
Emergency Brake .	Expanding on rear wheels	Transmission . . .	Selective sliding
		Gear Changes . . .	Three forward, one reverse
Cylinders	Six		
Arranged . . .	Vertically	Drive	Spiral bevel
Cast . . -.	En bloc	Rear Axle	Three-quarters floating
Horsepower	25.35 (N. A. C. C. Rating)	Steering Gear . . .	Worm and nut

In addition to above specifications, price includes top, top hood,
windshield, speedometer, ammeter and demountable rims

DORT MOTOR
CAR COMPANY

Price, $650

F L I N T
M I C H I G A N

DORT TOURING CAR—5

COLOR	Dark green and black		LUBRICATION	Splash with circulating pump
SEATING CAPACITY .	Five persons		RADIATOR	Tubular
POSITION OF DRIVER	Left side		COOLING	Thermo-syphon
WHEELBASE	105 inches		IGNITION	Storage battery
GAUGE	56 inches		STARTING SYSTEM . .	Two unit
WHEELS	Wood		STARTER OPERATED .	Gear to fly wheel
FRONT TIRES	30 x 3½ inches		LIGHTING SYSTEM . .	Electric
REAR TIRES	30 x 3½ inches, anti-skid		VOLTAGES	Six
			WIRING SYSTEM . . .	Single
SERVICE BRAKE . . .	Contracting on rear wheels		GASOLINE SYSTEM . .	Gravity
			CLUTCH	Cone
EMERGENCY BRAKE .	Expanding on rear wheels		TRANSMISSION . . .	Selective sliding
			GEAR CHANGES . . .	Three forward, one reverse
CYLINDERS	Four			
ARRANGED	Vertically		DRIVE	Plain bevel
CAST	En bloc		REAR AXLE	Three-quarters floating
HORSEPOWER	16.9 (N. A. C. C. Rating)		STEERING GEAR . .	Worm and nut
BORE AND STROKE .	3¼ x 5 inches			

In addition to above specifications, price includes top,
top hood, windshield, speedometer and demountable rims

Price, $445

ARGO MOTOR
COMPANY, Inc.
**JACKSON
MICHIGAN**

ARGO ROADSTER

COLOR	Body, Brewster green; wheels, black
SEATING CAPACITY .	Two persons
POSITION OF DRIVER	Left side
WHEELBASE	96 inches
GAUGE	56 inches
WHEELS	Wood
FRONT TIRES	30 x 3 inches
REAR TIRES	30 x 3 inches
SERVICE BRAKE . . .	Contracting on rear wheels
EMERGENCY BRAKE .	Contracting on transmission
CYLINDERS	Four
ARRANGED	Vertically
CAST	En bloc
HORSEPOWER	15.63
(N. A. C. C. Rating)	
BORE AND STROKE .	3⅛ x 4 inches

LUBRICATION	Splash with circulating pump
RADIATOR	Cellular
COOLING	Thermo-syphon
IGNITION	Storage battery
STARTING SYSTEM . .	Single unit
STARTER OPERATED .	Chain to crank shaft
LIGHTING SYSTEM . .	Electric
VOLTAGES	Twelve
WIRING SYSTEM . . .	Single
GASOLINE SYSTEM . .	Gravity
CLUTCH	Cone
TRANSMISSION . . .	Progressive sliding
GEAR CHANGES . . .	Two forward, one reverse
DRIVE	Plain bevel
REAR AXLE	Semi-floating
STEERING GEAR . .	Worm

In addition to above specifications, price
includes top, top hood and windshield

G R A N T
M O T O R
C O M P A N Y

FINDLAY, OHIO

Price. $795
Three-Passenger Roadster . . . 795
Three-Passenger Cabriolet . . . 1025

GRANT TOURING CAR—V

COLOR	Body, Brewster green; running gear, black		BORE AND STROKE .	3 x 4¼ inches
			LUBRICATION	Splash with circulating pump
SEATING CAPACITY .	Five persons		RADIATOR	Tubular
POSITION OF DRIVER	Left side		COOLING	Thermo-syphon
WHEELBASE	112 inches		IGNITION	Storage battery
GAUGE	56 inches		STARTING SYSTEM . .	Single unit
WHEELS	Wood		STARTER OPERATED .	Chain to crank shaft
FRONT TIRES	32 x 3½ inches		LIGHTING SYSTEM . .	Electric
REAR TIRES	32 x 3½ inches, anti-skid		VOLTAGES	Six
SERVICE BRAKE . . .	Contracting on rear wheels		WIRING SYSTEM . .	Single
			GASOLINE SYSTEM . .	Gravity
EMERGENCY BRAKE .	Expanding on rear wheels		CLUTCH	Cone
			TRANSMISSION . . .	Selective sliding
CYLINDERS	Six		GEAR CHANGES . . .	Three forward, one reverse
ARRANGED	Vertically		DRIVE	Plain bevel
CAST	En bloc		REAR AXLE	Full floating
HORSEPOWER	21.6		STEERING GEAR . . .	Worm
(N. A. C. C. Rating)				

In addition to above specifications, price includes top, top hood, windshield, speedometer, ammeter, voltmeter, and demountable rims

**B R I G G S -
D E T R O I T E R
C O M P A N Y**

D E T R O I T
M I C H I G A N

Price $985
Five-Passenger Sedan . 1150

DETROITER TOURING CAR—F

COLOR	Body, Kimball green; running gear, black
SEATING CAPACITY .	Five persons
POSITION OF DRIVER	Left side
WHEELBASE	112 inches
GAUGE	56 inches
WHEELS	Wood
FRONT TIRES	33 x 4 inches
REAR TIRES	33 x 4 inches, anti-skid
SERVICE BRAKE . . .	Contracting on rear wheels
EMERGENCY BRAKE .	Expanding on rear wheels
CYLINDERS	Four
ARRANGED	Vertically
CAST	En bloc
HORSEPOWER	22.5
(N. A. C. C. Rating)	
BORE AND STROKE .	3¾ x 4¼ inches

LUBRICATION	Splash with circulating pump
RADIATOR	Tubular
COOLING	Thermo-syphon
IGNITION	High-tension magneto
STARTING SYSTEM . .	Single unit
STARTER OPERATED .	Chain to crankshaft
LIGHTING SYSTEM . .	Electric
VOLTAGES	Twelve
WIRING SYSTEM . .	Single
GASOLINE SYSTEM . .	Gravity
CLUTCH	Multiple disc in oil
TRANSMISSION . . .	Selective sliding
GEAR CHANGES . . .	Three forward, one reverse
DRIVE	Spiral bevel
REAR AXLE	Full floating
STEERING GEAR . .	Worm and sector

In addition to above specifications, price includes top,
top hood, windshield, speedometer and demountable rims

ILLUSTRATIONS AND
SPECIFICATIONS
ELECTRIC
VEHICLES

ANDERSON
ELECTRIC CAR
COMPANY

DETROIT
MICHIGAN

Price	$2175
Three-Passenger Cabriolet . .	2075
Five-Passenger Duplex Drive . .	2275
Five-Passenger Forward Drive .	2250
Five-Passenger Rear Drive . . .	2225
Four-Passenger Rear Drive . .	1975

DETROIT ELECTRIC BROUGHAM—57

COLOR	Blue, green or maroon		BRAKE SYSTEMS . . .	Expanding on rear wheels; also magnetic controller brake
SEATING CAPACITY .	Four persons			
BODY:				
LENGTH ALL OVER	142 inches		BATTERY	42 cells, 15 plate
WIDTH ALL OVER .	67 inches			
WHEELBASE	100 inches		SPEED	21 miles per hour
GAUGE	56 inches		NO. FORWARD SPEEDS	Five
WHEELS	Optional		NO. REVERSE SPEEDS	Five
FRONT TIRES	34 x 4 inches, pneumatic		CONTROL	Lever operated
REAR TIRES	36 x 4½ inches, anti-skid cushion		STEERING	Lever

**OHIO ELECTRIC
CAR COMPANY**

TOLEDO, OHIO

Price	$3250
Single-Drive Brougham .	2900
Single-Drive Coupe . . .	2400
Roadster	2650

OHIO ELECTRIC BROUGHAM—62

COLOR	Coach blue	BRAKE SYSTEMS . .	Double contracting on rear wheels with magnetic brake on motor
SEATING CAPACITY .	Five persons		
BODY:			
LENGTH ALL OVER	147½ inches		
WIDTH ALL OVER	65 inches	BATTERY	40 cells, 13 plate
WHEELBASE	103 inches	SPEED	Twenty-eight miles per hour
GAUGE	56 inches		
WHEELS	Optional		
FRONT TIRES	34 x 4½ inches, pneumatic, or 36 x 4½ inches cushion	NO. FORWARD SPEEDS	Five
		NO. REVERSE SPEEDS	Three
REAR TIRES	34 x 4½ inches, pneumatic, or 36 x 4½ inches, cushion	CONTROL	Magnetic
		STEERING	Lever

**WOODS MOTOR
V E H I C L E
C O M P A N Y**

**C H I C A G O
I L L I N O I S**

Price, $2850

WOODS ELECTRIC—16-1522

COLOR	Optional		BRAKE SYSTEMS . . .	Contracting on armature shaft and expanding on rear wheels
SEATING CAPACITY .	Four persons			
BODY:				
LENGTH ALL OVER	119⅞ inches		BATTERY	42 cells, 13 plate
WIDTH ALL OVER .	60⅜ inches			
WHEELBASE	100 inches		SPEED	25 miles per hour
GAUGE	56 inches			
WHEELS	Wood		NO. FORWARD SPEEDS	Five
FRONT TIRES	34 x 4 inches, cushion or pneumatic		NO. REVERSE SPEEDS	Five
REAR TIRES	38 x 4½ inches, cushion or pneumatic		CONTROL	Lever operator
			STEERING	Lever

THE BAKER
R. & L. CO.

Price. $3000

CLEVELAND, OHIO

RAUCH & LANG COACH—J-6

COLOR	Optional	REAR TIRES	33 x 4½ inches; or 36 x 4½ inches, cushion
SEATING CAPACITY	Five persons		
BODY:		BRAKE SYSTEMS	Contracting on motor and expanding on rear wheels; also electric brake
LENGTH ALL OVER	144 inches		
WIDTH ALL OVER	64 inches		
WHEELBASE	100 inches	BATTERY	42 cells, 11 plate
GAUGE	56 inches	SPEED	26 miles per hour
WHEELS	Optional	NO. FORWARD SPEEDS	Six
		NO. REVERSE SPEEDS	Three
FRONT TIRES	34 x 4½ inches; or 36 x 4½ inches, cushion	CONTROL	Dual lever
		STEERING	Lever

**THE BAKER
R. & L. CO.**

CLEVELAND, OHIO

BAKER COUPE D. A.—6

COLOR . . . . Optional

SEATING CAPACITY . Four persons

BODY:

    LENGTH ALL OVER   126 inches

    WIDTH ALL OVER .   66½ inches

WHEELBASE . . . . 90 inches

GAUGE . . . . . . 56 inches

WHEELS . . . . . . Optional

FRONT TIRES . . . . 32 x 4 inches,
                 pneumatic

REAR TIRES . . . . 34 x 4 inches,
                 cushion

BRAKE SYSTEMS . . Internal expand-
                 ing on rear wheels

BATTERY . . . . . . 36 cells, 11 plate

SPEED . . . . 23 miles per hour

NO. FORWARD SPEEDS Seven

NO. REVERSE SPEEDS Three

CONTROL . . . . . Lever operated

STEERING . . . . . Optional

**THE WAVERLEY
C O M P A N Y**

**INDIANAPOLIS
I N D I A N A**

Price $2150
Four-Chair Brougham . . 2200

WAVERLEY ELECTRIC—110

COLOR	Black	
SEATING CAPACITY .	Four persons	
BODY:		
LENGTH ALL OVER	124 inches	
WIDTH ALL OVER .	56 inches	
WHEELBASE	95 inches	
GAUGE	56 inches	
WHEELS	Wood	
FRONT TIRES	32 x 4 inches, pneumatic or cushion	

REAR TIRES	32 x 4 inches, pneumatic or cushion
BRAKE SYSTEMS . . .	Hub brakes
BATTERY	42 cells, 11 plate
SPEED	20 miles per hour
No. FORWARD SPEEDS	Four
No. REVERSE SPEEDS	Two
CONTROL	Lever operated
STEERING	Lever

G E N E R A L
V E H I C L E
COMPANY, INC.

Price, Chassis, $2600

LONG ISLAND CITY
N E W   Y O R K

G. V. ELECTRIC TWO-TON TRUCK

COLOR	Lead
CARRYING CAPACITY .	4000 pounds
BODY:	
LENGTH ALL OVER	120 inches
WIDTH ALL OVER .	56 inches
WHEELBASE	111 inches
GAUGE	61 inches
WHEELS	Wood
FRONT TIRES	36 x 4 inches, single solid
REAR TIRES	36 x 3 inches, dual solid

BRAKE SYSTEMS . .	Expanding on rear wheels and contracting on countershaft
BATTERY	44 cells, 17 plate
SPEED	9 miles per hour
No. FORWARD SPEEDS	Five
No. REVERSE SPEEDS	Two
CONTROL	Lever operated
STEERING	Wheel

M I L B U R N
W A G O N
C O M P A N Y

TOLEDO, OHIO

Price $1485
Roadster . . 1285

MILBURN LIGHT ELECTRIC COUPE—15

Color	Blue	
Seating Capacity .	Four persons	
Wheelbase	100 inches	
Gauge	50 inches	
Wheels	Wood	
Front Tires	30 x 3½ inches, pneumatic	
Rear Tires	30 x 3½ inches, pneumatic	

Brake Systems . .	Contracting and expanding on rear wheels
Battery	22 cells, 15 plate
Speed	20 miles per hour
No. Forward Speeds	Four
No. Reverse Speeds	Two
Control	Lever
Steering	Lever

**ARGO ELECTRIC
V E H I C L E
C O M P A N Y**

**S A G I N A W
M I C H I G A N**

Price, Chassis, $1200

AMERICAN-ARGO—K-10

COLOR	Optional		BRAKE SYSTEMS . .	Double expanding on rear wheels
CARRYING CAPACITY .	1000 pounds			
BODY:			BATTERY	40 cells, 11 plate
LENGTH ALL OVER	129½ inches			
WIDTH ALL OVER .	68 inches		SPEED	16 miles per hour
WHEELBASE	86 inches		NO. FORWARD SPEEDS	Four
GAUGE	54 inches			
TIRE DIMENSIONS:			NO. REVERSE SPEEDS	Two
FRONT	34 x 3 inches (cushion or solid)		CONTROL	Lever operated
REAR	34 x 3 inches (cushion or solid)		STEERING	Wheel

**B O R L A N D -
G R A N N I S
C O M P A N Y**

S A G I N A W
M I C H I G A N

Price $2550
Roadster . . 2250
Limousine 5500

AMERICAN-BORLAND—50

COLOR	Optional	BRAKE SYSTEMS . . .	Internal expanding on rear wheels
SEATING CAPACITY .	Four persons		
BODY:		BATTERY	40 cells, 11 plate
LENGTH ALL OVER	120¾ inches		
WIDTH ALL OVER .	67½ inches	SPEED	22 miles per hour
WHEELBASE	96 inches		
GAUGE	56 inches	NO. FORWARD SPEEDS	Six
TIRE DIMENSIONS:		NO. REVERSE SPEEDS	Three
FRONT	34 x 4 inches (pneumatic or cushion)	CONTROL	Lever operated
REAR	34 x 4 inches (pneumatic or cushion)	STEERING	Lever

AMERICAN ELECTRIC CAR COMPANY
SAGINAW MICHIGAN

Price $3200
Model 33 Rear-Drive Brougham . 3100
Model 34 Rear-Drive Brougham . 3150

AMERICAN-BROC DOUBLE-DRIVE BROUGHAM—36

COLOR	Optional
SEATING CAPACITY .	Five persons
BODY:	
LENGTH ALL OVER	123 inches
WIDTH ALL OVER .	68 inches
WHEELBASE	96 inches
GAUGE	56 inches
TIRE DIMENSIONS:	
FRONT	34 x 4 inches (pneumatic), or 36 x 4 inches (cushion)
REAR	34 x 4 inches (pneumatic), or 36 x 4 inches (cushion)

BRAKE SYSTEMS . .	Contracting on drive shaft and expanding on rear wheels
BATTERY	40 cells, 11 plate
SPEED	24 miles per hour
NO. FORWARD SPEEDS	Five
NO. REVERSE SPEEDS	Five
CONTROL	Lever operated
STEERING	Lever

AMERICAN
ELECTRIC CAR
COMPANY
SAGINAW
MICHIGAN

AMERICAN-BROC DOUBLE DRIVE BROUGHAM

ILLUSTRATIONS AND
SPECIFICATIONS
GASOLINE
COMMERCIAL
VEHICLES

**G E N E R A L
M O T O R S
T R U C K   C O.**

P O N T I A C
M I C H I G A N

Price, $1205

G. M. C. 1500-POUND TRUCK—15

COLOR	G. M. C. gray, Brewster green, or dark red	HORSEPOWER . . . . (N. A. C. C. Rating)	19.6
CARRYING CAPACITY .	1500 pounds	BORE AND STROKE .	3½ x 5 inches
POSITION OF DRIVER	Left side	LUBRICATION	Force feed and splash
WHEELBASE	122 inches	RADIATOR	Tubular
GAUGE	56 inches	COOLING	Water pump
WHEELS	Wood	IGNITION	High-tension magneto
FRONT TIRES	35 x 5 inches, pneumatic	GASOLINE SYSTEM . .	Gravity
REAR TIRES	35 x 5 inches, pneumatic	CLUTCH	Cone
		TRANSMISSION . . .	Selective sliding
SERVICE BRAKE . . .	Contracting on rear wheels	GEAR CHANGES . . .	Three forward, one reverse
EMERGENCY BRAKE .	Expanding on rear wheels	DRIVE	Plain bevel
CYLINDERS	Four	REAR AXLE	Three-quarters floating
ARRANGED	Vertically		
CAST	En bloc	STEERING GEAR . . .	Screw and nut

In addition to above specifications,
price includes body and canopy top

**GENERAL
VEHICLE
COMPANY, INC.**

**LONG ISLAND CITY
NEW YORK**

G. V. MERCEDES FIVE- TO SIX-TON TRUCK—FV

COLOR	Lead		CAST	In pairs
CARRYING CAPACITY .	Six tons		HORSEPOWER	28.9
POSITION OF DRIVER	Right side			(N. A. C. C. Rating)
WHEELBASE	169 inches		BORE AND STROKE . .	4¼ x 5⁹⁄₁₀ inches
GAUGE	61 inches		LUBRICATION	Force feed
WHEELS	Cast steel		RADIATOR	Cellular
FRONT TIRES	34 x 5 inches, single solid		COOLING	Water pump
			IGNITION	High-tension magneto
REAR TIRES	40 x 6 inches, dual solid		GASOLINE SYSTEM . .	Pressure
SERVICE BRAKE . . .	Contracting on transmission		CLUTCH	Cone
			TRANSMISSION . . .	Selective sliding
EMERGENCY BRAKE .	Contracting on rear wheels		GEAR CHANGES . . .	Four forward, one reverse
			DRIVE	Internal gear
CYLINDERS	Four		REAR AXLE	Dead
ARRANGED	Vertically		STEERING GEAR . . .	Screw and nut

**VELIE MOTOR
V E H I C L E
C O M P A N Y**
M O L I N E
I L L I N O I S

Price, Chassis . . $3350

VELIE THREE-AND-ONE-HALF-TON TRUCK—26

COLOR	Optional
CARRYING CAPACITY .	7000 pounds
POSITION OF DRIVER	Right side
WHEELBASE	172 inches
GAUGE	Front, 58 inches; rear, 66 inches
WHEELS	Wood
FRONT TIRES	36 x 5 inches solid
REAR TIRES	40 x 5 inches dual solid
SERVICE BRAKE . . .	External on rear axle
EMERGENCY BRAKE .	Internal on rear axle
CYLINDERS	Four
ARRANGED	Vertically
CAST	In pairs

HORSEPOWER	32.4 (N. A. C. C. Rating)
BORE AND STROKE . .	4½ x 5½ inches
LUBRICATION	Force feed and splash
RADIATOR	Tubular
COOLING	Water pump
IGNITION	High tension
GASOLINE SYSTEM . .	Vacuum
CLUTCH	Dry multiple disc
TRANSMISSION . . .	Selective sliding
GEAR CHANGES . . .	Four forward, one reverse
DRIVE	Worm
REAR AXLE	Full floating
STEERING GEAR . . .	Worm and gear

In addition to above specifications, price includes top, seat, prestolite tank and lamps

**STERLING
MOTOR TRUCK
COMPANY**

**WEST ALLIS
WISCONSIN**

Price	$895
Flare Board Express, with Top	1005
Flare Board Express, with Storm Curtains	1020
Full Panel Body	1030

STERLING 1500-POUND TRUCK

COLOR	Optional	HORSEPOWER	15.63	
CARRYING CAPACITY .	1500 pounds		(N. A. C. C. Rating)	
POSITION OF DRIVER .	Behind motor	BORE AND STROKE . .	3⅛ x 4½ inches	
WHEELBASE . . .	127 inches	LUBRICATION	Pump over and	
GAUGE	56 inches		splash	
WHEELS	Wood	RADIATOR	Tubular	
FRONT TIRES	34 x 4 inches, pneumatic	COOLING	Thermo-syphon	
REAR TIRES	34 x 4 inches, anti-skid, pneumatic	IGNITION	High tension magneto and storage battery	
SERVICE BRAKE . . .	Expanding on rear wheels	GASOLINE SYSTEM . .	Gravity	
		CLUTCH	Dry multiple disc	
EMERGENCY BRAKE .	Expanding on rear wheels	TRANSMISSION . . .	Selective sliding	
CYLINDERS	Four	GEAR CHANGES . . .	Three forward	
ARRANGED	Vertically	DRIVE	Worm	
CAST	En bloc	REAR AXLE	Semi-floating	
		STEERING GEAR . .	Worm and nut	

In addition to above specifications, price includes windshield and hubometer

PIERCE-ARROW
M O T O R C A R
C O M P A N Y

B U F F A L O
N E W Y O R K

Price, Chassis . . $3000

PIERCE-ARROW TWO-TON TRUCK—X-2

COLOR . . . . . . Optional

CARRYING CAPACITY . Two tons

POSITION OF DRIVER . Right side

WHEELBASE . . . . 150 or 180 inches

GAUGE . . . . . . 56 inches

WHEELS . . . . . . Wood

FRONT TIRES . . . . 36 x 4 inches, single solid

REAR TIRES . . . . 36 x 4 inches, dual solid

SERVICE BRAKE . . . Contracting on transmission

EMERGENCY BRAKE . Expanding on rear wheels

CYLINDERS . . . . . Four

ARRANGED . . . . . Vertically

CAST . . . . . . In pairs

HORSEPOWER . . . 25.6
(N. A. C. C. Rating)

BORE AND STROKE . 4 x 5½ inches

LUBRICATION . . . . Force feed

RADIATOR . . . . . Tubular

COOLING . . . . . . Water

IGNITION . . . . . . High tension magneto

GASOLINE SYSTEM . . Gravity

CLUTCH . . . . . . Cone

TRANSMISSION . . . Selective sliding

GEAR CHANGES . . . Three forward, one reverse

DRIVE . . . . Worm

REAR AXLE . . . . Full floating

STEERING GEAR . . Screw and nut

PIERCE-ARROW
MOTOR CAR
COMPANY

B U F F A L O
N E W   Y O R K

Price, Chassis . . $4500

PIERCE-ARROW FIVE-TON TRUCK—R-5

COLOR	Optional
CARRYING CAPACITY .	Five tons
POSITION OF DRIVER .	Right side
WHEELBASE	168 or 204 inches
GAUGE	64 inches
WHEELS	Wood
FRONT TIRES	36 x 5 inches, single solid
REAR TIRES	40 x 6 inches, dual solid
SERVICE BRAKE . . .	Contracting on transmission
EMERGENCY BRAKE .	Expanding on rear wheels
CYLINDERS	Four
ARRANGED	Vertically
CAST	In pairs

HORSEPOWER	38.03 (N. A. C. C. Rating)
BORE AND STROKE .	4⅞ x 6 inches
LUBRICATION	Force feed
RADIATOR	Tubular
COOLING	Water
IGNITION	High tension magneto and dry batteries
GASOLINE SYSTEM . .	Gravity
CLUTCH	Cone
TRANSMISSION . . .	Selective sliding
GEAR CHANGES . . .	Three forward, one reverse
DRIVE	Worm
REAR AXLE	Full floating
STEERING GEAR . .	Screw and nut

**THE AUTOCAR
COMPANY**

**ARDMORE
PENNSYLVANIA**

Price, Chassis. $1650
With Coal or Contractor Body
  with Power Hoist Attach-
  ment   2150
With Open Body.   1800
With Express Body   1875

AUTOCAR TWO-TON TRUCK—XXI-F

COLOR	Optional
CARRYING CAPACITY.	4000 pounds
POSITION OF DRIVER.	Right side over motor
WHEELBASE. . . .	97 inches
GAUGE	58 inches
WHEELS	Wood
FRONT TIRES	34 x 4 inches, solid, or 36 x 5 inches, pneumatic
REAR TIRES	34 x 5 inches, solid, or 36 x 5 inches, pneumatic
SERVICE BRAKE. . .	Contracting on rear wheels
EMERGENCY BRAKE .	Expanding on rear wheels
CYLINDERS	Two
ARRANGED	Horizontally

CAST	Separately
HORSEPOWER	18 (N. A. C. C. Rating)
BORE AND STROKE. .	4¾ x 4½ inches
LUBRICATION	Full splash
RADIATOR	Tubular
COOLING	Water
IGNITION	High-tension magneto
GASOLINE SYSTEM. .	Gravity
CLUTCH	Three plate
TRANSMISSION . . .	Progressive sliding
GEAR CHANGES . . .	Three forward, one reverse
DRIVE	Shaft
REAR AXLE	Full floating
STEERING GEAR. . .	Bevel pinion and sector

FEDERAL
MOTOR TRUCK
COMPANY

DETROIT
MICHIGAN

Price, Chassis . . $1800

FEDERAL ONE-AND-ONE-HALF-TON TRUCK

COLOR	Lead	HORSEPOWER	27.23
CARRYING CAPACITY .	3000 pounds		(N. A. C. C. Rating)
POSITION OF DRIVER .	Left side	BORE AND STROKE .	4⅛ x 5¼ inches
WHEELBASE	120 or 144 inches	LUBRICATION	Splash with circulating pump
GAUGE	Front, 56 inches; rear, 58¼ inches	RADIATOR	Cellular
WHEELS	Wood	COOLING	Water pump
FRONT TIRES	36 x 3½ inches	IGNITION	High-tension magneto
REAR TIRES	36 x 5 inches	GASOLINE SYSTEM . .	Gravity
SERVICE BRAKE . . .	Expanding on rear wheels	CLUTCH	Cone
EMERGENCY BRAKE .	Expanding on rear wheels	TRANSMISSION . . .	Selective sliding
CYLINDERS	Four	GEAR CHANGES . . .	Three forward, one reverse
ARRANGED	Vertically	DRIVE	Worm
CAST	En bloc	REAR AXLE	Full floating
		STEERING GEAR . .	Worm and wheel

Price, Chassis . . $2800

**FEDERAL
MOTOR TRUCK
COMPANY**

**DETROIT
MICHIGAN**

FEDERAL THREE-AND-ONE-HALF-TON TRUCK—L

COLOR	Lead	HORSEPOWER . . . . 32.4 (N. A. C. C. Rating)	
CARRYING CAPACITY .	7000 pounds	BORE AND STROKE .	4½ x 5½ inches
POSITION OF DRIVER	Right side	LUBRICATION	Splash with circulating pump
WHEELBASE	146 inches		
GAUGE	Front, 66½ inches; rear, 67¾ inches	RADIATOR	Cellular
		COOLING	Water pump
WHEELS	Wood	IGNITION	High-tension magneto
FRONT TIRES	36 x 5 inches, single solid		
REAR TIRES	36 x 5 inches, dual solid	GASOLINE SYSTEM . .	Gravity
		CLUTCH	Dry multiple disc
SERVICE BRAKE . . .	Expanding on rear wheels	TRANSMISSION . . .	Selective sliding
EMERGENCY BRAKE .	Expanding on rear wheels	GEAR CHANGES . . .	Three forward, one reverse
		DRIVE	Worm
CYLINDERS	Four	REAR AXLE	Full floating
ARRANGED	Vertically	STEERING GEAR . . .	Worm and wheel
CAST	In pairs		

**LOCOMOBILE
COMPANY
OF AMERICA**

Price, Chassis, $3500

**BRIDGEPORT
CONNECTICUT**

LOCOMOBILE THREE-TON TRUCK—B

COLOR	Optional	BORE AND STROKE	4¼ x 6 inches
CARRYING CAPACITY	6000 pounds	LUBRICATION	Pressure and internal circulating system
POSITION OF DRIVER	Right side		
WHEELBASE	150 or 170 inches		
GAUGE	Front, 60 inches; rear, 66 inches	RADIATOR	Cellular
		COOLING	Water pump
WHEELS	Wood	IGNITION	High-tension magneto and storage battery
FRONT TIRES	36 x 5 inches, single solid		
REAR TIRES	36 x 5 inches, dual solid	STARTING SYSTEM	Two unit
		STARTER OPERATED	Gear to fly wheel
SERVICE BRAKE	Contracting on propeller shaft	LIGHTING SYSTEM	Oil
		VOLTAGES	Six
EMERGENCY BRAKE	Expanding on rear wheels	WIRING SYSTEM	Single
		GASOLINE SYSTEM	Gravity
CYLINDERS	Four	CLUTCH	Cone
ARRANGED	Vertically	TRANSMISSION	Selective sliding
CAST	In pairs	GEAR CHANGES	Four forward
HORSEPOWER	28.9	DRIVE	Worm
(N. A. C. C. Rating)		REAR AXLE	Full floating
		STEERING GEAR	Worm and gear

Price includes driver's seat and cushion, and lamps

LOCOMOBILE
COMPANY
OF AMERICA

BRIDGEPORT
CONNECTICUT

Price, Chassis . . $3650

LOCOMOBILE FOUR-TON TRUCK—BB

COLOR	Optional
CARRYING CAPACITY .	8000 pounds
POSITION OF DRIVER .	Right side
WHEELBASE	150 or 170 inches
GAUGE	Front, 60 inches; rear, 66 inches
WHEELS	Wood
FRONT TIRES	36 x 5 inches, single solid
REAR TIRES	36 x 6 inches, dual solid
SERVICE BRAKE . . .	Contracting on propeller shaft
EMERGENCY BRAKE .	Expanding on rear wheels
CYLINDERS	Four
ARRANGED	In pairs
CAST	Vertically
HORSEPOWER	28.9 (N. A. C. C. Rating)
BORE AND STROKE .	4¼ x 6 inches

LUBRICATION	Pressure and internal circulating system
RADIATOR	Cellular
COOLING	Water pump
IGNITION	High-tension magneto and storage battery
STARTING SYSTEM . .	Two unit
STARTER OPERATED .	Gear to fly wheel
LIGHTING SYSTEM . .	Oil
VOLTAGES	Six
WIRING SYSTEM . . .	Single
GASOLINE SYSTEM . .	Gravity
CLUTCH	Cone
TRANSMISSION . . .	Selective sliding
GEAR CHANGES . . .	Four forward
DRIVE	Worm
REAR AXLE	Full floating
STEERING GEAR . . .	Worm and gear

Price includes driver's seat and cushion, and lamps

BUICK MOTOR
C O M P A N Y

F   L   I   N   T
M I C H I G A N

Price, $1225

BUICK ONE-TON TRUCK—D-4

COLOR	Body red, running gear black		LUBRICATION	Splash with circulating pump
CARRYING CAPACITY	2000 pounds		RADIATOR	Cellular
POSITION OF DRIVER	Left side		COOLING	Water pump
WHEELBASE	122 inches		IGNITION	Storage battery
GAUGE	56 inches		STARTING SYSTEM	Single unit
WHEELS	Wood		STARTER OPERATED	Gear to fly wheel
FRONT TIRES	35 x 5 inches, pneumatic		LIGHTING SYSTEM	Electric
REAR TIRES	35 x 5 inches, pneumatic		VOLTAGES	Six
			WIRING SYSTEM	Single
SERVICE BRAKE	Contracting on rear wheels		GASOLINE SYSTEM	Vacuum
EMERGENCY BRAKE	Expanding on rear wheels		CLUTCH	Cone
			TRANSMISSION	Selective sliding
CYLINDERS	Four		GEAR CHANGES	Three forward, one reverse
ARRANGED	Vertically			
CAST	In pairs		DRIVE	Bevel
HORSEPOWER	22.5		REAR AXLE	Three-quarters floating
(N. A. C. C. Rating)				
BORE AND STROKE	3¾ x 5 inches		STEERING GEAR	Split nut and worm

In addition to above specifications, price includes top,
windshield, speedometer, ammeter and demountable rims

WALTER
MOTOR TRUCK
COMPANY

49-51 WEST 66th ST.
NEW YORK, N. Y.

Price, Chassis $4750
Six-Ton 5000
Seven and One-half Ton . 5250

WALTER FOUR WHEEL DRIVE FIVE-TON TRUCK

COLOR	Lead
CARRYING CAPACITY .	Five tons
POSITION OF DRIVER	Left side
WHEELBASE	96 to 168 inches
GAUGE	Front, 66 inches; rear, 66 inches
WHEELS	Wood
FRONT TIRES . . .	40 x 6 inches, single solid
REAR TIRES	40 x 5 inches, dual solid
SERVICE BRAKE . . .	Contracting on transmission shaft
EMERGENCY BRAKE .	Contracting on rear wheels
CYLINDERS	Four
ARRANGED	Vertically, under hood

CAST	En bloc
HORSEPOWER	30.63 (N. A. C. C. Rating)
BORE AND STROKE .	4⅜ x 6 inches
LUBRICATION	Splash with circulating pump
RADIATOR	Tubular
COOLING	Water pump
IGNITION	High-tension magneto
GASOLINE SYSTEM . .	Gravity
CLUTCH	Cone
TRANSMISSION . . .	Selective sliding
GEAR CHANGES . . .	Four and reverse
DRIVE	Spur gear to wheels
REAR AXLE	Dead
STEERING GEAR . . .	Worm and gear

In addition to above specifications, price includes cab

**S A U R E R
M O T O R
C O M P A N Y**

WEST END AVE. &
64th STREET
NEW YORK, N. Y.

Price, Chassis . . $4800

SAURER FIVE-TON TRUCK

COLOR	Lead	BORE AND STROKE	4⅜ x 5½ inches
CARRYING CAPACITY	10,000 pounds	LUBRICATION	Pump over and splash and gravity
POSITION OF DRIVER	Right side		
WHEELBASE	153½ inches		
GAUGE	66¼ inches	RADIATOR	Honeycomb
WHEELS	Wood	COOLING	Water pump
FRONT TIRES	36 x 5 inches, single solid	IGNITION	High-tension magneto
REAR TIRES	42 x 5 inches, dual solid	GASOLINE SYSTEM	Gravity
SERVICE BRAKE	On differential	CLUTCH	Cone
EMERGENCY BRAKE	Expanding on rear wheels	TRANSMISSION	Selective sliding
CYLINDERS	Four	GEAR CHANGES	Four forward, one reverse
ARRANGED	Vertically, under hood	DRIVE	Chain
CAST	In pairs	REAR AXLE	Dead
HORSEPOWER	30.63 (N. A. C. C. Rating)	STEERING GEAR	Worm and sector

MACK BROTHERS MOTOR CAR COMPANY

64th STREET AND WEST END AVE., NEW YORK, N. Y.

Price, Chassis . . $2700

MACK TWO-TON TRUCK—AB

COLOR	Lead
CARRYING CAPACITY .	4000 pounds
POSITION OF DRIVER	Back of motor
WHEELBASE	144 or 162 inches
GAUGE	58½ inches
WHEELS	Wood
FRONT TIRES	36 x 4 inches, single solid
REAR TIRES	36 x 4 inches, dual solid
SERVICE BRAKE . . .	Contracting on rear wheels
EMERGENCY BRAKE .	Expanding on rear wheels
CYLINDERS	Four
ARRANGED	Vertically
CAST	In pairs

HORSEPOWER	25.6 (N. A. C. C. Rating)
BORE AND STROKE .	4 x 5 inches
LUBRICATION	Pump over and splash and gravity
RADIATOR	Honeycomb
COOLING	Water pump
IGNITION	High-tension magneto
GASOLINE SYSTEM .	Gravity
CLUTCH	Dry multiple disc
TRANSMISSION . . .	Selective sliding
GEAR CHANGES . . .	Three forward, one reverse
DRIVE	Worm
REAR AXLE	Full floating
STEERING GEAR . . .	Worm and sector

KELLY-SPRINGFIELD MOTOR TRUCK COMPANY
SPRINGFIELD
OHIO

Price, $2000

KELLY-SPRINGFIELD ONE-AND-ONE-HALF-TON TRUCK—K-30

COLOR	Optional	CAST	En bloc
CARRYING CAPACITY	3000 pounds	HORSEPOWER	22.5 (N. A. C. C. Rating)
POSITION OF DRIVER	Back of motor	BORE AND STROKE	3¾ x 5¼ inches
WHEELBASE	120, 144, 168 and 180 inches	LUBRICATION	Force feed
GAUGE	Front, 56 inches; rear, 60 inches	RADIATOR	Cellular
		COOLING	Water pump
WHEELS	Wood	IGNITION	High-tension magneto
FRONT TIRES	36 x 3½ inches, single solid		
REAR TIRES	36 x 5 inches, single solid	GASOLINE SYSTEM	Gravity
		CLUTCH	Cone
SERVICE BRAKE	Contracting on rear wheels	TRANSMISSION	Selective sliding
		GEAR CHANGES	Three forward, one reverse
EMERGENCY BRAKE	Expanding on rear wheels	DRIVE	Side chain
CYLINDERS	Four	REAR AXLE	Dead
ARRANGED	Vertically	STEERING GEAR	Worm and gear

Price, $3400

KELLY-
SPRINGFIELD
MOTOR TRUCK
COMPANY

SPRINGFIELD
O   H   I   O

KELLY-SPRINGFIELD THREE-AND-ONE-HALF-TON TRUCK—K-40

COLOR	Optional	CAST	In pairs
CARRYING CAPACITY	7000 pounds	HORSEPOWER	32.4
POSITION OF DRIVER	Back of motor		(N. A. C. C. Rating)
WHEELBASE	150, 172, 194 or 208 inches	BORE AND STROKE	4½ x 6½ inches
		LUBRICATION	Force feed
GAUGE	Front, 68 inches; rear, 73 inches	RADIATOR	Cellular
		COOLING	Water pump
WHEELS	Wood	IGNITION	High-tension magneto
FRONT TIRES	36 x 5 inches, single solid	GASOLINE SYSTEM	Gravity
REAR TIRES	40 x 5 inches, dual solid	CLUTCH	Cone
		TRANSMISSION	Selective sliding
SERVICE BRAKE	Contracting on rear wheels	GEAR CHANGES	Three forward, one reverse
EMERGENCY BRAKE	Expanding on rear wheels	DRIVE	Side chain
		REAR AXLE	Dead
CYLINDERS	Four	STEERING GEAR	Worm and gear
ARRANGED	Vertically		

**K E L L Y -
SPRINGFIELD
MOTOR TRUCK
C O M P A N Y**

SPRINGFIELD
O   H   I   O

Price, $4250

KELLY-SPRINGFIELD FIVE-TON TRUCK—K-50

COLOR	Optional	CAST	In pairs
CARRYING CAPACITY .	10,000 pounds	HORSEPOWER	32.4
POSITION OF DRIVER	Back of motor		(N. A. C. C. Rating)
WHEELBASE	150, 172, 194 or 208 inches	BORE AND STROKE . .	4½ x 6½ inches
		LUBRICATION	Force feed
GAUGE	Front, 68 inches; rear, 75½ inches	RADIATOR	Cellular
		COOLING	Water pump
WHEELS	Wood	IGNITION	High-tension magneto
FRONT TIRES	36 x 6 inches, single solid	GASOLINE SYSTEM . .	Gravity
REAR TIRES	40 x 6 inches, dual solid	CLUTCH	Cone
SERVICE BRAKE . .	Contracting on rear wheels	TRANSMISSION . . .	Selective sliding
		GEAR CHANGES . . .	Three forward, one reverse
EMERGENCY BRAKE .	Expanding on rear wheels	DRIVE	Side chain
CYLINDERS	Four	REAR AXLE	Dead
ARRANGED	Vertically	STEERING GEAR . . .	Worm and gear

STUDEBAKER CORPORATION OF AMERICA

DETROIT MICHIGAN

Price, Chassis	. . . .	$785
Express Body	. . . .	850
Panel Body	. . . .	875
Combination Passenger and Express	. . . .	875
One-Ton Express	. . . . . .	1200
One-Ton Stake Body	. . . .	1250
Sixteen-Passenger Bus	. . .	1400

STUDEBAKER 1000-POUND COMMERCIAL CAR—SF

COLOR	Body, blue; running gear, black		LUBRICATION	Splash with circulating pump
CARRYING CAPACITY .	1000 pounds		RADIATOR	Tubular
POSITION OF DRIVER	Left side		COOLING	Water pump
WHEELBASE	112 inches		IGNITION	Storage battery
GAUGE	56 inches		STARTING SYSTEM . .	Two unit
WHEELS	Wood		STARTER OPERATED .	Chain to crank shaft
FRONT TIRES	34 x 4 inches		LIGHTING SYSTEM . .	Electric
REAR TIRES	34 x 4 inches, anti-skid		VOLTAGES	Six
SERVICE BRAKE . . .	Contracting on rear wheels		WIRING SYSTEM . . .	Single
EMERGENCY BRAKE .	Expanding on rear wheels		GASOLINE SYSTEM . .	Vacuum
			CLUTCH	Cone
CYLINDERS	Four		TRANSMISSION . . .	Selective sliding
ARRANGED	Vertically		GEAR CHANGES . . .	Three forward, one reverse
CAST	En bloc		DRIVE	Plain bevel
HORSEPOWER . . . . (N. A. C. C. Rating)	24.03		REAR AXLE	Full floating
BORE AND STROKE .	3⅞ x 5 inches		STEERING GEAR . . .	Worm and gear

In addition to above specifications, price includes top, windshield, speedometer, battery indicator and demountable rims.

PACKARD
MOTOR CAR
COMPANY

DETROIT
MICHIGAN

Price, Chassis. $2200
With Electric Starting and
   Lighting 2425
One and One-half Ton . . . 2500
Two-Ton 2800

PACKARD ONE-TON TRUCK—ID

Color	Body, Packard blue with Packard light derby red striping; wheels, blue; chassis black
Carrying Capacity .	2000 pounds
Position of Driver .	Left side
Wheelbase	126 or 144 inches
Gauge	56 inches
Wheels	Wood
Front Tires	34 x 3½ inches, single solid
Rear Tires	34 x 6 inches, single solid
Service Brake . . .	Propeller shaft
Emergency Brake .	Expanding on rear wheels
Cylinders	Four
Arranged	Vertically

Cast	En bloc
Horsepower	25.6 (N. A. C. C. Rating)
Bore and Stroke . .	4 x 5½ inches
Lubrication	Force feed
Radiator	Cellular
Cooling	Water pump
Ignition	High-tension magneto and storage battery
Gasoline System . .	Pressure
Clutch	Dry multiple disc
Transmission . . .	Progressive sliding
Gear Changes . . .	Three forward, one reverse
Drive	Worm
Rear Axle	Full floating
Steering Gear . . .	Worm and wheel

**PACKARD
MOTOR CAR
COMPANY**

D E T R O I T
M I C H I G A N

Price, Chassis $3400
With Electric Light-
ing and Starting . 3625
Four-Ton 3800

PACKARD THREE-TON TRUCK—3D

COLOR	Body, Packard blue, with Packard light derby red striping; wheels, Packard light derby red, with Packard blue striping; chassis, black	CYLINDERS	Four
		ARRANGED	Vertically
		CAST	En bloc
		HORSEPOWER	32.4
		(N. A. C. C. Rating)	
		BORE AND STROKE .	4½ x 5½ inches
		LUBRICATION	Full force feed
CARRYING CAPACITY.	6000 pounds	RADIATOR	Cellular
POSITION OF DRIVER.	Left side	COOLING	Water pump
WHEELBASE	156 or 186 inches	IGNITION	High-tension magneto and storage battery
GAUGE	Rear wheels, 66 inches; front wheels, 69¾ inches		
		GASOLINE SYSTEM . .	Pressure
WHEELS	Wood	CLUTCH	Dry multiple disc
FRONT TIRES	36 x 5 inches, single solid	TRANSMISSION . . .	Progressive sliding
REAR TIRES	36 x 5 inches, dual solid	GEAR CHANGES . . .	Three forward, one reverse
SERVICE BRAKE. . .	Propeller shaft	DRIVE	Worm
EMERGENCY BRAKE .	Expanding on rear wheels	REAR AXLE	Full floating
		STEERING GEAR. . .	Worm and wheel

AMERICAN-LA FRANCE FIRE ENGINE COMPANY, INC.

ELMIRA N. Y.

Price, $9000

AMERICAN-LA FRANCE PUMPING ENGINE—TYPE 12

COLOR	Optional
POSITION OF DRIVER	Right side
WHEELBASE	156¾ inches
GAUGE	Front, 62 inches; rear, 71¼ inches
WHEELS	Wood
FRONT TIRES	38 x 4½ inches, single cushion
REAR TIRES	38 x 4½ inches, dual cushion
SERVICE BRAKE . . .	Expanding on rear wheels
EMERGENCY BRAKE .	Expanding on rear wheels
CYLINDERS	Six
ARRANGED	Vertically
CAST	In pairs
HORSEPOWER . . . . 72.6 (N. A. C. C. Rating)	
BORE AND STROKE . .	5½ x 6 inches

LUBRICATION	Force feed and splash
RADIATOR	Cellular
COOLING	Water pump
IGNITION	High tension magneto and storage battery
STARTING SYSTEM . .	Two unit
STARTER OPERATED .	Gear to fly wheel
LIGHTING SYSTEM . .	Electric
VOLTAGES	Six
WIRING SYSTEM . . .	Single
GASOLINE SYSTEM . .	Gravity
CLUTCH	Dry multiple disc
TRANSMISSION . . .	Selective sliding
GEAR CHANGES . . .	Three forward, one reverse
DRIVE	Side chain
REAR AXLE	Dead
STEERING GEAR . . .	Worm and gear

In addition to above specifications, price includes speedometer, ammeter, voltmeter and demountable rims

**AMERICAN-
LA FRANCE
FIRE ENGINE
COMPANY, INC.**

Price, $5500

ELMIRA   N. Y.

AMERICAN-LA FRANCE CHEMICAL ENGINE AND HOSE CAR—
TYPE 10

COLOR	Optional	LUBRICATION	Force feed and splash
POSITION OF DRIVER	Right side	RADIATOR	Cellular
WHEELBASE . . .	156¾ inches	COOLING	Water pump
GAUGE	Front, 62 inches; rear, 71¼ inches	IGNITION	High tension magneto and storage battery
WHEELS	Wood		
FRONT TIRES	38 x 4½ inches, single cushion	STARTING SYSTEM . .	Two unit
REAR TIRES	38 x 4½ inches, dual cushion	STARTER OPERATED .	Gear to fly wheel
		LIGHTING SYSTEM . .	Electric
SERVICE BRAKE . . .	Expanding on rear wheels	VOLTAGES	Six
		WIRING SYSTEM . . .	Single
EMERGENCY BRAKE .	Expanding on rear wheels	GASOLINE SYSTEM . .	Gravity
		CLUTCH	Dry multiple disc
CYLINDERS	Four	TRANSMISSION . . .	Selective sliding
ARRANGED	Vertically	GEAR CHANGES . . .	Three forward, one reverse
CAST	In pairs		
HORSEPOWER	48.4 (N. A. C. C. Rating)	DRIVE	Side chain
		REAR AXLE	Dead
BORE AND STROKE . .	5½ x 6 inches	STEERING GEAR . . .	Worm and gear

In addition to above specifications, price includes
speedometer, ammeter, voltmeter and demountable rims

AMERICAN-LA FRANCE FIRE ENGINE COMPANY, INC.
ELMIRA   N. Y.

Price, $10,000

AMERICAN-LA FRANCE PUMPING ENGINE—TYPE 19

COLOR	Optional	LUBRICATION	Force feed and splash
POSITION OF DRIVER	Right side	RADIATOR	Cellular
WHEELBASE	165 inches	COOLING	Water pump
GAUGE	Front, 71¼ inches; rear, 81⅜ inches	IGNITION	High tension magneto and storage battery
WHEELS	Wood	STARTING SYSTEM	Two unit
FRONT TIRES	38 x 5 inches, single solid	STARTER OPERATED	Chain to crank shaft
REAR TIRES	38 x 4 inches, dual solid	LIGHTING SYSTEM	Electric
SERVICE BRAKE	Expanding on rear wheels	VOLTAGES	Twelve
		WIRING SYSTEM	Single
EMERGENCY BRAKE	Expanding on rear wheels	GASOLINE SYSTEM	Gravity
CYLINDERS	Six	CLUTCH	Dry multiple disc
ARRANGED	Vertically	TRANSMISSION	Selective sliding
CAST	In pairs	GEAR CHANGES	Three forward, one reverse
HORSEPOWER	93.7 (N. A. C. C. Rating)	DRIVE	Side chain
		REAR AXLE	Dead
BORE AND STROKE	6¼ x 8 inches	STEERING GEAR	Worm and gear

In addition to above specifications, price includes speedometer, ammeter, voltmeter and demountable rims

AMERICAN-LA FRANCE FIRE ENGINE COMPANY, INC.
ELMIRA   N. Y.

Price, $4500

AMERICAN-LA FRANCE CHEMICAL ENGINE AND HOSE CAR— TYPE 20

COLOR	Optional
POSITION OF DRIVER.	Right side
WHEELBASE	140¾ inches
GAUGE	Front, 62 inches; rear, 71¼ inches
WHEELS	Wood
FRONT TIRES	38 x 4 inches, single cushion
REAR TIRES	38 x 3½ inches, dual cushion
SERVICE BRAKE. . .	Expanding on rear wheels
EMERGENCY BRAKE .	Expanding on rear wheels
CYLINDERS	Six
ARRANGED	Vertically
CAST	In threes
HORSEPOWER	38.4 (N. A. C. C. Rating)
BORE AND STROKE .	4 x 5½ inches

LUBRICATION	Force feed and splash
RADIATOR	Cellular
COOLING	Water pump
IGNITION	High-tension magneto and storage battery
STARTING SYSTEM . .	Two unit
STARTER OPERATED .	Gear to fly wheel
LIGHTING SYSTEM . .	Electric
VOLTAGES	Six
WIRING SYSTEM . . .	Single
GASOLINE SYSTEM . .	Gravity
CLUTCH	Dry multiple disc
TRANSMISSION . . .	Selective sliding
GEAR CHANGES . . .	Three forward, one reverse
DRIVE	Side chain
REAR AXLE	Dead
STEERING GEAR. . .	Worm and gear

In addition to above specifications, price includes speedometer, ammeter, voltmeter and demountable rims

AMERICAN-
LA FRANCE
FIRE ENGINE
COMPANY, INC.

ELMIRA   N. Y.

Price, $3000

AMERICAN-LA FRANCE COMBINATION CHEMICAL ENGINE AND HOSE CAR—TYPE B

COLOR . . . . . . Optional
POSITION OF DRIVER Left side
WHEELBASE . . . . 140 inches
GAUGE . . . . . . 58 inches
WHEELS . . . . . . Wood
FRONT TIRES . . . . 36 x 4 inches, single cushion
REAR TIRES . . . . 36 x 5 inches, dual cushion
SERVICE BRAKE . . . Contracting on rear wheels
EMERGENCY BRAKE . Expanding on rear wheels
CYLINDERS . . . . . Four
ARRANGED . . . . . Vertically
CAST . . . . En bloc
HORSEPOWER 27.23
            (N. A. C. C. Rating)
BORE AND STROKE . 4⅛ x 5¼ inches

LUBRICATION . . . . Force feed and splash
RADIATOR . . . . . Cellular
COOLING . . . . . . Water pump
IGNITION . . . . . . High tension magneto
STARTING SYSTEM . . Two unit
STARTER OPERATED . Gear to fly wheel
LIGHTING SYSTEM . . Gas
VOLTAGES . . . . . Six
WIRING SYSTEM . . . Single
GASOLINE SYSTEM . . Gravity
CLUTCH . . . . . . Cone
TRANSMISSION . . . Selective sliding
GEAR CHANGES . . . Three forward, one reverse
DRIVE . . . . Side chain
REAR AXLE . . . . Dead
STEERING GEAR . . . Worm and gear

In addition to above specifications, price includes
speedometer, ammeter, voltmeter and demountable rims

**AMERICAN-
LA FRANCE
FIRE ENGINE
COMPANY, INC.**

ELMIRA   N. Y.

Price, $6000

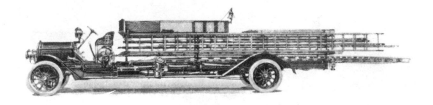

AMERICAN-LA FRANCE SERVICE HOOK AND LADDER TRUCK—
TYPE 14

COLOR.	Optional
POSITION OF DRIVER.	Right side
WHEELBASE	246 inches
GAUGE	Front, 62 inches; rear, 71¼ inches
WHEELS	Wood
FRONT TIRES	38 x 4½ inches, single cushion
REAR TIRES	38 x 4½ inches, dual cushion
SERVICE BRAKE. . .	Expanding on rear wheels
EMERGENCY BRAKE .	Expanding on rear wheels
CYLINDERS	Four
ARRANGED	Vertically
CAST	In pairs
HORSEPOWER . . .	48.4 (N. A. C. C. Rating)
BORE AND STROKE .	5½ x 6 inches

LUBRICATION	Force feed and splash
RADIATOR	Cellular
COOLING	Water pump
IGNITION	High-tension magneto and storage battery
STARTING SYSTEM . .	Two unit
STARTER OPERATED .	Gear to fly wheel
LIGHTING SYSTEM . .	Electric
VOLTAGES	Six
WIRING SYSTEM. . .	Single
GASOLINE SYSTEM . .	Gravity
CLUTCH	Dry multiple disc
TRANSMISSION . . .	Selective sliding
GEAR CHANGES . . .	Three forward, one reverse
DRIVE	Side chain
REAR AXLE	Dead
STEERING GEAR. . .	Worm and gear

In addition to above specifications, price includes
speedometer, ammeter, voltmeter and demountable rims

AMERICAN-
LA FRANCE
FIRE ENGINE
COMPANY, INC.

ELMIRA   N. Y.

Price . . $9500 to $11,000

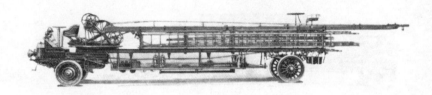

AMERICAN LA-FRANCE AERIAL HOOK AND LADDER TRUCK—TYPE 31

COLOR	Optional	LUBRICATION	Force feed and splash
POSITION OF DRIVER .	Right side	RADIATOR	Cellular
WHEELBASE	333 inches	COOLING	Water pump
GAUGE	Front inner, 67¼ inches; front outer, 76¾ inches; rear, 62 inches	IGNITION	High tension magneto and storage battery
WHEELS	Front, cast steel; rear, wood	STARTING SYSTEM . .	Two unit
FRONT TIRES	38 x 4 inches dual solid	STARTER OPERATED .	Gear to fly wheel
		LIGHTING SYSTEM .	Electric
REAR TIRES	42 x 4 inches single solid	VOLTAGES	Six
		WIRING SYSTEM . . .	Single
SERVICE BRAKE . . .	Expanding on front wheels	GASOLINE SYSTEM . .	Gravity
		CLUTCH	Dry multiple disc
EMERGENCY BRAKE .	Expanding on front wheels	TRANSMISSION . . .	Selective sliding
		GEAR CHANGES . . .	Three forward, one reverse
CYLINDERS	Four		
ARRANGED	Vertically	DRIVE	Side chain
CAST	In pairs	REAR AXLE	Dead
HORSEPOWER . . .	48.4	STEERING GEAR . . .	Front, worm and sleeve; rear, worm and sector
(N. A. C. C. Rating)			
BORE AND STROKE .	5½ x 6 inches		

In addition to above specifications, price includes
speedometer, ammeter, voltmeter and demountable rims

AMERICAN-LA FRANCE FIRE ENGINE COMPANY, INC.
ELMIRA N.Y.

Price, $8500

AMERICAN-LA FRANCE MOTOR STEAM FIRE ENGINE—TYPE 31

COLOR	Optional
POSITION OF DRIVER.	Right side
WHEELBASE	126 inches
GAUGE	Front inner, 67¼ inches; front outer, 76¾ inches; rear, 62 inches
WHEELS	Front, cast steel; rear, wood
FRONT TIRES	38 x 4 inches dual solid
REAR TIRES	60 x 4 inches single solid
SERVICE BRAKE. . .	Expanding on front wheels
EMERGENCY BRAKE .	Expanding on front wheels
CYLINDERS	Four
ARRANGED	Vertically
CAST	In pairs
HORSEPOWER	48.4 (N. A. C. C. Rating)

BORE AND STROKE .	5½ x 6 inches
LUBRICATION	Force feed and splash
RADIATOR	Cellular
COOLING	Water pump
IGNITION	High tension magneto and storage battery
STARTING SYSTEM . .	Two unit
STARTER OPERATED .	Gear to fly wheel
LIGHTING SYSTEM . .	Electric
VOLTAGES	Six
WIRING SYSTEM. . .	Single
GASOLINE SYSTEM. .	Gravity
CLUTCH	Dry multiple disc
TRANSMISSION . . .	Selective sliding
GEAR CHANGES . . .	Three forward, one reverse
DRIVE	Side chain
REAR AXLE	Dead
STEERING GEAR. . .	Worm and sleeve

In addition to above specifications, price includes speedometer, ammeter, voltmeter and demountable rims

**REO MOTOR
CAR COMPANY**

**L A N S I N G
M I C H I G A N**

Price, Chassis	$1650
With Low Stake Body	1800
With High Stake Body	1825
With Express Body	1810
Express Body with Top	1960
Express Body with Top and Screen Sides	2035

REO TWO-TON TRUCK—J

COLOR	Lead
CARRYING CAPACITY	4000 pounds
POSITION OF DRIVER	Left side
WHEELBASE	146 inches
GAUGE	Front, 59¾ inches; rear, 62⅞ inches
WHEELS	Wood
FRONT TIRES	36 x 4 inches, solid
REAR TIRES	36 x 3½ inches, dual solid
SERVICE BRAKE	Contracting on jack shaft
EMERGENCY BRAKE	Contracting on rear wheels
CYLINDERS	Four
ARRANGED	Vertically

CAST	In pairs
HORSEPOWER	27.23 (N. A. C. C. Rating)
BORE AND STROKE	4⅛ x 4½ inches
LUBRICATION	Splash with circulating pump
RADIATOR	Tubular
COOLING	Water pump
IGNITION	Low tension magneto and dry cells
GASOLINE SYSTEM	Gravity
CLUTCH	Dry multiple disc
TRANSMISSION	Selective sliding
GEAR CHANGES	Three forward, one reverse
DRIVE	Side chain drive to rear wheels
REAR AXLE	Dead
STEERING GEAR	Pinion and sector

In addition to above specifications, price includes cab

REO MOTOR
CAR COMPANY

L A N S I N G
M I C H I G A N

REO THREE-QUARTER-TON TRUCK—F

COLOR	Body, golden olive, running gear, red
CARRYING CAPACITY .	1500 pounds
POSITION OF DRIVER	Left side
WHEELBASE	120 inches
GAUGE	56 inches
WHEELS	Wood
FRONT TIRES	34 x 4½ inches
REAR TIRES	34 x 4½ inches, anti-skid
SERVICE BRAKE . . .	Contracting on rear wheels
EMERGENCY BRAKE .	Expanding on rear wheels
CYLINDERS	Four
ARRANGED	Vertically
CAST	In pairs
HORSEPOWER	27.23
(N. A. C. C. Rating)	
BORE AND STROKE .	4⅛ x 4½ inches

LUBRICATION	Splash with circulating pump
RADIATOR	Tubular
COOLING	Water pump
IGNITION	Storage battery
STARTING SYSTEM . .	Two unit
STARTER OPERATED .	Chain to transmission shaft
LIGHTING SYSTEM . .	Electric
VOLTAGES	Six
WIRING SYSTEM . . .	Double
GASOLINE SYSTEM . .	Gravity
CLUTCH	Dry multiple disc
TRANSMISSION . . .	Selective sliding
GEAR CHANGES . . .	Three forward, one reverse
DRIVE	Plain bevel
REAR AXLE	Full floating
STEERING GEAR . . .	Pinion and sector

In addition to above specifications, price includes top, windshield, speedometer, ammeter and demountable rims

**THE GRAMM
MOTOR TRUCK
CO., MANUFAC-
TURERS OF
GARFORD
M O T O R
T R U C K S**

L I M A ,   O H I O

Price, Chassis . $1800
One-Ton. . . . 1450
Two-Ton. . . . 2300

GARFORD ONE-AND-ONE-HALF-TON TRUCK—66

COLOR	Optional		CAST	En bloc
CARRYING CAPACITY .	3000 pounds		HORSEPOWER	22.5
POSITION OF DRIVER.	Optional			(N. A. C. C. Rating)
WHEELBASE	142 or 166 inches		BORE AND STROKE .	3¾ x 5½ inches
GAUGE.	Front, 56½ inches; rear, 58¾ inches		LUBRICATION	Splash with circulating pump
			RADIATOR	Cellular
WHEELS	Wood		COOLING	Water pump
FRONT TIRES	36 x 3½ inches, solid		IGNITION	High-tension magneto
			GASOLINE SYSTEM . .	Gravity
REAR TIRES	36 x 5 inches, solid		CLUTCH	Dry multiple disc
SERVICE BRAKE . . .	Expanding on rear wheels		TRANSMISSION . . .	Selective sliding
			GEAR CHANGES . . .	Three forward, one reverse
EMERGENCY BRAKE .	Contracting on rear wheels		DRIVE	Worm
CYLINDERS	Four		REAR AXLE	Full floating
ARRANGED	Vertically		STEERING GEAR . . .	Worm and nut

THE GRAMM
MOTOR TRUCK
CO., MANUFAC-
TURERS OF
GARFORD
MOTOR
TRUCKS

LIMA, OHIO

Price, Chassis $4300
Three-Ton . .   3400
Six-Ton . . .   4500

GARFORD FIVE-TON TRUCK—D

COLOR	Optional		CAST	In pairs
CARRYING CAPACITY .	Five tons		HORSEPOWER	36.1
POSITION OF DRIVER	Right side			(N. A. C. C. Rating)
WHEELBASE	128 or 150 inches		BORE AND STROKE .	4¾ x 5½ inches
GAUGE	Front, 62½ inches; rear, 71 inches		LUBRICATION	Splash with circulating pump
			RADIATOR	Cellular
WHEELS	Wood		COOLING	Water pump
FRONT TIRES	30 x 6 inches, single solid		IGNITION	High-tension magneto
REAR TIRES	40 x 6 inches, dual solid		GASOLINE SYSTEM . .	Gravity
			CLUTCH	Dry multiple disc
SERVICE BRAKE . . .	Contracting on transmission countershaft		TRANSMISSION . . .	Selective sliding
			GEAR CHANGES . . .	Four forward, one reverse
EMERGENCY BRAKE .	Expanding on rear wheels		DRIVE	Plain bevel
CYLINDERS	Four		REAR AXLE	Dead
ARRANGED	Vertically		STEERING GEAR . . .	Worm and nut

VIM MOTOR TRUCK COMPANY
PHILADELPHIA, PA.

Price $725
With Jitney Body   975
With Undertaker's Body . .   875
With Express Body   775

VIM HALF-TON DE LUXE DELIVERY

COLOR	Body, blue; wheels, red	BORE AND STROKE .	3 x 4½ inches
CARRYING CAPACITY	1000 pounds	LUBRICATION	Full splash
POSITION OF DRIVER	Left side	RADIATOR	Cellular
WHEELBASE	100 inches	COOLING	Water
GAUGE	56 inches	IGNITION	High-tension magneto
WHEELS	Wood		
FRONT TIRES	31 x 4 inches	LIGHTING SYSTEM . .	Gas
REAR TIRES	31 x 4 inches	GASOLINE SYSTEM . .	Gravity
SERVICE BRAKE . . .	Contracting on rear wheels	CLUTCH	Cone
EMERGENCY BRAKE .	Expanding on rear wheels	TRANSMISSION . . .	Selective sliding
		GEAR CHANGES . . .	Three forward, one reverse
CYLINDERS	Four		
ARRANGED	Vertically	DRIVE	Plain bevel
CAST	En bloc	REAR AXLE	Three-quarters floating
HORSEPOWER	14.4 (N. A. C. C. Rating)	STEERING GEAR. . .	Worm and sector

In addition to above specifications, price includes
top, top hood, windshield and demountable rims

**KISSEL MOTOR
CAR COMPANY**

**H A R T F O R D
W I S C O N S I N**

Price, Chassis	$950
With Standard Stake or Express Body.	1075

KISSEL-KAR ONE-THOUSAND-POUND DELIVERY

COLOR	Lead	HORSEPOWER	24.03 (N. A. C. C. Rating)
CARRYING CAPACITY.	1000 pounds		
POSITION OF DRIVER	Left side	BORE AND STROKE .	3⅞ x 5½ inches
WHEELBASE	115 inches	LUBRICATION	Splash with circulating pump
GAUGE	56 inches		
WHEELS	Wood	RADIATOR	Square tube
FRONT TIRES	32 x 4 inches	COOLING	Water pump
REAR TIRES	32 x 4 inches, anti-skid	IGNITION	High-tension magneto
SERVICE BRAKE. . .	Contracting on rear wheels	GASOLINE SYSTEM. .	Vacuum
		CLUTCH	Cone
EMERGENCY BRAKE .	Contracting on rear wheels	TRANSMISSION . . .	Selective sliding
		GEAR CHANGES . . .	Three
CYLINDERS	Four	DRIVE	Spiral bevel
ARRANGED	Vertically	REAR AXLE	Full floating
CAST	En bloc	STEERING GEAR. . .	Split nut and worm

**KISSEL MOTOR
CAR COMPANY**

**HARTFORD
WISCONSIN**

Price, Chassis $2100
With Standard Stake or Express
    Body 2250

KISSEL-KAR TWO-TON TRUCK

COLOR	Lead
CARRYING CAPACITY .	Two tons
POSITION OF DRIVER	Left side
WHEELBASE	144 inches
GAUGE	56 inches
WHEELS	Wood
FRONT TIRES	34 x 3½ inches, single solid
REAR TIRES	36 x 6 inches, single solid
SERVICE BRAKE . . .	Expanding on rear wheels
EMERGENCY BRAKE .	Expanding on rear wheels
CYLINDERS	Four
ARRANGED	Vertically
CAST	En bloc

HORSEPOWER	28.9 (N. A. C. C. Rating)
BORE AND STROKE .	4¼ x 5½ inches
LUBRICATION	Splash with circulating pump
RADIATOR	Square tube
COOLING	Water pump
IGNITION	High-tension magneto
GASOLINE SYSTEM . .	Vacuum
CLUTCH	Cone
TRANSMISSION . . .	Selective sliding
GEAR CHANGES . . .	Four
DRIVE	Worm
REAR AXLE	Full floating
STEERING GEAR . .	Split nut and worm

**KISSEL MOTOR
CAR COMPANY**

HARTFORD
WISCONSIN

Price, Chassis $1250
With Standard Stake or Express
body 1400

KISSEL-KAR ONE-TON TRUCK

COLOR	Lead
CARRYING CAPACITY .	One ton
POSITION OF DRIVER	Left side
WHEELBASE	132 inches
GAUGE	56 inches
WHEELS	Wood
FRONT TIRES	35 x 4½ inches, plain, or 34 x 3 inches, solid
REAR TIRES	35 x 4½ inches, anti-skid, or 34 x 4 inches, solid
SERVICE BRAKE . .	Expanding on rear wheels
EMERGENCY BRAKE .	Expanding on rear wheels
CYLINDERS	Four
ARRANGED	Vertically

CAST	En bloc
HORSEPOWER	24.03 (N. A. C. C. Rating)
BORE AND STROKE .	3⅞ x 5½ inches
LUBRICATION	Splash with circulating pump
RADIATOR	Square tube
COOLING	Water pump
IGNITION	High-tension magneto
GASOLINE SYSTEM . .	Vacuum
CLUTCH	Cone
TRANSMISSION . . .	Selective sliding
GEAR CHANGES . .	Three
DRIVE	Worm
REAR AXLE	Semi-floating
STEERING GEAR . .	Worm and sector

**PEERLESS
MOTOR CAR
COMPANY**

CLEVELAND, OHIO

Price, Chassis, $3000

PEERLESS TWO-TON TRUCK—TC-2

COLOR	Lead		HORSEPOWER	32.4
CARRYING CAPACITY	Two tons			(N. A. C. C. Rating)
POSITION OF DRIVER	Right side		BORE AND STROKE . .	4½ x 6½ inches
WHEELBASE	145 inches		LUBRICATION	Full splash
GAUGE	68 inches		RADIATOR	Tubular
WHEELS	Wood		COOLING	Water pump
FRONT TIRES	36 x 4 inches, single solid		IGNITION	High-tension magneto and storage battery
REAR TIRES	36 x 4 inches, dual solid		GASOLINE SYSTEM . .	Gravity
SERVICE BRAKE . . .	Expanding on rear wheels		CLUTCH	Cone
EMERGENCY BRAKE .	Expanding on rear wheels		TRANSMISSION . . .	Selective sliding
			GEAR CHANGES . . .	Three forward, one reverse
CYLINDERS	Four		DRIVE	Worm
ARRANGED	Vertically		REAR AXLE	Live
CAST	In pairs		STEERING GEAR . . .	Worm and sector

P E E R L E S S
M O T O R   C A R
C O M P A N Y

CLEVELAND, OHIO

Price, Chassis . $4500
Three-Ton . . .   3700
Four-Ton . . .   4000
Six-Ton 6000

PEERLESS FIVE-TON TRUCK—TC-5

COLOR	Lead	HORSEPOWER . . . . 32.4 (N. A. C. C. Rating)	
CARRYING CAPACITY	10,000 pounds	BORE AND STROKE . .	4½ x 6½ inches
POSITION OF DRIVER	Right side	LUBRICATION.	Full splash
WHEELBASE	151 inches	RADIATOR	Tubular
GAUGE	68 inches	COOLING	Water pump
WHEELS	Wood	IGNITION	High-tension magneto and storage battery
FRONT TIRES	38 x 6 inches, single solid		
REAR TIRES	42 x 6 inches, dual solid	GASOLINE SYSTEM . .	Gravity
		CLUTCH	Cone
SERVICE BRAKE. . .	Contracting on jack shaft	TRANSMISSION . . .	Selective sliding
EMERGENCY BRAKE .	Expanding on rear wheels	GEAR CHANGES . . .	Four forward, one reverse
CYLINDERS	Four	DRIVE	Side chain
ARRANGED	Vertically	REAR AXLE	Dead
CAST	In pairs	STEERING GEAR. . .	Worm and sector

**THE WHITE
COMPANY**

CLEVELAND, OHIO

Price, Chassis $2100
With Standard Body 2250

WHITE THREE-QUARTER-TON TRUCK—GBBE

Color	Chassis, red; body, dark green	Horsepower . . . . (N. A. C. C. Rating)	22.5
Carrying Capacity .	1500 pounds	Bore and Stroke .	3¾ x 5⅛ inches
Position of Driver	Left side	Lubrication	Force feed and splash
Wheelbase	133½ inches	Radiator	Honeycomb
Gauge	56 inches	Cooling	Water pump
Wheels	Wood	Ignition	High-tension magneto
Front Tires	34 x 4 inches, pneumatic	Lighting System . .	Gas
Rear Tires	34 x 4 inches, pneumatic	Gasoline System . .	Gravity
Service Brake . . .	Contracting on rear wheels	Clutch	Single plate in oil
Emergency Brake .	Expanding on rear wheels	Transmission . . .	Selective sliding
		Gear Changes . . .	Four
Cylinders	Four	Drive	Plain bevel
Arranged	Vertically	Rear Axle	Semi-floating
Cast	En bloc	Steering Gear . .	Worm and sector

In addition to above specifications, price includes prestolite tank and demountable rims

THE WHITE COMPANY
CLEVELAND, OHIO

Price, Chassis $3000
With Standard Body . . 3150

WHITE ONE-AND-ONE-HALF-TON TRUCK—TBC

COLOR	Red	BORE AND STROKE .	3¾ x 5⅛ inches
CARRYING CAPACITY .	3000 pounds	LUBRICATION	Force feed and splash
POSITION OF DRIVER	Left side		
WHEELBASE	145½ inches	RADIATOR	Honeycomb
GAUGE	56 inches	COOLING	Water pump
WHEELS	Wood	IGNITION	High-tension magneto
FRONT TIRES	36 x 4½ inches		
REAR TIRES	36 x 4½ inches, dual solid	LIGHTING SYSTEM . .	Gas
		GASOLINE SYSTEM . .	Gravity
SERVICE BRAKE . . .	Contracting on rear wheels	CLUTCH	Single plate in oil
EMERGENCY BRAKE .	Expanding on rear wheels	TRANSMISSION . . .	Selective sliding
		GEAR CHANGES . . .	Four
CYLINDERS	Four	DRIVE	Plain bevel
ARRANGED	Vertically	REAR AXLE	Semi-floating
CAST	En bloc	STEERING GEAR . .	Worm and sector
HORSEPOWER	22.5 (N. A. C. C. Rating)		

In addition to above specifications, price includes demountable rims

T H E   W H I T E
C O M P A N Y

Price, Chassis, ... $3700
With Standard Body . 3850

CLEVELAND, OHIO

WHITE THREE-TON TRUCK—TAD

COLOR	Red		BORE AND STROKE .	3¾ x 5⅛ inches
CARRYING CAPACITY .	Three tons		LUBRICATION	Force feed and splash
POSITION OF DRIVER	Left side			
WHEELBASE	163 inches		RADIATOR	Honeycomb
GAUGE	Front, 64 inches		COOLING	Water pump
WHEELS	Cast steel		IGNITION	High-tension magneto
FRONT TIRES	36 x 5 inches, single solid			
REAR TIRES	40 x 5 inches, dual solid		LIGHTING SYSTEM . .	Gas
			GASOLINE SYSTEM . .	Gravity
SERVICE BRAKE . . .	Contracting on jack shaft drums		CLUTCH	Single plate in oil
EMERGENCY BRAKE .	Expanding on rear wheels		TRANSMISSION . . .	Selective sliding
			GEAR CHANGES . . .	Four
CYLINDERS	Four		DRIVE	Double side chain
ARRANGED	Vertically			
CAST	En bloc		REAR AXLE	Dead
HORSEPOWER	22.5 (N. A. C. C. Rating)		STEERING GEAR . .	Worm and sector

THE WHITE
COMPANY

Price, $5000

CLEVELAND, OHIO

WHITE FIVE-TON POWER DUMPING TRUCK—ATCD

COLOR	Red		BORE AND STROKE .	4¼ x 6⅜ inches
CARRYING CAPACITY .	Five tons		LUBRICATION	Force feed and splash
POSITION OF DRIVER	Left side			
WHEELBASE	149 inches		RADIATOR	Honeycomb
GAUGE	Front, 64 inches		COOLING	Water pump
WHEELS	Cast steel		IGNITION	High-tension magneto
FRONT TIRES	36 x 5 inches, single solid		LIGHTING SYSTEM . .	Gas
REAR TIRES	40 x 6 inches, dual solid		GASOLINE SYSTEM . .	Gravity
SERVICE BRAKE . . .	Contracting on jack shaft drums		CLUTCH	Single plate in oil
EMERGENCY BRAKE .	Expanding on rear wheels		TRANSMISSION . . .	Selective sliding
			GEAR CHANGES . . .	Four
CYLINDERS	Four		DRIVE	Double side chain
ARRANGED	Vertically			
CAST	En bloc		REAR AXLE	Dead
HORSEPOWER	28.9		STEERING GEAR . .	Worm and sector
(N. A. C. C. Rating)				

**S E L D E N
M O T O R
V E H I C L E
C O M P A N Y**

**R O C H E S T E R
N E W   Y O R K**

Price, Chassis, $1700

SELDEN ONE-TON TRUCK—T

COLOR	Optional	HORSEPOWER	19.6 (N. A. C. C. Rating)
CARRYING CAPACITY	One and one-quarter tons	BORE AND STROKE	3½ x 5 inches
POSITION OF DRIVER	Right side	LUBRICATION	Splash with circulating pump
WHEELBASE	126½ inches	RADIATOR	Tubular
GAUGE	Front, 56 inches; rear, 58 inches	COOLING	Thermo-syphon
WHEELS	Wood	IGNITION	High-tension magneto
FRONT TIRES	34 x 3 inches, solid	GASOLINE SYSTEM	Gravity
REAR TIRES	34 x 4 inches, solid	CLUTCH	Dry multiple disc
SERVICE BRAKE	Expanding on rear wheels	TRANSMISSION	Selective sliding
EMERGENCY BRAKE	Expanding on rear wheels	GEAR CHANGES	Three forward, one reverse
CYLINDERS	Four	DRIVE	Worm
ARRANGED	Vertically	REAR AXLE	Full floating
CAST	En bloc	STEERING GEAR	Worm and nut

**S E L D E N
M O T O R
V E H I C L E
C O M P A N Y**

R O C H E S T E R
N E W   Y O R K

Price, Chassis, $2250

SELDEN TWO-TON TRUCK—JWL

COLOR	Optional		HORSEPOWER . . .	27.23
CARRYING CAPACITY .	Two tons		(N. A. C. C. Rating)	
POSITION OF DRIVER	Left side		BORE AND STROKE .	4⅛ x 5¼ inches
WHEELBASE	150 inches		LUBRICATION	Splash with circulating pump
GAUGE	Front, 56 inches; rear, 58¼ inches		RADIATOR	Cellular
WHEELS	Wood		COOLING	Water pump
FRONT TIRES	36 x 4 inches, solid		IGNITION	High-tension magneto
REAR TIRES	36 x 6 inches, solid		GASOLINE SYSTEM . .	Gravity
SERVICE BRAKE . . .	Contracting on rear wheels		CLUTCH	Dry multiple disc
EMERGENCY BRAKE .	Expanding on rear wheels		TRANSMISSION . . .	Selective sliding
CYLINDERS	Four		GEAR CHANGES . . .	Three forward, one reverse
ARRANGED	Vertically		DRIVE	Worm
CAST	En bloc		REAR AXLE	Full floating
			STEERING GEAR . . .	Worm and nut

**S E L D E N
M O T O R
V E H I C L E
C O M P A N Y**

**R O C H E S T E R
N E W   Y O R K**

Price, Chassis, $2000

SELDEN TWO-TON TRUCK—JC

COLOR	Optional	HORSEPOWER	22.5
CARRYING CAPACITY .	Two tons		(N. A. C. C. Rating)
POSITION OF DRIVER	Left side	BORE AND STROKE .	3¾ x 5¼ inches
WHEELBASE	150 inches	LUBRICATION	Splash with cir-culating pump
GAUGE	Front, 56 inches; rear, 58¾ inches	RADIATOR	Tubular
WHEELS	Wood	COOLING	Water pump
FRONT TIRES	36 x 4 inches, solid	IGNITION	High-tension magneto
REAR TIRES	36 x 6 inches, solid	GASOLINE SYSTEM . .	Gravity
SERVICE BRAKE . . .	Contracting on rear wheels	CLUTCH	Dry multiple disc
EMERGENCY BRAKE .	Expanding on rear wheels	TRANSMISSION . . .	Selective sliding
		GEAR CHANGES . . .	Three forward, one reverse
CYLINDERS	Four	DRIVE	Internal gear
ARRANGED	Vertically	REAR AXLE	Dead
CAST	En bloc	STEERING GEAR . . .	Worm and nut

S E L D E N
M O T O R
V E H I C L E
C O M P A N Y

R O C H E S T E R
N E W   Y O R K

Price, Chassis, $2950

SELDEN THREE-AND-ONE-HALF-TON TRUCK—N

COLOR	Optional	HORSEPOWER . . . . 32.4 (N. A. C. C. Rating)	
CARRYING CAPACITY .	3½ tons		
POSITION OF DRIVER	Right side	BORE AND STROKE .	4½ x 5½ inches
WHEELBASE	164 inches	LUBRICATION	Splash with circulating pump
GAUGE	Front, 61 inches; rear, 66¾ inches	RADIATOR	Cellular
WHEELS	Wood	COOLING	Water pump
FRONT TIRES	36 x 5 inches, solid	IGNITION	High-tension magneto
REAR TIRES	36 x 5 inches, dual solid	GASOLINE SYSTEM . .	Gravity
SERVICE BRAKE . . .	Expanding on rear wheels	CLUTCH	Dry multiple disc
		TRANSMISSION . . .	Selective sliding
EMERGENCY BRAKE .	Expanding on rear wheels	GEAR CHANGES . . .	Four forward, one reverse
CYLINDERS	Four	DRIVE	Worm
ARRANGED	Vertically	REAR AXLE	Full floating
CAST	In pairs	STEERING GEAR . . .	Worm and nut

**D E N B Y
MOTOR TRUCK
C O M P A N Y**

**D E T R O I T
M I C H I G A N**

Price	$890
With Electric Starter, Generator, Battery and Lights	975
With Removable Panel Body and Windshield	980
With Full Tarpaulin Top and Windshield	950

DENBY THREE-QUARTER-TON TRUCK WITH EXPRESS BODY— TYPE U

COLOR	Body, blue; chassis, red
CARRYING CAPACITY .	¾ tons
POSITION OF DRIVER	Left side
WHEELBASE	119 inches
GAUGE	56 inches
WHEELS	Wood
FRONT TIRES	34 x 3 inches, solid
REAR TIRES	34 x 3½ inches solid
SERVICE BRAKE . . .	Contracting on rear wheels
EMERGENCY BRAKE .	Expanding on rear wheels
CYLINDERS	Four
ARRANGED	Vertically

CAST	En bloc
HORSEPOWER	15.63 (N. A. C. C. Rating)
BORE AND STROKE .	3⅛ x 4½ inches
LUBRICATION	Splash with circulating pump
RADIATOR	Tubular
COOLING	Thermo-syphon
IGNITION	High-tension magneto
GASOLINE SYSTEM . .	Gravity
CLUTCH	Dry multiple disc
TRANSMISSION . . .	Selective sliding
GEAR CHANGES . . .	Three
DRIVE	Internal gear
REAR AXLE	Dead
STEERING GEAR . . .	Worm and nut

**D E N B Y
MOTOR TRUCK
C O M P A N Y**

**D E T R O I T
M I C H I G A N**

Price, Chassis $1685
With Standard Stake Body . 1845
With Baggage Transfer Body 1840
With Coal and Coke Body . . 2000

DENBY ONE-AND-ONE-HALF-TON TRUCK WITH STANDARD STAKE BODY—TYPE D

COLOR	Lead	HORSEPOWER	22.5 (N. A. C. C. Rating)
CARRYING CAPACITY .	1½ tons		
POSITION OF DRIVER	Left side	BORE AND STROKE .	3¾ x 5 inches
WHEELBASE	144 inches	LUBRICATION	Splash with circulating pump
GAUGE	Front, 56½ inches; rear, 59½ inches		
		RADIATOR	Tubular
WHEELS	Wood	COOLING	Thermo-syphon
FRONT TIRES	36 x 3½ inches, solid	IGNITION	High-tension magneto
REAR TIRES	36 x 5 inches solid	GASOLINE SYSTEM . .	Gravity
SERVICE BRAKE . . .	Contracting on rear wheels	CLUTCH	Dry multiple disc
		TRANSMISSION . . .	Selective sliding
EMERGENCY BRAKE .	Expanding on rear wheels	GEAR CHANGES . . .	Three
CYLINDERS	Four	DRIVE	Internal gear
ARRANGED	Vertically	REAR AXLE	Dead
CAST	En bloc	STEERING GEAR . . .	Worm and wheel